Pro SpringSource dm Server™

Gary Mak, Daniel Rubio

Apress®

Pro SpringSource dm Server™

Copyright © 2009 by Gary Mak, Daniel Rubio

ISBN-13 (pbk): 978-1-4302-1640-7

ISBN-13 (electronic): 978-1-4302-1641-4

SpringSource is the company behind Spring, the de facto standard in enterprise Java. SpringSource is a leading provider of enterprise Java infrastructure software and delivers enterprise-class software, support, and services to help organizations utilize Spring. The open source-based Spring Portfolio is a comprehensive enterprise application framework designed on long-standing themes of simplicity and power. With more than five million downloads to date, Spring has become an integral part of the enterprise application infrastructure at organizations worldwide. For more information, visit www.springsource.com.

Lead Editors: Steve Anglin, Tom Welsh
Technical Reviewers: Oleg Zhurakousky, Manuel Jordan
Editorial Board: Clay Andres, Steve Anglin, Mark Beckner, Ewan Buckingham, Tony Campbell, Gary Cornell, Jonathan Gennick, Jonathan Hassell, Michelle Lowman, Matthew Moodie, Jeffrey Pepper, Frank Pohlmann, Douglas Pundick, Ben Renow-Clarke, Dominic Shakeshaft, Matt Wade, Tom Welsh
Project Manager: Kylie Johnston
Copy Editor: James A. Compton
Associate Production Director: Kari Brooks-Copony
Compositor: Bookmakers
Indexer: BIM Indexing
Cover Designer: Anna Ishchenko
Manufacturing Director: Tom Debolski

Distributed to the book trade worldwide by Springer New York, Inc., 233 Spring Street, 6th Floor, New York, NY 10013. Phone 1-800-SPRINGER, fax 201-348-4505, e-mail orders-ny@springer-sbm.com, or visit http://www.springeronline.com.

Contents at a Glance

Contents

About the Authors

Gary Mak, founder and chief consultant of Meta-Archit Software Technology Limited, has been a technical architect and application developer on the enterprise Java platform for over seven years. He is the author of the Apress book *Spring Recipes: A Problem-Solution Approach* and coauthor of *Pro SpringSource dm Server*. In his career, Gary has developed a number of Java-based software projects, most of which are application frameworks, system infrastructures, and software tools. He enjoys designing and implementing the complex parts of software projects. Gary has a master's degree in computer science. His research interests include object-oriented technology, aspect-oriented technology, design patterns, software reuse, and domain-driven development.

Gary specializes in building enterprise applications on technologies including Spring, Hibernate, JPA, JSF, Portlet, AJAX, and OSGi. He has been using the Spring Framework in his projects for five years, since Spring version 1.0. Gary has been an instructor of courses on enterprise Java, Spring, Hibernate, Web Services, and agile development. He has written a series of Spring and Hibernate tutorials as course materials, parts of which are open to the public, and they're gaining popularity in the Java community. In his spare time, he enjoys playing tennis and watching tennis competitions.

Daniel Rubio is a consultant with over 10 years of experience in enterprise and web technologies. Specializing in web-based architectures that integrate with back-end systems such as relational databases, ERPs, and CICS, he's relied on Java, CORBA, and .NET technology throughout his career to deliver cost-effective solutions to the financial and manufacturing industries.

He is the author of the Apress book *Pro Spring Dynamic Modules for OSGi* and coauthor of *Pro SpringSource dm Server*. Additionally, he writes articles on emerging technologies for various content networks in this same space, which include TheServerSide.com, Oracle Technology Network, SearchSOA.com, and his own blog WebForefront.com. More recently, Daniel is founder and technical lead of MashupSoft.com.

About the Technical Reviewer

Oleg Zhurakousky is a Senior Consultant with SpringSource and a committer to several Spring portfolio projects (including Spring Integration and Spring-DM). He is an IT professional with 14+ years of experience in software engineering across multiple disciplines including software architecture and design, consulting, business analysis, and application development. He currently focuses on delivering simple but powerful Spring based solutions and training to the North American market.

After starting his career in the world of COBOL and CICS, Oleg has been focusing on professional Java and Java EE development since 1999. Before joining SpringSource, Oleg was heavily involved in using several open source technologies and platforms with Spring Framework at the forefront, while working on a number of projects around the world and spanning industries such as telecommunication, banking, law enforcement, US DOD, and others.

Oleg' current passions include event driven architecture (EDA), grid computing, test-driven development, and aspect-oriented programming, while his Spring passions are aligned with OSGi, Spring-DM and dm Server, Spring integration and Spring Web Services, a combination that he believes will evolve into a simple, lightweight, yet powerful SOA platform.

You can regularly spot Oleg on the Spring Forums contributing to a number of topics. A resident of the Philadelphia area, Oleg enjoys windsurfing, scuba diving, snowboarding, hockey, and traveling when he can find some spare time.

Acknowledgments

I'd like to thank my family, especially my wife, Ivy. Writing books is an intensive job, both mentally and physically. She gave me mental support in writing this book and took care of my health. Most thankfully, she encouraged me and tried to give me suggestions each time when I got into trouble, although she didn't know any technical subjects in this book. Without her love and support, I could never have finished this book.

Additionally, I'd like to thank the team who worked on this book, in particular the following individuals:

Steve Anglin, my acquisition editor, who believed in my writing this book and offered many ideas and suggestions for this book.

Tom Welsh, my development editor, who improved the book both literarily and technically.

Kylie Johnston, my project manager, who managed the book schedule and responded to my requests very quickly.

Manuel Jordan, my other technical reviewer, who reviewed an earlier draft of this book technically, pointed out my faults, and gave valuable suggestions.

Jim Compton, my copy editor, who corrected my grammatical mistakes, improved my words, and kept the conventions consistent throughout the book.

Candace English, my production editor, who produced a nice look for this book.

Other Apress people who were involved in making this a great book.

Gary Mak

First off I would like to thank everyone at Apress, many of whom I had already had the opportunity to work with in my first book project, *Spring Dynamic Modules for OSGi*. They include Steve Anglin, Dominic Shakeshaft, Kylie Johnston, Tom Welsh, Jim Compton, and Laura Cheu. And of course, every other person at Apress who had a role in this book and with whom I didn't have the opportunity to interact directly.

On the technical front, special thanks go to Gary Mak, who laid the foundations for this book, and to Oleg Zhurakousky, who served as the book's technical reviewer.

In addition, thanks go to the many people that make up SpringSource and provide timely information in both support forums and blog posts. These include Adrian Colyer, Rob Harrop, Andy Wilkinson, Christian Dupuis, Ben Hale, Christopher Frost and Glyn Normington. And of course, the many other active people in these areas who have surely influenced my thinking, and whom I unfortunately can't remember.

And finally special thanks to my family and friends, who provided the essential moral support needed to complete a project of this nature.

Daniel Rubio

Introduction

I have been a big fan of the Spring Framework since its first release in 2004 and have been using it in almost all my projects. When the application server written by the same company—the SpringSource dm Server—first came out in April 2008, even though it was in the beta release, I immediately installed it on my machine and tried it out. Note that when it was in the beta release, the dm Server was named the SpringSource Application Platform. When it came to the final release, the name was changed to the SpringSource dm Server, and the SpringSource Application Platform's scope was extended to include a set of SpringSource tools, frameworks, and servers, which includes the dm Server as a core component.

When I was trying out the dm Server, I could see already that it was to bring an evolution to enterprise Java application development. The dm Server is built on top of OSGi, a technology specially designed for building dynamic and modular systems in Java. OSGi brings many benefits to Java developers: first, it allows you to divide a system into multiple modules, each of which can be installed, uninstalled, updated, started, and stopped independently; second, it allows different versions of a module to be deployed at the same time so that different applications can choose a version to import at runtime. The OSGi technology brings great benefits by itself, but the dm Server makes it even more valuable by extending it and integrating it with other technologies that you need for building enterprise Java applications. Moreover, the dm Server is the first application server that directly exposes OSGi's dynamic and modular capabilities to application developers. These are the reasons why I believed the dm Server would succeed and why I decided to write this book.

Because of the positive comments I received for my book *Spring Recipes: A Problem-Solution Approach*, I decide to write another book on this exciting dm Server topic using a similar approach. In this book, each development topic is introduced by a complete and real-world code example that you can follow step by step. Also, instead of abstract descriptions of complex concepts, you will find live examples and easy-to-understand diagrams in this book.

Gary Mak

I was introduced to the dm Server when I started researching OSGi in the context of enterprise Java applications. At the time, Spring Dynamic Modules (Spring-DM) was in its initial release, offering Spring framework techniques—like POJO design and dependency injection—to OSGi developers.

While Spring-DM offers enterprise Java developers a way of *building* OSGi applications using Spring framework techniques, the dm Server fulfills an important role as an enterprise environment for *running* OSGi applications.

Two of OSGi's main features—versioning and services—are not designed to operate in the context of Java EE application servers or web containers, at least not in their out-of-the-box of state. Similarly, though OSGi operates on a run-time environment or container to support versioning and services, such an environment lacks many of the features needed in enterprise Java environments. So emerged the dm Server as a run-time environment for enterprise OSGi applications.

When I wrote a book on the topic of Spring-DM, the dm Server was in its initial 1.0 release, built on the foundations of OSGi's Equinox container, Apache Tomcat's standard web container, Spring-DM, and other custom artifacts. It was a first-generation enterprise OSGi server.

Fast-forward to the dm Server's 2.0 release covered in this book. It is substantially different from the initial dm Server's 1.0 version. Since then, OSGi's standards body has published a series of specifications dedicated to enterprise scenarios; chief among them is one charged with defining an OSGi standard web container. The dm Server is now built on such an OSGi web container, unlike its first release, which used a Java web container with ad hoc provisions to run OSGi applications.

Being built on an OSGi web container, the dm Server guarantees that all your enterprise Java applications based on OSGi are standard-compliant, just like applications relying on Java EE application servers or web containers.

In addition to being built on a set of enterprise OSGi specifications, the dm Server has also incorporated other advances to make the development of enterprise Java application with OSGi easier. These include the use of bundle cloning—which addresses a general OSGi problem that can be more prevalent in enterprise cases—as well as tools designed for the Eclipse IDE or SpringSource Tools Suite to streamline the development of enterprise OSGi Java applications, and support for special artifacts like SpringSource Slices to deal with certain peculiarities of enterprise Java applications in the context of OSGi.

If you're starting to take advantage of OSGi in your Java EE projects, the dm Server is sure to be on your to-do list as one of the first run-time environments to support OSGi applications in the enterprise. This book will take you from its basic operation to exploring some of its more advanced features.

Daniel Rubio

Who This Book Is For

This book is mainly for application developers who would like to develop OSGi-based applications that run on the dm Server, and ideally for Java developers who are already familiar with the Spring Framework and want to enhance the modularity and dynamics of their applications with OSGi and the dm Server. System administrators who need to deploy and trace applications on the server and administrate the server will also find this book useful.

How This Book Is Structured

This book covers both application development and system administration topics of the dm Server. It's divided into eight chapters:

- *Chapter 1: Introduction to OSGi*: This chapter explains why you need OSGi and introduces the OSGi basics that you need for learning about the dm Server. If you are already familiar with OSGi, feel free to skip this chapter.

- *Chapter 2: Developing Bundles with Spring Dynamic Modules*: This chapter introduces the common features and mechanisms of Spring-DM and demonstrates how to develop bundles with it. Understanding Spring-DM is a prerequisite to learning about application development for the dm Server.

- *Chapter 3: Introduction to the dm Server*: This chapter gives you an overview of the dm Server's components, solutions, features, and architecture to provide a general understanding of it.

- *Chapter 4: Getting Started with the dm Server*: This chapter familiarizes you with the dm Server's general concepts and guides you in getting started with its installation, administration, configuration, and deployment.

- *Chapter 5: Developing Applications for the dm Server*: This chapter demonstrates how to develop modular and OSGi-based enterprise applications to run on the dm Server, using the dm Server tools installed in Eclipse or the SpringSource Tool Suite.
- *Chapter 6: Migrating Web Applications to the dm Server*: This chapter demonstrates how to migrate an existing Java EE web application from a standard WAR file to OSGi web bundles in the form of shared libraries WARs and shared services WARs, as well as the dm Server's Platform Archive (PAR) format.
- *Chapter 7: Tracing Applications on the dm Server*: This chapter introduces the dm Server's serviceability and discusses how to trace applications running on the dm Server.
- *Chapter 8: Managing Application Growth on the dm Server:* This chapter provides an in-depth look at more advanced topics related to the dm Server, including plan files, configuration provisioning, cloning, the Bundlor tool, and SpringSource Slices.

Each of Chapters 1, 2, 5, 6, 7, and 8 demonstrates a topic with a complete real-world example. The example within a chapter is self-contained, but examples are independent between chapters with the exception of Chapter 8, which illustrates growth scenarios for the example presented in chapter 5.

Conventions

Sometimes when you should pay particular attention to a part within a code example, that part will appear in **boldface**. Please note that boldface doesn't necessarily reflect a change from the previous version of the code. In cases where a code line is too long to fit the page width, it is broken with a code continuation character (~CCC). Please note that when you try out the code, you need to concatenate the line by yourself without adding any space.

Prerequisites

Before reading this book, you should already be familiar with basic Spring Framework concepts and usage. You should also have a basic knowledge of Java EE topics including Java Persistence API (JPA), transaction management, web application development, and Spring's support for them. If you are new to these topics, I suggest reading Chapters 1, 2, 3, 8, 9, and 10 of *Spring Recipes: A Problem-Solution Approach*, which was published by Apress in June 2008.

Also note that although Spring-DM is covered in Chapter 2, the development model offered by Spring-DM (which is heavily used by dm Server applications) has more depth than can be presented in a book focused on the dm Server. If you're interested in an in-depth look at Spring-DM, please consult *Spring Dynamic Modules for OSGi*, which was published by Apress in February 2009.

Downloading the Code

The source code for this book is available to readers at www.apress.com in the Downloads section of this book's home page The source code is organized by chapters, each of which includes one or more independent Eclipse projects. Please refer to readme.txt, located in the root, for setting up and running the source code.

Contacting the Authors

I always welcome your questions and feedback regarding to the contents of this book. You can send your comments to prodmserver@metaarchit.com and access the book discussion and updates on http://www.metaarchit.com.

Gary Mak

I welcome your comments and feedback on the contents of this book. You can send your comments to osgi@webforefront.com.

Daniel Rubio

CHAPTER 1

■ ■ ■

Introduction to OSGi

OSGi (Open Services Gateway initiative) is a technology for building dynamic and modular systems in Java. OSGi is one of the core technologies underlying the dm Server. Therefore, before you start learning about the dm Server, you have to understand the concepts, mechanisms, and uses of OSGi. In this chapter, you will learn about the OSGi basics that are prerequisite to working with the dm Server. This chapter covers the following topics:

- Why you need OSGi for building modular systems
- Introducing the OSGi technology, OSGi bundles, and OSGi containers
- Developing OSGi bundles using Eclipse
- Starting the Equinox OSGi container and deploying OSGi bundles
- Versioning packages in OSGi bundles
- Developing OSGi services and using them across bundles

When reading this chapter, keep in mind that OSGi is a huge topic in itself, one that may need an entire book to cover. This chapter aims only at familiarizing you with the OSGi basics that you need for learning about the dm Server, without the need to read the entire OSGi specification (available at http://www.osgi.org/Specifications/). If you are already familiar with OSGi, feel free to skip to Chapter 2, "Developing Bundles with Spring Dynamic Modules."

Setting Up the Development Environment

The first thing you must do is set up the environment for developing OSGi-based applications. Because Java is a cross-platform technology, there's no restriction on the target platform on which you set up your development environment. Throughout this book I will use Microsoft Windows as my platform to develop sample applications.

Installing JDK

Prior to developing applications for the Java platform, you should have a Java Development Kit (JDK) installed on your machine. You can download JDK from the Java SE downloads web site:

http://java.sun.com/javase/downloads/index.jsp

Note that the dm Server requires Java SE 6 or higher as its runtime environment. For this book, I will use JDK 1.6 Update 13 to develop and run sample applications. Upon finishing the JDK installation, you can simply run the following command for verification:

java -version

1

If JDK has been installed on your machine successfully, you will be able to see the current Java version as follows:

```
java version "1.6.0_13"
Java(TM) 2 Runtime Environment, Standard Edition (build 1.6.0_13-b03)
Java HotSpot(TM) Client VM (build 11.3-b02, mixed mode, sharing)
```

Installing Eclipse or SpringSource Tools Suite (STS)

Although a Java IDE is not absolutely required for developing Java applications, installing one will make development easier. For this book, I strongly recommend one of two options: Eclipse, for its powerful features that support OSGi and its built-in OSGi container (Equinox), or the SpringSource Tools Suite (STS), which is also an Eclipse-based IDE.

The difference between these two IDEs is subtle, especially when you consider that both are based on the same code base (Eclipse), both are free, and an Eclipse IDE can be upgraded—with plug-ins—to provide the same functionality as STS.

STS, though, comes preinstalled with a series of Spring-related plug-ins—among them dm Server tools—as well as a copy of the dm Server and tc Server. By contrast, the Eclipse IDE requires these additional pieces to be installed separately. Moreover, when you learn about developing applications for the dm Server in later chapters, you will find the dm Server tools plug-in for Eclipse to be very helpful.

At this point, you can use either Eclipse or STS, for you will only be using a basic set of OSGi features available in both IDEs. When the time comes to use the dm Server and with it the dm Server tools plug-in, I will describe the plug-in's installation for an Eclipse IDE in case you opted for this choice; STS, as already mentioned, comes preinstalled with this plug-in.

To use Eclipse as your IDE, you first have to download an Eclipse package from the Eclipse downloads web site:

`http://www.eclipse.org/downloads/`

At the time of writing, the current annual release of Eclipse projects is Eclipse Ganymede, which contains three major packages, as shown in Figure 1-1.

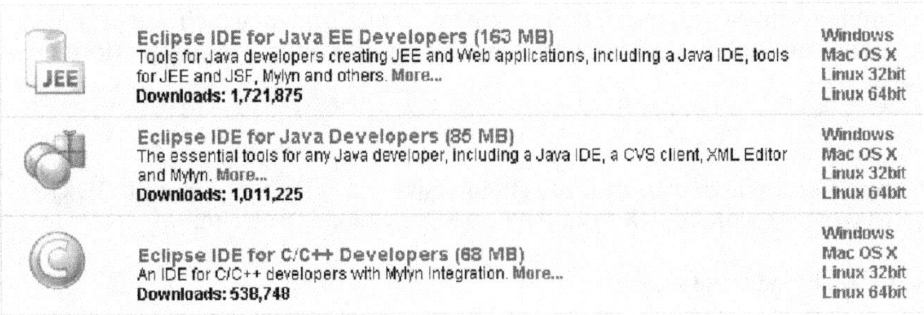

Eclipse IDE for Java EE Developers (163 MB)
Tools for Java developers creating JEE and Web applications, including a Java IDE, tools for JEE and JSF, Mylyn and others. More...
Downloads: 1,721,875
Windows / Mac OS X / Linux 32bit / Linux 64bit

Eclipse IDE for Java Developers (85 MB)
The essential tools for any Java developer, including a Java IDE, a CVS client, XML Editor and Mylyn. More...
Downloads: 1,011,225
Windows / Mac OS X / Linux 32bit / Linux 64bit

Eclipse IDE for C/C++ Developers (68 MB)
An IDE for C/C++ developers with Mylyn Integration. More...
Downloads: 538,748
Windows / Mac OS X / Linux 32bit / Linux 64bit

Figure 1-1. Downloading an Eclipse package from the Eclipse downloads web site

To use STS as your IDE, you first have to download the STS package from the SpringSource downloads web site:

`http://www.springsource.com/products/sts/`

At the time of writing, the current release of the STS project is STS 2.1.

When the download completes for either Eclipse or STS, simply extract the file into a directory of your choice (e.g., `c:\eclipse`) and then run the Eclipse executable file in the top-level directory (`eclipse.exe` for the Windows platform). If this is the first time you are using Eclipse, consider referring to its Help menu for the basic features and usages.

Since both IDEs are based on the same code base, their menus and navigation screens are identical, so you should have no trouble following the steps outlined in the remainder of the chapter if you use either Eclipse or STS.

Why You Need OSGi

Before you are introduced to what OSGi is and how it works, you have to understand why you need OSGi. Consider the following example, which consists of multiple modules.

Creating a System with Multiple Modules

Suppose you have to develop a system for an online bookshop, one of whose functions is to export several kinds of data from the system for analysis and statistics purposes. Following object-oriented design practices, the first thing you would do is define an interface containing the primary operations of the system, such as a data export service belonging to an export package like the one that follows:

```
package com.apress.prodmserver.bookshop.export;

import java.io.IOException;

public interface ExportService {

    public void export(String filename, Object[][] data) throws IOException;
}
```

This `ExportService` interface—which will make up part of the system's first module—defines the `export()` method signature, which takes two input values: a `filename` argument to define the actual file name and a two-dimensional `Object` array to export the data.

Because it would be common to export the data in various report formats, such as plain text, HTML, XML, Excel, and PDF, it's also convenient to define another interface—ReportGenerator—that would form part of the system's second module in a separate package named report, as illustrated next:

```
package com.apress.prodmserver.bookshop.report;

public interface ReportGenerator {

    public String getExtension();
    public byte[] generate(Object[][] data);
}
```

This last interface has two method signatures, getExtension() and generate(). The getExtension() method will allow a class implementation to specify its file extension, such as txt, html, xml, xls, and pdf. The generate() method will allow a class implementation to generate a report in the target format; this generated report will in turn return the report contents in a byte array.

With these two interfaces in hand, we can move ahead and start creating implementation classes for the first two modules of the online bookshop. Let's create two simple ReportGenerator implementations, one for plain-text reports and one for HTML reports. The TextReportGenerator implementation will be located in the text subpackage, as illustrated next:

```
package com.apress.prodmserver.bookshop.report.text;

import com.apress.prodmserver.bookshop.report.ReportGenerator;

public class TextReportGenerator implements ReportGenerator {

    private String delimiter;

    public TextReportGenerator(String delimiter) {
        this.delimiter = delimiter;
    }

    public String getExtension() {
        return "txt";
    }

    public byte[] generate(Object[][] data) {
        StringBuffer buffer = new StringBuffer();
        for (int row = 0; row < data.length; row++) {
            for (int column = 0; column < data[row].length; column++) {
                if (column != 0) {
                    buffer.append(delimiter);
                }
                buffer.append(data[row][column]);
            }
            buffer.append("\r\n");
        }
        return buffer.toString().getBytes();
    }
}
```

Notice that this last class implements the two method signatures for the ReportGenerator interface, in addition to defining a delimiter field that is instantiated in the class's constructor and is later used inside the generate() method.

The HtmlReportGenerator implementation, on the other hand, will be placed in the html subpackage as follows:

```
package com.apress.prodmserver.bookshop.report.html;

import com.apress.prodmserver.bookshop.report.ReportGenerator;

public class HtmlReportGenerator implements ReportGenerator {

    private String title;

    public HtmlReportGenerator(String title) {
        this.title = title;
    }

    public String getExtension() {
        return "html";
    }

    public byte[] generate(Object[][] data) {
        StringBuffer buffer = new StringBuffer();
        buffer.append("<html><head><title>");
        buffer.append(title);
        buffer.append("</title></head><body><table>");
        for (int row = 0; row < data.length; row++) {
            buffer.append("<tr>");
            for (int column = 0; column < data[row].length; column++) {
                buffer.append("<td>");
                buffer.append(data[row][column]);
                buffer.append("</td>");
            }
            buffer.append("</tr>");
        }
        buffer.append("</table></body></html>");
        return buffer.toString().getBytes();
    }
}
```

Notice that this class also implements the two method signatures for the ReportGenerator interface, and it defines a similar title field that is instantiated in the class's constructor and is later used in the generate() method.

If you are an experienced Java web application developer, you should be aware that using a template language (such as JSP or Apache Velocity) to generate the HTML reports would be more reasonable. However, here I'm using in-line HTML reports for simplicity.

With these two ReportGenerator implementations designed for text and HTML reports, you can now address an implementation for the remaining ExportService interface. The implementation class for the ExportService interface will be defined inside the impl subpackage as follows:

```
package com.apress.prodmserver.bookshop.export.impl;

import java.io.File;
import java.io.FileOutputStream;
import java.io.IOException;
import java.io.OutputStream;

import com.apress.prodmserver.bookshop.export.ExportService;
import com.apress.prodmserver.bookshop.report.ReportGenerator;
import com.apress.prodmserver.bookshop.report.text.TextReportGenerator;

public class ExportServiceImpl implements ExportService {

    private ReportGenerator reportGenerator = new TextReportGenerator(",");
    private String path;

    public ExportServiceImpl(String path) {
        this.path = path;
    }

    public void export(String filename, Object[][] data) throws IOException {
        OutputStream out = null;
        try {
            File file = new File(path + "/" + filename + "."
                    + reportGenerator.getExtension());
            out = new FileOutputStream(file);
            out.write(reportGenerator.generate(data));
        } finally {
            if (out != null) {
                out.close();
            }
        }
    }
}
```

Notice the way this last class implements the ExportService interface's export method. This particular implementation is charged with exporting data to a file in text format, given the use of the report generator implementation TextReportGenerator. However, keep in mind that a similar implementation could be created for an HTML format if the report generator implementation HtmlReportGenerator were used.

We have now finished the first two modules of the online bookstore, one that takes care of exporting reports and the other one with generating them. We will get to how you would package these modules in the context of OSGi shortly. Next, you will set out to create another module for the online bookstore, to track sales ranking. It will also leverage these earlier modules.

Just as the export and report module relied on their own unique interfaces, let's begin by defining a new interface for the sales ranking module, one within the ranking package as follows:

```
package com.apress.prodmserver.bookshop.ranking;

import java.io.IOException;

public interface RankingService {

    public void exportRanking() throws IOException;
}
```

The exportRanking() method signature simply exports a current book's ranking, which in a production system would be loaded and summarized from a database. However, for testing purposes you can hard-code the ranking, as in the following implementation in the impl subpackage:

```
package com.apress.prodmserver.bookshop.ranking.impl;

import java.io.IOException;

import com.apress.prodmserver.bookshop.export.ExportService;
import com.apress.prodmserver.bookshop.export.impl.ExportServiceImpl;
import com.apress.prodmserver.bookshop.ranking.RankingService;

public class RankingServiceImpl implements RankingService {

    private ExportService exportService = new ExportServiceImpl("c:/bookshop");

    public void exportRanking() throws IOException {
        Object[][] ranking = { { "Rank", "Book" }, { 1, "Spring Recipes" },
                { 2, "Pro SpringSource dm Server" } };

        exportService.export("ranking", ranking);
    }
}
```

Notice that this class implements the exportRanking() method and declares a hard-coded Object[][] array. More importantly though, look at how this last array is used to invoke exportService.export(îrankingî,ranking), which in itself is a reference to the interface ExportService, which is based on ExportServiceImpl—part of the export module.

Next, and to complete the logic of the sales ranking module, suppose you need to export a book's rankings regularly; for example, every hour in a production system or every 60 seconds for testing purposes. You can create the following Main class in the root package using the JDK Timer API for scheduling:

```
package com.apress.prodmserver.bookshop;

import java.util.Timer;
import java.util.TimerTask;

import com.apress.prodmserver.bookshop.ranking.RankingService;
import com.apress.prodmserver.bookshop.ranking.impl.RankingServiceImpl;

public class Main {

    public static void main(String[] args) {
        final RankingService rankingService = new RankingServiceImpl();

        new Timer().schedule(new TimerTask() {

            public void run() {
                try {
                    rankingService.exportRanking();
                } catch (Exception e) {
                    e.printStackTrace();
                }
            }
        }, 0, 60000);
    }
}
```

This class instantiates the RankingServiceImpl class and then invokes the exportRanking() method inside a try/catch block.

Given that this last class relies on the export module, it's necessary to ensure the presence of certain file system directories that are required by the export module. Therefore you must create the directory c:/bookshop for storing the output files. Then you will see that the books' rankings are exported to the file ranking.txt, and that file is updated every 60 seconds.

Now let's consider one final module for the bookstore, one for checking a book's stock value (whether it is in stock or not). Like the ranking module, the stock module will also rely on the export module. So let's start by defining this last module's interface in the stock package as follows:

```
package com.apress.prodmserver.bookshop.stock;

import java.io.IOException;

public interface StockService {

    public void exportStock() throws IOException;
}
```

Similarly, and for testing purposes, you can implement this interface in the impl subpackage with hard-coded stock values:

```
package com.apress.prodmserver.bookshop.stock.impl;

import java.io.IOException;

import com.apress.prodmserver.bookshop.export.ExportService;
import com.apress.prodmserver.bookshop.export.impl.ExportServiceImpl;
import com.apress.prodmserver.bookshop.stock.StockService;

public class StockServiceImpl implements StockService {

    private ExportService exportService = new ExportServiceImpl("c:/bookshop");

    public void exportStock() throws IOException {
        Object[][] stock = { { "Book", "Stock" }, { "Spring Recipes", "10" },
                { "Pro SpringSource dm Server", "20" } };

        exportService.export("stock", stock);
    }
}
```

Notice that the exportStock() method—similar to exportRanking()—also defines an array. This array invokes exportService.export(ìstockî, stock), which in itself is a reference to the interface ExportService that is based on ExportServiceImpl—part of the export module.

Next, and to establish the same functionality as the sales ranking module, you can add the following code to the Main class to export the stock values at regular intervals; for example, every 60 seconds for testing purposes:

```
package com.apress.prodmserver.bookshop;
...
import com.apress.prodmserver.bookshop.stock.StockService;
import com.apress.prodmserver.bookshop.stock.impl.StockServiceImpl;

public class Main {

    public static void main(String[] args) {
        ...
        final StockService stockService = new StockServiceImpl();

        new Timer().schedule(new TimerTask() {

            public void run() {
                try {
                    stockService.exportStock();
                } catch (Exception e) {
                    e.printStackTrace();
                }
            }
        }, 0, 60000);
    }
}
```

When you run this class, you can inspect the file c:/bookshop/stock.txt for the exported stock values.

Now your bookshop system has four modules in total. The module dependencies are illustrated in Figure 1-2.

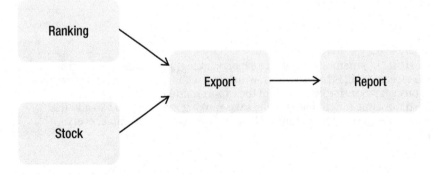

Figure 1-2. *The module dependencies in the bookshop example*

A simplified version of the UML package and class diagram is shown in Figure 1-3, so that you can better understand the system architecture.

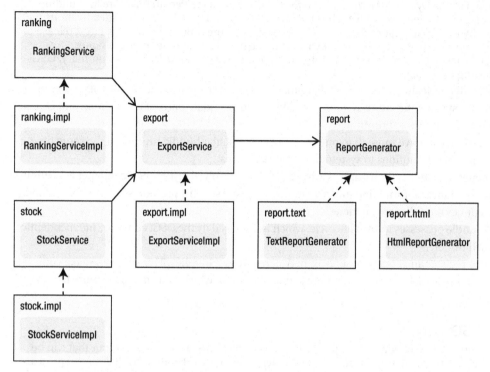

Figure 1-3. *A simplified UML package and class diagram*

Problems When Updating the System

From the system design point of view, the bookshop system is divided into multiple modules. However, from the deployment point of view, it is deployed as a single application. You must redeploy and restart the entire system whenever you have updated even a single module. For example, you might update the export module to include the current time in the file name so that the export service will export data to a different file each time. As you know, in a large system there may be hundreds or thousands of modules, so a system restart may be very time-consuming. Moreover, the system may have to provide 24/7 services. Such a restart may not always be possible.

On the other hand, suppose you have updated a single module (e.g., the export module), which is being used by two or more other modules (e.g., the ranking and stock modules). You can't have some of the modules use the new module version while others stick to the old version at the same time. However, you may often need to do just that for system upgrade transitions when you are not going to upgrade all involved modules in one shot.

In the upcoming sections, I will introduce how to solve all these problems in a reasonable way with OSGi.

Introducing OSGi

OSGi, also known as *the Dynamic Module System for Java,* defines a layered architecture for building dynamic and modular systems with Java. The OSGi architecture is defined by a set of specifications that are maintained by the OSGi Alliance (http://www.osgi.org/). At the time of writing, the latest release of the OSGi specifications is version 4.1, which I will use in creating the examples of this chapter.

With OSGi, you can divide a system into multiple modules, called *bundles.* In summary, OSGi offers the following advantages:

- You can dynamically install, uninstall, update, start, and stop different bundles of your system without restarting the entire system. This allows you to update parts of your system and change some of its behaviors at runtime.

- Your system can have more than one version of a particular bundle running at the same time. This offers good solutions to system upgrade transitions.

- The dependencies between bundles are managed and resolved by the OSGi container at runtime, taking versioning information into account while doing so. This promotes better encapsulation and reduces module dependencies.

- Each bundle possesses its own life cycle, which is managed by the OSGi container independently for each bundle.

- You can register and consume services between different bundles. This can help make your system more loosely coupled and more service-oriented, which in turn make it more flexible, dynamic, and adaptive.

Introducing OSGi Bundles

A system built with OSGi is divided into multiple bundles, each of which is a modular unit that can be installed, uninstalled, updated, started, and stopped independently and dynamically. If designed properly, bundles can be reused across multiple projects and you can accumulate a bundle repository. A bundle can export packages and services to other bundles, as well as importing packages and services from other bundles. Thus, there are two types of dependencies between bundles:

Package dependency: A bundle exports its packages so that other bundles can import the packages and then access the classes, interfaces, and resources in the packages.

Service dependency: A bundle registers its objects to the service registry provided by the OSGi container as OSGi services, so that other bundles can consume the services.

A bundle contains Java class files and resource files, and it is packaged and distributed as a normal JAR file. Most importantly, what makes a regular JAR different is that a valid OSGi bundle must include a MANIFEST.MF file in the META-INF directory, and this file can contain bundle manifest headers in addition to standard manifest headers for describing the bundle. The OSGi specifications define a set of bundle manifest headers, the most common of which are described in Table 1-1.

Table 1-1. *Common Bundle Manifest Headers*

Header	Description
Bundle-ManifestVersion	The OSGi specification version to which this bundle conforms; required. The default value 1 is for OSGi Release 3, while the value 2 is for OSGi Release 4 and higher.
Bundle-Name	The human-readable name of this bundle; required.
Bundle-SymbolicName	The unique identifier of this bundle, usually in a form similar to Java package names; required.
Bundle-Version	The version of this bundle in the form of *major.minor.micro.qualifier*, where *major*, *minor*, and *micro* are numbers, while *qualifier* can contain alphabets, numbers, underscores, and hyphens. Only the *major* part is required.
Bundle-Vendor	The vendor name of this bundle; optional.
Bundle-RequiredExecutionEnvironment	The required execution environments to run this bundle in a comma-separated list, such as J2SE-1.5, JavaSE-1.6, and CDC-1.1/Foundation-1.1; optional.
Bundle-Activator	The activator class that controls this bundle's life cycle; optional.
Import-Package	The packages imported by this bundle in a comma-separated list. Each package may include a version or a version range separated by a semicolon; optional.
Export-Package	The packages exported by this bundle in a comma-separated list. Each package may include a version separated by a semicolon; optional.
Require-Bundle	The bundles all of whose exported packages are required by this bundle; optional.

When deployed to an OSGi container, an OSGi bundle has its own life cycle and can be in one of the following states:

INSTALLED: The bundle has been successfully installed to the container.

RESOLVED: All interfaces and classes that the bundle needs are resolved and available. This state indicates that the bundle is either ready to be started or has been stopped from the ACTIVE state.

STARTING: The bundle is being started and the activator's start() method is being called but has not yet returned.

ACTIVE: The bundle has been successfully activated and is running.

STOPPING: The bundle is being stopped and the activator's stop() method is being called but has not yet returned.

UNINSTALLED: The bundle has been uninstalled from the container.

At runtime, a bundle's state can be changed by different actions applied to the bundle, as shown in Figure 1-4.

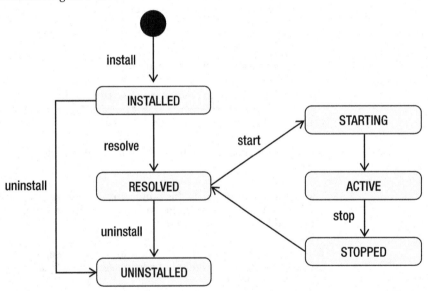

Figure 1-4. *An OSGi bundle's state diagram*

When you *install* a bundle to an OSGi container, it's stored in the container's storage and has the INSTALLED state. When you *start* the bundle, it will first be resolved internally by the OSGi container and has the RESOLVED state once resolved successfully. Then, if a bundle has an activator class—which is a class containing instructions executed when a bundle is activated—the activator's start() method will be called (at this time the bundle has the STARTING state), and the bundle will have the ACTIVE state on success, whether it has an activator class or not. When you *stop* a running bundle, the OSGi container will call the activator's stop() method (at this time the bundle has the STOPPING state). Once stopped, the bundle will return to the RESOLVED state. You can either start the bundle again or *uninstall* the bundle so that it will have the UNINSTALL state.

Don't worry about the significance of these particular bundle states right now; you will explore them in detail shortly. Next, I will describe OSGi containers, the environment that takes care of managing bundles and their corresponding states.

Introducing OSGi Containers

Like most components, such as servlets and EJBs, OSGi bundles also need to run within a container. An OSGi container is responsible for managing the package dependencies and life cycles of bundles, and also for providing bundles with the standard services defined by the OSGi specifications. At the time of writing, there are the following popular open-source OSGi containers:

Equinox (`http://www.eclipse.org/equinox/`): This is an Eclipse project and the reference implementation (RI) of the OSGi Release 4 core framework specification. Equinox is used internally by the Eclipse IDE to manage its plug-ins. In fact, each Eclipse plug-in is an OSGi bundle with additional Eclipse-specific code.

Apache Felix (`http://felix.apache.org/`): This is an open-source OSGi container from the Apache Software Foundation that implements the core OSGi framework and standard container services. Felix targets the OSGi Release 4 specification, but at the time of writing it's still in progress for full compliance.

Knopflerfish (`http://www.knopflerfish.org/`): This is another leading open-source OSGi container that has a long history. Knopflerfish version 2 is designed to be compliant with the OSGi Release 4 specification, while version 1 is available as an OSGi Release 3 option.

As the dm Server relies on the Eclipse Equinox OSGi container, I will use Equinox to run all examples in this chapter as well. However, keep in mind that these standard OSGi examples can also run in any OSGi-compliant container.

Developing OSGi Bundles

With OSGi, you can divide a system into multiple bundles, each of which can be installed, uninstalled, updated, started, and stopped dynamically and independently. As a comprehensive Java/Java EE IDE, Eclipse provides powerful OSGi support features that allow you to develop bundles. For example, you can create bundles using Eclipse's plug-in wizard and edit the `MANIFEST.MF` file visually with Eclipse's plug-in GUI. Eclipse also embeds the Equinox OSGi container for you to execute and debug bundles. In this section I will demonstrate how to create a bundle for each module of the bookshop system.

Creating the Report Bundle

Currently there are four modules in the bookshop system. Since the report module has no dependencies to other modules, let's create an OSGi bundle for it first. To develop a bundle using Eclipse, you first create a plug-in project by choosing File ➤ New ➤ Project ➤ Plug-in Development ➤ Plug-in Project, as shown in Figure 1-5.

Then, in the New Plug-in Project dialog, enter `com.apress.prodmserver.bookshop.report` as the project name and select An OSGi Framework ➤ Standard as the target platform, as shown in Figure 1-6. As mentioned earlier, each Eclipse plug-in is actually an OSGi bundle with additional Eclipse-specific code that can run only within Eclipse. By selecting the standard OSGi framework as the target platform, you guarantee that your bundle will be able to run in any OSGi-compliant container.

Figure 1-5. *Creating a new plug-in project*

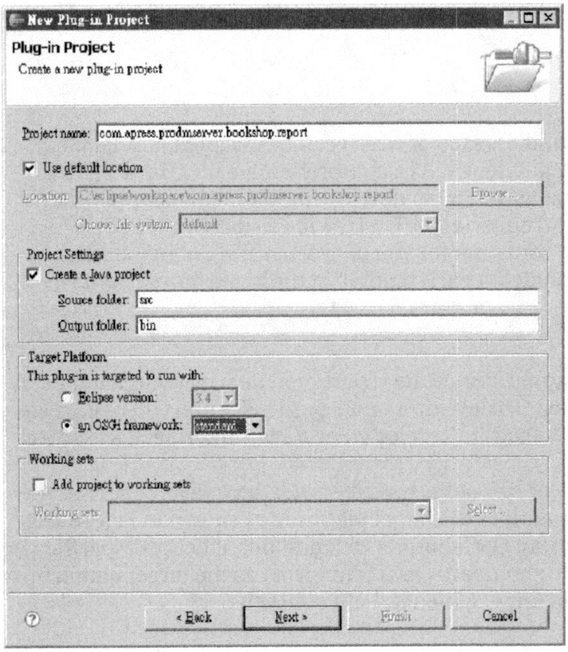

Figure 1-6. *Selecting the target plug-in platform*

In the next screen, you can edit the default bundle manifest headers generated by Eclipse. Each OSGi bundle can have an `Activator` class that can participate in the bundle's life cycle and execute code at each step in the cycle for different purposes. This class allows you to perform custom tasks during bundle start and stop. For the report bundle, you needn't perform such tasks, so you can uncheck the Generate an Activator check box, as shown in Figure 1-7.

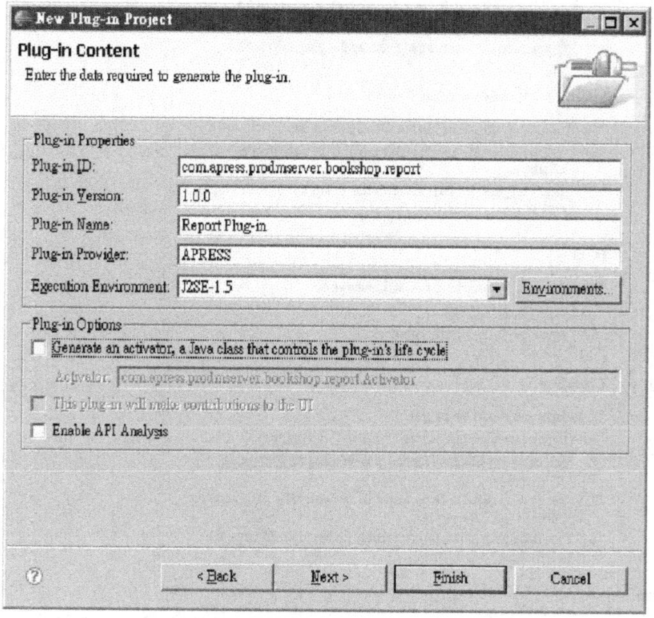

Figure 1-7. *Editing the bundle manifest headers*

When you finish the project wizard, your Eclipse workspace will automatically switch to the Plug-in Development perspective. Now you can use Eclipse's GUI to edit the `MANIFEST.MF` file visually, as shown in Figure 1-8. Note that there are several tabs at the bottom for you to edit different categories of bundle manifest headers.

The report bundle should contain interfaces and implementation classes related to report generation, and it should export these for other bundles to use. Copy the `ReportGenerator` interface and the `TextReportGenerator` and `HtmlReportGenerator` classes from the previous bookshop project to the same packages of this plug-in project. Then export these packages by adding them to the Exported Packages list in the Runtime tab, as shown in Figure 1-9.

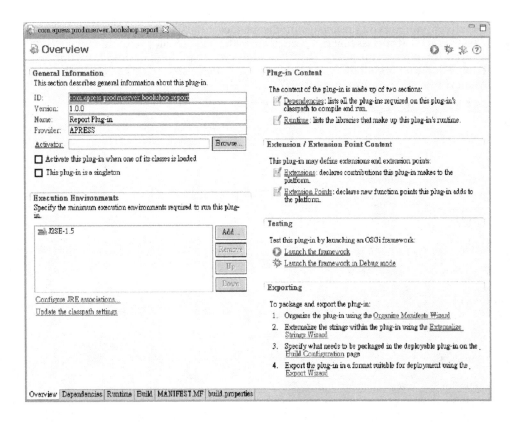

Figure 1-8. *Eclipse's GUI for editing bundle manifest headers visually*

After you save the file, the report bundle is complete. If you open the MANIFEST.MF tab to view the source, you will see the following contents:

```
Manifest-Version: 1.0
Bundle-ManifestVersion: 2
Bundle-Name: Report Plug-in
Bundle-SymbolicName: com.apress.prodmserver.bookshop.report
Bundle-Version: 1.0.0
Bundle-Vendor: APRESS
Bundle-RequiredExecutionEnvironment: J2SE-1.5
Export-Package: com.apress.prodmserver.bookshop.report,
 com.apress.prodmserver.bookshop.report.html,
 com.apress.prodmserver.bookshop.report.text
```

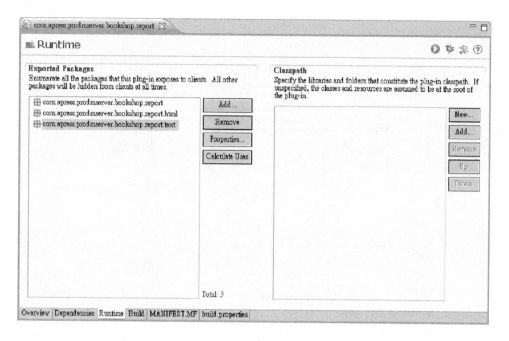

Figure 1-9. *Exporting the report interface and implementation packages*

Creating the Export Bundle

Next, let's create a new plug-in project for the export bundle, following essentially the same steps as the report bundle. This time, use the name `com.apress.prodmserver.bookshop.export` for the bundle. Then copy the `ExportService` interface and the `ExportServiceImpl` class from the previous bookshop project to this plug-in project. However, you will then see errors reporting that the `com.apress.prodmserver.bookshop.report` package and its `text` or `html` subpackage cannot be resolved. To solve this problem, simply add these packages to the Imported Packages list in the Dependencies tab, as shown in Figure 1-10.

At runtime, the OSGi container will automatically look for other bundles that export the packages (the report bundle in this case). Once such bundles are found, the OSGi container will import the interfaces and classes exported from these bundles. Also note that you can directly import the report bundle to the Required Plug-ins list on the left side of the Dependencies tab, but this practice is not recommended, because it will introduce direct dependencies between bundles, making it hard to update individual bundles. However, in some cases when it's necessary to import all packages of a bundle and there are many packages, you may consider requiring the entire bundle.

The export module also has to export its interfaces and implementations for other bundles to use. In the Runtime tab, add the `com.apress.prodmserver.bookshop.export` package and its `impl` sub-package to the Exported Packages list.

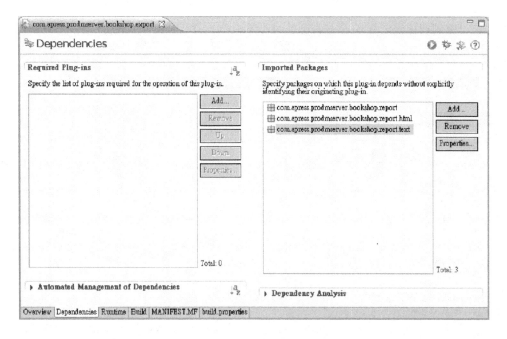

Figure 1-10. Importing the report interface and implementation packages

Now the export bundle is complete. To view its source code, open the MANIFEST.MF tab and you will see the following contents:

```
Manifest-Version: 1.0
Bundle-ManifestVersion: 2
Bundle-Name: Export Plug-in
Bundle-SymbolicName: com.apress.prodmserver.bookshop.export
Bundle-Version: 1.0.0
Bundle-Vendor: APRESS
Bundle-RequiredExecutionEnvironment: J2SE-1.5
Import-Package: com.apress.prodmserver.bookshop.report,
 com.apress.prodmserver.bookshop.report.html,
 com.apress.prodmserver.bookshop.report.text
Export-Package: com.apress.prodmserver.bookshop.export,
 com.apress.prodmserver.bookshop.export.impl
```

Creating the Ranking Bundle

Now it's time to create a new plug-in project for the ranking bundle, whose name should be com.apress.
prodmserver.bookshop.ranking. Since this bundle needs to start and stop a timer task when it starts and
stops, you should check the Generate an Activator check box so that Eclipse will generate an Activator
class for you to control the bundle's life cycle, as shown in Figure 1-11.

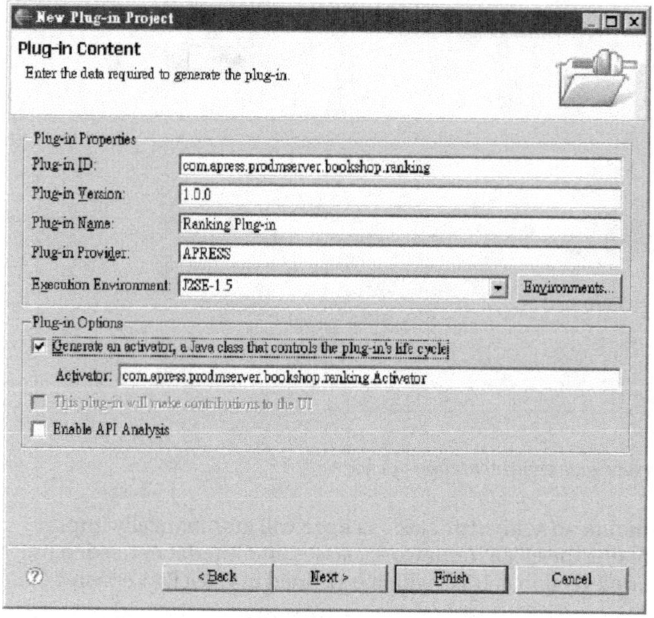

Figure 1-11. *Generating an Activator class*

The purpose of the Activator class is to execute certain tasks when a bundle enters or exits certain
states. In this case, since the ranking module is required to export a book's rankings regularly; the
Activator class becomes the ideal place to trigger the execution of this logic once the bundle is started
(enters its STARTING/ACTIVE state) and be terminated once the bundle is stopped(enters its STOPPING/
RESOLVED state).

When the project is created, you will notice the Activator class skeleton generated by
Eclipse. Before implementing its methods, you have to copy the RankingService interface and the
RankingServiceImpl class from the previous bookshop project to this plug-in project. Then import the
com.apress.prodmserver.bookshop.export package and its impl subpackage to the Imported Packages
list in the Dependencies tab, as shown in Figure 1-12.

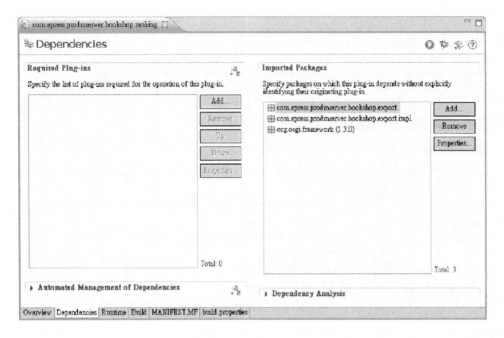

Figure 1-12. *Importing the export service's interface and implementation packages*

Note that if you have chosen to generate an Activator class, Eclipse will automatically import the org.osgi.framework package, which contains the OSGi framework classes and interfaces needed by the Activator. Also note that the default imported version is 1.3.0, which is defined in OSGi R4 Version 4.0, while 1.4.0 is defined in OSGi R4 Version 4.1.

Finally, migrate the ranking export code from the Main class in the ranking module to this activator's start() method. By doing so, you instruct the OSGi container to trigger this method automatically and invoke its logic once the bundle starts. In this method, you can start a JDK Timer to export the ranking regularly (every 60 seconds). Correspondingly, you should stop the timer in the stop() method, which will be called by the OSGi container when this bundle stops.

```
package com.apress.prodmserver.bookshop.ranking;

import java.util.Timer;
import java.util.TimerTask;

import org.osgi.framework.BundleActivator;
import org.osgi.framework.BundleContext;

import com.apress.prodmserver.bookshop.ranking.impl.RankingServiceImpl;
```

```
public class Activator implements BundleActivator {

    private Timer timer = new Timer();

    public void start(BundleContext context) throws Exception {
        final RankingService rankingService = new RankingServiceImpl();

        timer.schedule(new TimerTask() {

            public void run() {
                try {
                    rankingService.exportRanking();
                } catch (Exception e) {
                    e.printStackTrace();
                }
            }
        }, 0, 60000);
    }

    public void stop(BundleContext context) throws Exception {
        timer.cancel();
    }
}
```

If you view the MANIFEST.MF source code, you should see the following contents:

```
Manifest-Version: 1.0
Bundle-ManifestVersion: 2
Bundle-Name: Ranking Plug-in
Bundle-SymbolicName: com.apress.prodmserver.bookshop.ranking
Bundle-Version: 1.0.0
Bundle-Activator: com.apress.prodmserver.bookshop.ranking.Activator
Bundle-Vendor: APRESS
Bundle-RequiredExecutionEnvironment: J2SE-1.5
Import-Package: com.apress.prodmserver.bookshop.export,
 com.apress.prodmserver.bookshop.export.impl,
 org.osgi.framework;version="1.3.0"
```

Note that the Activator class is specified in the Bundle-Activator manifest header. So even if you forgot to generate an Activator class in the project wizard, you can manually define it in the Overview tab's Activator field, which will generate a Bundle-Activator header in the MANIFEST.MF source code.

Creating the Stock Bundle

Following steps similar to those for creating the ranking plug-in project, you can create a project for the stock bundle, giving it the name com.apress.prodmserver.bookshop.stock. Then copy the StockService interface and the StockServiceImpl class from the previous bookshop project to this plug-in project, and import the com.apress.prodmserver.bookshop.export package and its impl subpackage in the Dependencies tab.

Similarly, you can export the stock values regularly by starting a JDK Timer in the start() method of the Activator class as shown in the following code. Also, don't forget to stop the timer in the stop() method.

```java
package com.apress.prodmserver.bookshop.stock;

import java.util.Timer;
import java.util.TimerTask;

import org.osgi.framework.BundleActivator;
import org.osgi.framework.BundleContext;

import com.apress.prodmserver.bookshop.stock.impl.StockServiceImpl;

public class Activator implements BundleActivator {

    private Timer timer = new Timer();

    public void start(BundleContext context) throws Exception {
        final StockService stockService = new StockServiceImpl();

        timer.schedule(new TimerTask() {

            public void run() {
                try {
                    stockService.exportStock();
                } catch (Exception e) {
                    e.printStackTrace();
                }
            }
        }, 0, 60000);
    }

    public void stop(BundleContext context) throws Exception {
        timer.cancel();
    }
}
```

The MANIFEST.MF source code for this stock bundle should contain the following lines:

```
Manifest-Version: 1.0
Bundle-ManifestVersion: 2
Bundle-Name: Stock Plug-in
Bundle-SymbolicName: com.apress.prodmserver.bookshop.stock
Bundle-Version: 1.0.0
Bundle-Activator: com.apress.prodmserver.bookshop.stock.Activator
Bundle-Vendor: APRESS
Bundle-RequiredExecutionEnvironment: J2SE-1.5
Import-Package: com.apress.prodmserver.bookshop.export,
 com.apress.prodmserver.bookshop.export.impl,
 org.osgi.framework;version="1.3.0"
```

Deploying OSGi Bundles

In the previous section, you created four OSGi bundles for your bookshop system, using Eclipse's rich OSGi support features. Now you can deploy these bundles to an OSGi container and control their life cycles individually. In this section, I will demonstrate how to deploy bundles to the Equinox OSGi container.

Starting Equinox in Eclipse

If you are using Eclipse to develop OSGi bundles, you can simply test and debug the bundles in the Equinox container embedded in Eclipse. First, choose Run Configurations from the Run menu, and then right-click on the OSGi Framework category and choose New to create a new OSGi configuration. By default, all bundles, including workspace bundles and platform bundles, are selected in the table. Since the bundles you developed don't depend on any platform bundles, you can deselect all but the System Bundle (the Equinox implementation itself) under the Target Platform category, as shown in Figure 1-13.

You can assign an arbitrary name to this configuration, such as Bookshop. When you run this configuration, you should see osgi> appear in your console. You can use the command ss to display the short status of all installed bundles.

```
osgi> ss

Framework is launched.

id   State       Bundle
0    ACTIVE      org.eclipse.osgi_3.4.2.R34x_v20080826-1230
1    ACTIVE      com.apress.prodmserver.bookshop.export_1.0.0
2    ACTIVE      com.apress.prodmserver.bookshop.stock_1.0.0
3    ACTIVE      com.apress.prodmserver.bookshop.report_1.0.0
4    ACTIVE      com.apress.prodmserver.bookshop.ranking_1.0.0
```

By default, Eclipse will install and start all the bundles you selected in the configuration dialog besides the OSGi system bundle. You can see that each bundle has an ID, state, and symbolic name.

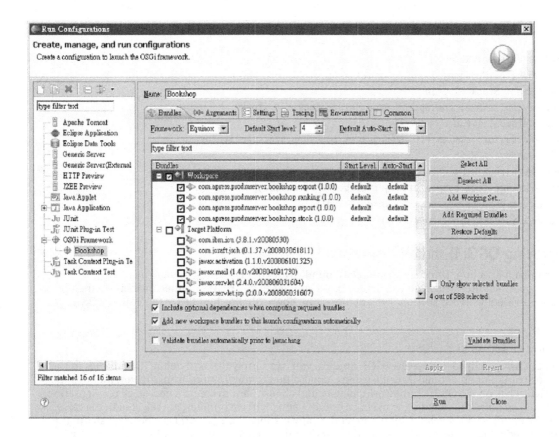

Figure 1-13. *Creating a run configuration for the OSGi bundles*

Starting Equinox from the Command Line

If you are an Eclipse user but would like to start the Equinox container outside Eclipse (for example, on a production server), you can directly execute the org.eclipse.osgi_[version].jar file, which is located in the plugins directory of the Eclipse IDE installation, using the following command:

```
java -jar org.eclipse.osgi_3.4.2.R34x_v20080826-1230.jar -console
```

Otherwise, if you are not using Eclipse but would like to use Equinox as your OSGi container, you can download it from the following web site:

```
http://download.eclipse.org/eclipse/equinox/
```

You can extract the downloaded ZIP file (e.g., eclipse-equinox-3.4.zip) to a directory of your choice and then execute the equivalent JAR file from the command line. Other JAR files in the downloaded ZIP files are mostly platform bundles.

By default, if you start Equinox from the command line, only the OSGi system bundle will be installed. You can install other bundles manually with the Equinox commands (e.g. install file: <*bundle_absolute_path*>). Now if you enter the ss command to view the short status, you will see that only the OSGi system bundle is active:

```
osgi> ss

Framework is launched.

id    State     Bundle
0     ACTIVE    org.eclipse.osgi_3.4.2.R34x_v20080826-1230
```

Exporting Bundles in the Deployable Format

To deploy the bundles you developed in Eclipse to a standalone OSGi container, you have to export them from Eclipse's workspace, usually in the form of JAR files. From Eclipse's File menu, choose Export and then select Deployable Plug-ins and Fragments under the Plug-in Development category, as shown in Figure 1-14.

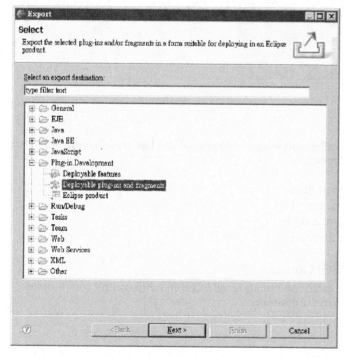

Figure 1-14. *Exporting bundles as deployable Eclipse plug-ins*

In the next screen, select the bundles you want to export and then specify the destination directory (e.g., C:\bookshop), as shown in Figure 1-15.

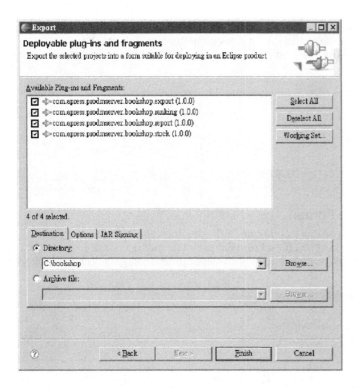

Figure 1-15. *Selecting the bundles to export*

When the wizard finishes, Eclipse will export the bundles you selected as the following JAR files to the destination directory's plugins subdirectory:

```
com.apress.prodmserver.bookshop.report_1.0.0.jar
com.apress.prodmserver.bookshop.export_1.0.0.jar
com.apress.prodmserver.bookshop.ranking_1.0.0.jar
com.apress.prodmserver.bookshop.stock_1.0.0.jar
```

Using Commands in the Equinox OSGi Console

In Equinox's OSGi console, you can use the basic commands listed in Table 1-2 to control your bundles. You can enter **?** or **help** to list all commands in the console.

Table 1-2. *Basic Equinox Commands*

Command	Description
ss	Displays the short status of all installed bundles.
start	Starts the bundle with the given ID or symbolic name.
stop	Stops the bundle with the given ID or symbolic name.
install	Installs the bundle from the given URL.
uninstall	Uninstalls the bundle with the given ID or symbolic name.
update	Updates the bundle with the given ID or symbolic name and the given URL.
refresh	Refreshes the packages of the bundle with the given ID or symbolic name.
help	Displays the entire list of Equinox console commands.

Now let's install the exported bundles one by one using the install command. You have to specify a URL as the command argument. This URL can be the location of a directory or a JAR file that contains the bundle files.

```
osgi> install↵
    file:c:/bookshop/plugins/com.apress.prodmserver.bookshop.report_1.0.0.jar
Bundle id is 1

osgi> install↵
    file:c:/bookshop/plugins/com.apress.prodmserver.bookshop.export_1.0.0.jar
Bundle id is 2

osgi> install↵
    file:c:/bookshop/plugins/com.apress.prodmserver.bookshop.ranking_1.0.0.jar
Bundle id is 3

osgi> install↵
    file:c:/bookshop/plugins/com.apress.prodmserver.bookshop.stock_1.0.0.jar
Bundle id is 4
```

Once installed, a bundle will have the INSTALLED state. You have to start the bundle using the start command, which first resolves the bundle's dependencies so that it has the RESOLVED state and then starts the bundle so that it has the ACTIVE state. You can specify either the bundle ID or the symbolic name as the command argument:

```
osgi> start 1

osgi> start 2

osgi> start 3

osgi> start 4
```

or

```
osgi> start com.apress.prodmserver.bookshop.report

osgi> start com.apress.prodmserver.bookshop.export

osgi> start com.apress.prodmserver.bookshop.ranking

osgi> start com.apress.prodmserver.bookshop.stock
```

To stop a bundle, you can use the stop command with either the bundle ID or the symbolic name:

```
osgi> stop 4
```

or

```
osgi> stop com.apress.prodmserver.bookshop.stock
```

When a running bundle is stopped, its state will change from ACTIVE to RESOLVED. You can again start the bundle.

You can uninstall a bundle using the uninstall command with either the bundle ID or the symbolic name as the command argument:

```
osgi> uninstall 4
```

or

```
osgi> uninstall com.apress.prodmserver.bookshop.stock
```

Suppose you would like to modify the ExportServiceImpl class to keep the last exported file for historical reference, instead of overwriting the file directly. To keep the last exported file, you can simply rename that file to another file with bak as the extension, as in the following code:

```
package com.apress.prodmserver.bookshop.export.impl;
...
public class ExportServiceImpl implements ExportService {
    ...
    public void export(String filename, Object[][] data) throws IOException {
        OutputStream out = null;
        try {
            File file = new File(path + "/" + filename + "."
                    + reportGenerator.getExtension());
            if (file.exists()) {
                File bak = new File(path + "/" + filename + ".bak");
                bak.delete();
                file.renameTo(bak);
            }
            out = new FileOutputStream(file);
            out.write(reportGenerator.generate(data));
        } finally {
            if (out != null) {
                out.close();
            }
        }
    }
}
```

Now you can export this bundle to com.apress.prodmserver.bookshop.export_1.0.0.jar in the destination directory's plugins subdirectory. To update a bundle deployed in Equinox, you can use the update command with either the bundle ID or the symbolic name, and the URL, as the command arguments:

```
osgi> update 2↵
        file:c:/bookshop/plugins/com.apress.prodmserver.bookshop.export_1.0.0.jar
```

Although the export bundle is updated, the ranking bundle and the stock bundle are still using the packages from the old export bundle. Bundles that are registered after the updated bundle (ID: 2) will be resolved to the packages of the update bundle, but bundles installed earlier will keep using older versions of the bundle. In order to update these earlier bundles you must use the refresh command with either the bundle ID or the symbolic name to trigger a package refresh:

```
osgi> refresh 2
```

The OSGi container will compute a graph of bundles that directly or indirectly import the packages exported by the specified bundle (in this case the ranking and stock bundles), and in turn refresh these bundles so that your changes will take effect.

Versioning Packages in Bundles

A highlight of OSGi is that it allows you to deploy more than one version of a bundle in the same OSGi container. This feature is very useful if some of your bundles need to use the new version of a library, while other bundles are using the old version. Besides supporting bundle versioning, OSGi supports versioning individual packages to export. For example, you can assign the value 1.0.0 to the version of both the com.apress.prodmserver.bookshop.export and com.apress.prodmserver.bookshop.export.impl packages in the preceding MANIFEST.MF file as follows:

```
Manifest-Version: 1.0
Bundle-ManifestVersion: 2
Bundle-Name: Export Plug-in
Bundle-SymbolicName: com.apress.prodmserver.bookshop.export
Bundle-Version: 1.0.0
Bundle-Vendor: APRESS
Bundle-RequiredExecutionEnvironment: J2SE-1.5
Import-Package: com.apress.prodmserver.bookshop.report,
 com.apress.prodmserver.bookshop.report.html,
 com.apress.prodmserver.bookshop.report.text
Export-Package: com.apress.prodmserver.bookshop.export;version="1.0.0",
 com.apress.prodmserver.bookshop.export.impl;version="1.0.0"
```

Now suppose you would like to modify the export bundle to accept a time in the export() method so that it will be included in the exported file's name. Before you modify the bundle for this purpose, rename the original project from com.apress.prodmserver.bookshop.export to com.apress.prodmserver.bookshop.export_1.0.0.

■ **Note** When renaming a plug-in project, remember to uncheck the Update References check box. Otherwise, the Bundle-SymbolicName manifest header will be renamed to the new project name also.

Copy this project to a new project named com.apress.prodmserver.bookshop.export_1.1.0. In this new project, modify the ExportService interface to accept a time argument as follows:

```
package com.apress.prodmserver.bookshop.export;

import java.io.IOException;
import java.util.Date;

public interface ExportService {

    public void export(String filename, Date time, Object[][] data)
            throws IOException;
}
```

Next, in the ExportServiceImpl class you can include the formatted time in the exported file's name as follows:

```
package com.apress.prodmserver.bookshop.export.impl;
...
import java.text.DateFormat;
import java.text.SimpleDateFormat;
import java.util.Date;

public class ExportServiceImpl implements ExportService {

    private DateFormat dateFormat = new SimpleDateFormat("yyyyMMddHHmmss");
    ...
    public void export(String filename, Date time, Object[][] data)
            throws IOException {
        OutputStream out = null;
        try {
            File file = new File(path + "/" + filename
                    + dateFormat.format(time) + "."
                    + reportGenerator.getExtension());
            out = new FileOutputStream(file);
            out.write(reportGenerator.generate(data));
        } finally {
            if (out != null) {
                out.close();
            }
        }
    }
}
```

Because you have made changes to this bundle, you should upgrade the bundle version as well as the package versions to 1.1.0.

```
Manifest-Version: 1.0
Bundle-ManifestVersion: 2
Bundle-Name: Export Plug-in
Bundle-SymbolicName: com.apress.prodmserver.bookshop.export
Bundle-Version: 1.1.0
Bundle-Vendor: APRESS
Bundle-RequiredExecutionEnvironment: J2SE-1.5
Import-Package: com.apress.prodmserver.bookshop.report,
 com.apress.prodmserver.bookshop.report.html,
 com.apress.prodmserver.bookshop.report.text
Export-Package: com.apress.prodmserver.bookshop.export;version="1.1.0",
 com.apress.prodmserver.bookshop.export.impl;version="1.1.0"
```

At this moment there are two bundles, the ranking bundle and the stock bundle, importing the export bundle's packages. If no version of the packages is explicitly specified, they will import the highest version (1.1.0 in this case) by default. For example, suppose the stock bundle is not going to use the export bundle's packages of the 1.1.0 version for some reason. In that case, you can explicitly specify the version of the packages to import in the stock bundle's Import-Package header:

```
Manifest-Version: 1.0
Bundle-ManifestVersion: 2
Bundle-Name: Stock Plug-in
Bundle-SymbolicName: com.apress.prodmserver.bookshop.stock
Bundle-Version: 1.0.0
Bundle-Activator: com.apress.prodmserver.bookshop.stock.Activator
Bundle-Vendor: APRESS
Bundle-RequiredExecutionEnvironment: J2SE-1.5
Import-Package: com.apress.prodmserver.bookshop.export;version="[1.0.0, 1.1.0)",
 com.apress.prodmserver.bookshop.export.impl;version="[1.0.0, 1.1.0)",
 org.osgi.framework;version="1.3.0"
```

Note that when you assign a specific value (e.g., 1.0.0) to the package version, you are actually specifying the lower bound of the package version, not the specific package version. In other words, you are asking for "at least" that version. The OSGi container will import a package with the highest version that is higher than or equal to that value (1.1.0 in this case). However, in your case what you actually expect is a package whose version is higher than or equal to 1.0.0 but lower than 1.1.0. The OSGi specifications allow you to specify a range of bundle versions using a mathematical interval notation, for example, [1.0.0, 1.1.0), where brackets [] indicate inclusive values, and parentheses () exclusive values.

For the ranking bundle, you can explicitly specify 1.1.0 (or don't specify any version, to import the highest available version) as the version of the export bundle's packages so that the OSGi container will import packages whose version is higher than or equal to 1.1.0 and has the highest value (1.1.0 in this case).

```
Manifest-Version: 1.0
Bundle-ManifestVersion: 2
Bundle-Name: Ranking Plug-in
Bundle-SymbolicName: com.apress.prodmserver.bookshop.ranking
Bundle-Version: 1.0.0
Bundle-Activator: com.apress.prodmserver.bookshop.ranking.Activator
Bundle-Vendor: APRESS
Bundle-RequiredExecutionEnvironment: J2SE-1.5
Import-Package: com.apress.prodmserver.bookshop.export;version="1.1.0",
 com.apress.prodmserver.bookshop.export.impl;version="1.1.0",
 org.osgi.framework;version="1.3.0"
```

Finally, you must modify the RankingServiceImpl class to pass the current time to the export service.

```
package com.apress.prodmserver.bookshop.ranking.impl;
...
import java.util.Date;

public class RankingServiceImpl implements RankingService {
    ...
    public void exportRanking() throws IOException {
        ...
        exportService.export("ranking", new Date(), ranking);
    }
}
```

For testing purposes, you can start the embedded Equinox container in Eclipse to run the export bundle versions 1.0.0 and 1.1.0 and other bundles. If you use the ss command to show the status of all installed bundles, you should see that there are two export bundles deployed at the same time, whose versions are 1.0.0 and 1.1.0, respectively:

```
osgi> ss

Framework is launched.

id   State      Bundle
0    ACTIVE     org.eclipse.osgi_3.4.2.R34x_v20080826-1230
1    ACTIVE     com.apress.prodmserver.bookshop.report_1.0.0
2    ACTIVE     com.apress.prodmserver.bookshop.export_1.0.0
3    ACTIVE     com.apress.prodmserver.bookshop.ranking_1.0.0
4    ACTIVE     com.apress.prodmserver.bookshop.stock_1.0.0
5    ACTIVE     com.apress.prodmserver.bookshop.export_1.1.0
```

You can also inspect the destination directory (e.g., c:/bookshop) to verify that the stock bundle is using the 1.0.0 packages to export data with a single backup file and the ranking bundle is using the 1.1.0 packages to export data to multiple files, each of which includes the current time in the file name.

In the future, if you decide to upgrade the package imports of the stock bundle to the 1.1.0 version, you can assign the value 1.1.0 to the package versions:

```
Manifest-Version: 1.0
Bundle-ManifestVersion: 2
Bundle-Name: Stock Plug-in
Bundle-SymbolicName: com.apress.prodmserver.bookshop.stock
Bundle-Version: 1.0.0
Bundle-Activator: com.apress.prodmserver.bookshop.stock.Activator
Bundle-Vendor: APRESS
Bundle-RequiredExecutionEnvironment: J2SE-1.5
Import-Package: com.apress.prodmserver.bookshop.export;version="1.1.0",
 com.apress.prodmserver.bookshop.export.impl;version="1.1.0",
 org.osgi.framework;version="1.3.0"
```

Then modify the StockServiceImpl class to pass the current time to the export service accordingly:

```
package com.apress.prodmserver.bookshop.stock.impl;
...
import java.util.Date;

public class StockServiceImpl implements StockService {
    ...
    public void exportStock() throws IOException {
        ...
        exportService.export("stock", new Date(), stock);
    }
}
```

Because you don't need the export bundle version 1.0.0 anymore, you can simply close the project or even delete it from the workspace so that it will not be included in the embedded Equinox container.

Developing OSGi Services

Up to this point, you only have exported and imported packages between bundles. In other words, you have been sharing static resources such as classes and interfaces between bundles. In fact, OSGi also supports exporting and importing dynamic resources—*services*. An OSGi service is simply a Java object that is registered by a bundle and is able to provide services to other bundles.

Each OSGi container maintains a *service registry* for its bundles to register their services. A service provider bundle registers a service object to the service registry under the names of one or more service interfaces and a set of service properties. As a result, the provider bundle can shield its consumers from the implementation details, such as implementation classes and service initialization. When a service consumer bundle needs a service, it simply looks up the service registry for a service reference, providing the service interface's name and optionally a filter string. With this approach, a service consumer can use a service without knowing who is providing it, while a service provider doesn't need to know who is consuming its service. In this way, your system will be more loosely coupled and service-oriented than with the package-sharing approach.

Registering an OSGi Service

First, let's go through an example of registering an OSGi service. From the export bundle, you can register an OSGi service for other bundles to export data from the system. As you can imagine, the best time to register the service to the registry is when the bundle starts. For this purpose you must create an Activator class for the bundle. Then, in its start() method, you have to create a service object and register this object to the registry, while in the stop() method you must remember to unregister the service. The following code performs those steps:

```
package com.apress.prodmserver.bookshop.export;

import org.osgi.framework.BundleActivator;
import org.osgi.framework.BundleContext;
import org.osgi.framework.ServiceRegistration;

import com.apress.prodmserver.bookshop.export.impl.ExportServiceImpl;

public class Activator implements BundleActivator {

    private ServiceRegistration exportServiceRegistration;

    public void start(BundleContext context) throws Exception {
        ExportService exportService = new ExportServiceImpl("c:/bookshop");
        exportServiceRegistration = context.registerService(
                ExportService.class.getName(), exportService, null);
    }

    public void stop(BundleContext context) throws Exception {
        exportServiceRegistration.unregister();
    }
}
```

In both the start() and stop() methods, you can get access to the bundle context through the BundleContext argument. A bundle context provides the registerService() method for a bundle to register a service under the names of one or more service interfaces. In the case of multiple service interfaces, you can pass their names as a string array. You can also specify a set of service properties, such as service description and service ranking, in the third method argument (where null can be passed if no service properties have to be specified). The return value of the registerService() method is a ServiceRegistration object, which you can use to unregister the service in the stop() method.

Before the `Activator` class can be compiled, you must import the `org.osgi.framework` package into this bundle; you can do this either by adding this package to the Imported Packages list in the Dependencies tab or by modifying the `MANIFEST.MF` file directly. Next, you must define the `Activator` class for this bundle. You can define it in the Overview tab's Activator field or by modifying the `MANIFEST.MF` file as follows:

```
Manifest-Version: 1.0
Bundle-ManifestVersion: 2
Bundle-Name: Export Plug-in
Bundle-SymbolicName: com.apress.prodmserver.bookshop.export
Bundle-Version: 1.1.0
Bundle-Activator: com.apress.prodmserver.bookshop.export.Activator
Bundle-Vendor: APRESS
Bundle-RequiredExecutionEnvironment: J2SE-1.5
Import-Package: com.apress.prodmserver.bookshop.report,
 com.apress.prodmserver.bookshop.report.html,
 com.apress.prodmserver.bookshop.report.text,
 org.osgi.framework;version="1.3.0"
Export-Package: com.apress.prodmserver.bookshop.export;version="1.1.0"
```

Most important is that after registering the export service as an OSGi service, you don't need to export the `com.apress.prodmserver.bookshop.export.impl` package to prevent other bundles from instantiating the `ExportServiceImpl` class directly.

Consuming an OSGi Service

Now the export bundle has registered a service to the service registry. Any bundles within the same OSGi container can look up the service by the interface name. Remember that until this moment, in order to use an export service the `RankingServiceImpl` class had to instantiate the `ExportServiceImpl` class and specify the export path; these actions introduced tight coupling between bundles, because the ranking bundle had to deal with the export bundle's implementation details. In terms of OSGi services, the ranking bundle can now simply look up the export service without having to know its implementation details, including the implementation class and service initialization.

Before looking up the service, you should modify the `RankingServiceImpl` class to accept an export service object via constructor injection or setter injection, instead of instantiating the `ExportServiceImpl` class. In the following code I choose constructor injection because the export service is a required dependency:

```
package com.apress.prodmserver.bookshop.ranking.impl;
...
import com.apress.prodmserver.bookshop.export.ExportService;

public class RankingServiceImpl implements RankingService {

    private ExportService exportService;
```

```
public RankingServiceImpl(ExportService exportService) {
        this.exportService = exportService;
    }
    ...
}
```

Then, in the start() method of the ranking bundle's Activator class, you can perform a service lookup and inject the service as follows:

```
package com.apress.prodmserver.bookshop.ranking;
...
import org.osgi.framework.ServiceReference;

import com.apress.prodmserver.bookshop.export.ExportService;

public class Activator implements BundleActivator {
    ...
    private ServiceReference exportServiceReference;

    public void start(BundleContext context) throws Exception {
        exportServiceReference =
                context.getServiceReference(ExportService.class.getName());
        ExportService exportService =
                (ExportService) context.getService(exportServiceReference);

        final RankingService rankingService =
                new RankingServiceImpl(exportService);
        ...
    }

    public void stop(BundleContext context) throws Exception {
        ...
        context.ungetService(exportServiceReference);
    }
}
```

In the start() method, you can call the bundle context's getServiceReference() method to get a service reference by the service interface's name. Note that this method returns only a ServiceReference object, not the actual service object. You can then ask the bundle context to resolve a service reference into a service object by calling its getService() method. Finally, when you won't use a service anymore, you must call the ungetService() method to release the service reference.

Since the ranking bundle doesn't need to instantiate the ExportServiceImpl class anymore, you can remove the com.apress.prodmserver.bookshop.export.impl package import from the MANIFEST.MF file:

```
Manifest-Version: 1.0
Bundle-ManifestVersion: 2
Bundle-Name: Ranking Plug-in
Bundle-SymbolicName: com.apress.prodmserver.bookshop.ranking
Bundle-Version: 1.0.0
Bundle-Activator: com.apress.prodmserver.bookshop.ranking.Activator
Bundle-Vendor: APRESS
Bundle-RequiredExecutionEnvironment: J2SE-1.5
Import-Package: com.apress.prodmserver.bookshop.export;version="1.1.0",
 org.osgi.framework;version="1.3.0"
```

For the stock bundle, you can make similar changes to the StockServiceImpl class, as follows:

```
package com.apress.prodmserver.bookshop.stock.impl;
...
import com.apress.prodmserver.bookshop.export.ExportService;

public class StockServiceImpl implements StockService {

    private ExportService exportService;

    public StockServiceImpl(ExportService exportService) {
        this.exportService = exportService;
    }
    ...
}
```

Then, in the Activator class, perform a service lookup, inject the service into the start() method, and release the service reference in the stop() method:

```
package com.apress.prodmserver.bookshop.stock;
...
import org.osgi.framework.ServiceReference;

import com.apress.prodmserver.bookshop.export.ExportService;

public class Activator implements BundleActivator {
    ...
```

```java
    private ServiceReference exportServiceReference;

    public void start(BundleContext context) throws Exception {
        exportServiceReference =
                context.getServiceReference(ExportService.class.getName());
        ExportService exportService =
                (ExportService) context.getService(exportServiceReference);

        final StockService stockService = new StockServiceImpl(exportService);
        ...
    }

    public void stop(BundleContext context) throws Exception {
        ...
        context.ungetService(exportServiceReference);
    }
}
```

Also, you can remove the `com.apress.prodmserver.bookshop.export.impl` package import from the `MANIFEST.MF` file, as follows:

```
Manifest-Version: 1.0
Bundle-ManifestVersion: 2
Bundle-Name: Stock Plug-in
Bundle-SymbolicName: com.apress.prodmserver.bookshop.stock
Bundle-Version: 1.0.0
Bundle-Activator: com.apress.prodmserver.bookshop.stock.Activator
Bundle-Vendor: APRESS
Bundle-RequiredExecutionEnvironment: J2SE-1.5
Import-Package: com.apress.prodmserver.bookshop.export;version="1.1.0",
 org.osgi.framework;version="1.3.0"
```

When you start the OSGi container to run these bundles, you must ensure that the export bundle is started before the ranking and stock bundles so that they can look up the service successfully. In OSGi, you can specify a *start level* for a bundle. A bundle with a lower start level will start prior to those with the higher level. You can specify a lower start level (e.g., 1) to the export bundle than to the ranking and stock bundles (e.g., 2).

If you start Equinox in Eclipse, you can specify the start levels in the Run Configurations dialog, as shown in Figure 1-16.

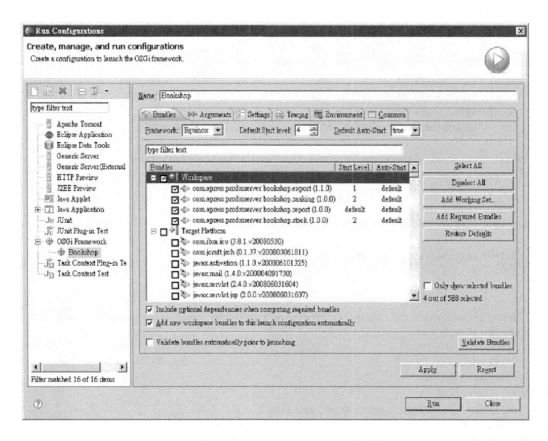

Figure 1-16. *Specifying the start levels in Eclipse's Run Configurations dialog*

If you start Equinox from the command line, you can use the setbsl (set bundle start level) command to set the start level. Note that the first argument of this command is the start level, while the second is either the bundle ID or the symbolic name.

```
osgi> ss

Framework is launched.

id    State        Bundle
0     ACTIVE       org.eclipse.osgi_3.4.2.R34x_v20080826-1230
1     RESOLVED     com.apress.prodmserver.bookshop.report_1.0.0
3     RESOLVED     com.apress.prodmserver.bookshop.ranking_1.0.0
4     RESOLVED     com.apress.prodmserver.bookshop.stock_1.0.0
5     RESOLVED     com.apress.prodmserver.bookshop.export_1.1.0

osgi> setbsl 1 5
Bundle 5 Start Level = 1
```

```
osgi> setbsl 2 3
Bundle 3 Start Level = 2

osgi> setbsl 2 4
Bundle 4 Start Level = 2
```

Switching Between OSGi Service Implementations

As mentioned at the beginning of this section, with OSGi services a consumer can simply use a service without knowing who the provider is. This allows you to switch between different service implementations in a transparent approach. A common pattern in designing an OSGi service is to encapsulate the service interface in a bundle and each service implementation in a separate bundle. You can simply install, uninstall, update, start, and stop bundles to switch between different service implementations.

Following this pattern, let's create a bundle for each ReportGenerator implementation. First, you create the com.apress.prodmserver.bookshop.report.text bundle for the plain text report generator implementation. Remember to check the Generate an Activator box in the wizard. Also, you must import the com.apress.prodmserver.bookshop.report package to this bundle. The MANIFEST.MF source code should look like this:

```
Manifest-Version: 1.0
Bundle-ManifestVersion: 2
Bundle-Name: Text Plug-in
Bundle-SymbolicName: com.apress.prodmserver.bookshop.report.text
Bundle-Version: 1.0.0
Bundle-Activator: com.apress.prodmserver.bookshop.report.text.Activator
Bundle-Vendor: APRESS
Bundle-RequiredExecutionEnvironment: J2SE-1.5
Import-Package: com.apress.prodmserver.bookshop.report,
 org.osgi.framework;version="1.3.0"
```

Then move the TextReportGenerator class from the previous report plug-in project to this project. In the Activator class, create a TextReportGenerator service object and register it to the service registry under the ReportGenerator interface when the bundle starts, and finally unregister the service when the bundle stops. The source code should look like this:

```
package com.apress.prodmserver.bookshop.report.text;

import org.osgi.framework.BundleActivator;
import org.osgi.framework.BundleContext;
import org.osgi.framework.ServiceRegistration;

import com.apress.prodmserver.bookshop.report.ReportGenerator;

public class Activator implements BundleActivator {
```

```
    private ServiceRegistration reportGeneratorRegistration;

    public void start(BundleContext context) throws Exception {
        ReportGenerator reportGenerator = new TextReportGenerator(",");
        reportGeneratorRegistration = context.registerService(
                ReportGenerator.class.getName(), reportGenerator, null);
    }

    public void stop(BundleContext context) throws Exception {
        reportGeneratorRegistration.unregister();
    }
}
```

Next, create the com.apress.prodmserver.bookshop.report.html bundle for the HTML report generator implementation and import the com.apress.prodmserver.bookshop.report package to this bundle. The MANIFEST.MF source code should look like this:

```
Manifest-Version: 1.0
Bundle-ManifestVersion: 2
Bundle-Name: Html Plug-in
Bundle-SymbolicName: com.apress.prodmserver.bookshop.report.html
Bundle-Version: 1.0.0
Bundle-Activator: com.apress.prodmserver.bookshop.report.html.Activator
Bundle-Vendor: APRESS
Bundle-RequiredExecutionEnvironment: J2SE-1.5
Import-Package: com.apress.prodmserver.bookshop.report,
 org.osgi.framework;version="1.3.0"
```

Similarly, move the HtmlReportGenerator class from the previous report plug-in project to this project. In the Activator class, create an HtmlReportGenerator service object and register it to the service registry when the bundle starts, and unregister the service when the bundle stops, as shown in the following code:

```
package com.apress.prodmserver.bookshop.report.html;

import org.osgi.framework.BundleActivator;
import org.osgi.framework.BundleContext;
import org.osgi.framework.ServiceRegistration;

import com.apress.prodmserver.bookshop.report.ReportGenerator;

public class Activator implements BundleActivator {

    private ServiceRegistration reportGeneratorRegistration;
```

```
public void start(BundleContext context) throws Exception {
    ReportGenerator reportGenerator = new HtmlReportGenerator("Export");
    reportGeneratorRegistration = context.registerService(
            ReportGenerator.class.getName(), reportGenerator, null);
}

public void stop(BundleContext context) throws Exception {
    reportGeneratorRegistration.unregister();
}
}
```

Because the report bundle contains only the report generator interface and no implementations, you should remove the html and text implementation packages from its exported packages as follows:

```
Manifest-Version: 1.0
Bundle-ManifestVersion: 2
Bundle-Name: Report Plug-in
Bundle-SymbolicName: com.apress.prodmserver.bookshop.report
Bundle-Version: 1.0.0
Bundle-Vendor: APRESS
Bundle-RequiredExecutionEnvironment: J2SE-1.5
Export-Package: com.apress.prodmserver.bookshop.report
```

Now you have to modify the export bundle to look up a report generator service instead of instantiating one in the ExportServiceImpl class directly. For this purpose, you modify the ExportServiceImpl class to accept a ReportGenerator object as a constructor argument, instead of instantiating one of the ReportGenerator implementations. This can help reduce coupling because the export bundle doesn't need to decide which report generator implementation to use. Even if you switch to another report generator implementation in the future, you needn't modify the ExportServiceImpl class at all. The modified code looks like this:

```
package com.apress.prodmserver.bookshop.export.impl;
...
public class ExportServiceImpl implements ExportService {
    ...
    private ReportGenerator reportGenerator;

    public ExportServiceImpl(ReportGenerator reportGenerator, String path) {
        this.reportGenerator = reportGenerator;
        this.path = path;
    }
    ...
}
```

Finally, in the start() method of the export bundle's Activator class, you can look up a report generator using the ReportGenerator interface's name and use this generator to create an ExportService object before registering it to the service registry. Now the export bundle is completely unaware of which report generator implementation is being used, as shown in the following code:

```java
package com.apress.prodmserver.bookshop.export;

import org.osgi.framework.BundleActivator;
import org.osgi.framework.BundleContext;
import org.osgi.framework.ServiceReference;
import org.osgi.framework.ServiceRegistration;

import com.apress.prodmserver.bookshop.export.impl.ExportServiceImpl;
import com.apress.prodmserver.bookshop.report.ReportGenerator;

public class Activator implements BundleActivator {

    private ServiceReference reportGeneratorReference;
    private ServiceRegistration exportServiceRegistration;

    public void start(BundleContext context) throws Exception {
        reportGeneratorReference =
                context.getServiceReference(ReportGenerator.class.getName());
        ReportGenerator reportGenerator =
                (ReportGenerator) context.getService(reportGeneratorReference);

        ExportService exportService =
                new ExportServiceImpl(reportGenerator, "c:/bookshop");
        exportServiceRegistration = context.registerService(
                ExportService.class.getName(), exportService, null);
    }

    public void stop(BundleContext context) throws Exception {
        exportServiceRegistration.unregister();
        context.ungetService(reportGeneratorReference);
    }
}
```

Since the export bundle no longer needs to instantiate a report generator implementation class, you can remove the imports of the com.apress.prodmserver.bookshop.report.html and com.apress.prodmserver.bookshop.report.text packages from the MANIFEST.MF file:

```
Manifest-Version: 1.0
Bundle-ManifestVersion: 2
Bundle-Name: Export Plug-in
Bundle-SymbolicName: com.apress.prodmserver.bookshop.export
Bundle-Version: 1.1.0
Bundle-Activator: com.apress.prodmserver.bookshop.export.Activator
Bundle-Vendor: APRESS
Bundle-RequiredExecutionEnvironment: J2SE-1.5
Import-Package: com.apress.prodmserver.bookshop.report,
 org.osgi.framework;version="1.3.0"
Export-Package: com.apress.prodmserver.bookshop.export;version="1.1.0"
```

When you start the OSGi container to run these bundles, you have to ensure that the start levels are set in the following order:

1. `com.apress.prodmserver.bookshop.report.text` or `com.apress.prodmserver.bookshop.report.html`
2. `com.apress.prodmserver.bookshop.export`
3. `com.apress.prodmserver.bookshop.ranking` and `com.apress.prodmserver.bookshop.stock`

Only in this order can the OSGi services be registered and looked up correctly. Moreover, you should only start either the text report bundle or the HTML report bundle, not both, since they are exclusive implementations for the current system. If both are started, the OSGi container will return the one with the highest service ranking (if the rankings have been specified, which is not the case here) or with the lowest service ID (a service registered first will have a lower service ID). If you start Equinox in Eclipse, you can prevent either of the bundles from auto-starting in the Run Configurations dialog, depending on which report format your system prefers.

In a running OSGi container, you can install, uninstall, update, start, and stop the bundles dynamically to switch between different report generator implementations, and even add new implementations without modifying an existing bundle and restarting the entire running system. For example, if you have installed both the text and HTML report bundles but only started the text report bundle, you can use the following commands to switch from a text report generator to an HTML report generator:

```
osgi> ss

Framework is launched.

id  State      Bundle
0   ACTIVE     org.eclipse.osgi_3.4.2.R34x_v20080826-1230
1   ACTIVE     com.apress.prodmserver.bookshop.report_1.0.0
3   ACTIVE     com.apress.prodmserver.bookshop.ranking_1.0.0
4   ACTIVE     com.apress.prodmserver.bookshop.stock_1.0.0
5   ACTIVE     com.apress.prodmserver.bookshop.export_1.1.0
6   ACTIVE     com.apress.prodmserver.bookshop.report.text_1.0.0
7   RESOLVED   com.apress.prodmserver.bookshop.report.html_1.0.0
```

```
osgi> start 7

osgi> stop 6

osgi> stop 5

osgi> start 5

osgi> stop 3

osgi> start 3

osgi> stop 4

osgi> start 4
```

Here you have to restart the export bundle because it looks up a report generator service once in the activator's start() method. So even if you stop the text report bundle and start the HTML report bundle, the export bundle won't be aware that a new report generator service is available, and the previous text report generator service will be still in use. When you restart the export bundle, it will look up a new report generator service from the registry in the activator's start() method, and this time the HTML report generator service will be returned. Also note that after the export bundle's restart, you must restart the ranking bundle and the stock bundle in turn for the same reason.

In a production system, there may be many bundles registering services and consuming services from each other. It won't be practical for you to restart each bundle in the service dependency graph in turn each time you update an OSGi service. This will also affect the dynamic nature of an OSGi-based system. A more reasonable way is to keep track of the changes of an OSGi service, instead of simply looking up the service once at bundle startup. Next you will see how to do that with a service tracker.

Tracking OSGi Services

OSGi services are dynamic in the sense that they can be registered and unregistered by bundles any time. So if your bundle looks up a service from the registry only once at startup and caches it to use throughout the entire life cycle, the cached service instance may become stale when the provider bundle has unregistered the service, and then you have to restart the bundle to look up a new service instance. Otherwise, if you look up a service from the registry each time you use it, you have to take the lookup overhead into account.

The OSGi specifications define that when an OSGi service is registered or unregistered, the OSGi container must trigger an event to notify every bundle. The best practice for accessing an OSGi service is to cache the service instance at bundle startup and listen to the container events about service registration and unregistration, and then look up and release the service reference accordingly. The OSGi specifications provide a ServiceTracker class for you to track OSGi services. A service tracker can automatically track a set of services that match the search criteria by listening to service events.

Now let's modify the export bundle to use a service tracker to track the report generator service. To use a service tracker, you must first import the org.osgi.util.tracker package. Modify the MANIFEST.MF file as follows:

```
Manifest-Version: 1.0
Bundle-ManifestVersion: 2
Bundle-Name: Export Plug-in
Bundle-SymbolicName: com.apress.prodmserver.bookshop.export
Bundle-Version: 1.1.0
Bundle-Activator: com.apress.prodmserver.bookshop.export.Activator
Bundle-Vendor: APRESS
Bundle-RequiredExecutionEnvironment: J2SE-1.5
Import-Package: com.apress.prodmserver.bookshop.report,
 org.osgi.framework;version="1.3.0",
 org.osgi.util.tracker;version="1.3.3"
Export-Package: com.apress.prodmserver.bookshop.export;version="1.1.0"
```

In the bundle activator, instead of looking up a service reference and getting a service via the bundle context, you can simply create a service tracker for your target service interface as follows:

```java
package com.apress.prodmserver.bookshop.export;

import org.osgi.framework.BundleActivator;
import org.osgi.framework.BundleContext;
import org.osgi.framework.ServiceRegistration;
import org.osgi.util.tracker.ServiceTracker;

import com.apress.prodmserver.bookshop.export.impl.ExportServiceImpl;
import com.apress.prodmserver.bookshop.report.ReportGenerator;

public class Activator implements BundleActivator {

    private ServiceTracker reportGeneratorTracker;
    private ServiceRegistration exportServiceRegistration;

    public void start(BundleContext context) throws Exception {
        reportGeneratorTracker =
                new ServiceTracker(context, ReportGenerator.class.getName(), null);
        reportGeneratorTracker.open();

        ExportService exportService =
                new ExportServiceImpl(reportGeneratorTracker, "c:/bookshop");
        exportServiceRegistration = context.registerService(
                ExportService.class.getName(), exportService, null);
    }
```

```
    public void stop(BundleContext context) throws Exception {
        exportServiceRegistration.unregister();
        reportGeneratorTracker.close();
    }
}
```

When you make a call to the open() method of a service tracker, it will prepare the initial set of services matched by the criteria and start tracking the target services by listening to the container events about service registration and unregistration. Finally, when the bundle stops, you must remember to stop the tracker from tracking the target services by calling its close() method.

Then you must pass a service tracker to the ExportServiceImpl class so that it can get a service instance from the tracker every time it has to use the service, as demonstrated in the following code:

```
package com.apress.prodmserver.bookshop.export.impl;
...
import org.osgi.util.tracker.ServiceTracker;

public class ExportServiceImpl implements ExportService {

    private ServiceTracker reportGeneratorTracker;
    ...
    public ExportServiceImpl(ServiceTracker reportGeneratorTracker, String path) {
        this.reportGeneratorTracker = reportGeneratorTracker;
        this.path = path;
    }

    public void export(String filename, Date time, Object[][] data)
            throws IOException {
        ReportGenerator reportGenerator =
                (ReportGenerator) reportGeneratorTracker.getService();
        if (reportGenerator == null) {
            throw new RuntimeException("Report generator service not available");
        }
        ...
    }
}
```

Note that in an OSGi environment, you can't ensure that a service is always available. In case of service unavailability, such as when the provider bundle has not been started yet or has unregistered its service, the service tracker will return null when you call its getService() method. In this case, you can choose to wait until the service becomes available by calling the service tracker's waitForService() method, or simply throw an exception to notify the caller of service unavailability. For the current bookshop system, this export() method is called by the timer tasks of the ranking and stock bundles, so this code simply throws a RuntimeException for the timer thread to handle, in order not to disturb the timers.

Thanks to the service tracker, you don't need to restart the export, ranking, and stock bundles in turn when switching to a different report generator implementation. The service tracker will listen to the container events about registration and unregistration of the report generator service and update its internal service reference automatically. Now you can simply start and stop the report generator bundles to complete the switch, as follows:

```
osgi> ss

Framework is launched.

id  State       Bundle
0   ACTIVE      org.eclipse.osgi_3.4.2.R34x_v20080826-1230
1   ACTIVE      com.apress.prodmserver.bookshop.report_1.0.0
3   ACTIVE      com.apress.prodmserver.bookshop.ranking_1.0.0
4   ACTIVE      com.apress.prodmserver.bookshop.stock_1.0.0
5   ACTIVE      com.apress.prodmserver.bookshop.export_1.1.0
6   ACTIVE      com.apress.prodmserver.bookshop.report.text_1.0.0
7   RESOLVED    com.apress.prodmserver.bookshop.report.html_1.0.0

osgi> start 7

osgi> stop 6
```

You can modify the ranking and stock bundles as well to utilize a service tracker to better access the export service. First, let's add the org.osgi.util.tracker package to their imported packages in the MANIFEST.MF files:

```
Manifest-Version: 1.0
Bundle-ManifestVersion: 2
Bundle-Name: Ranking Plug-in
Bundle-SymbolicName: com.apress.prodmserver.bookshop.ranking
Bundle-Version: 1.0.0
Bundle-Activator: com.apress.prodmserver.bookshop.ranking.Activator
Bundle-Vendor: APRESS
Bundle-RequiredExecutionEnvironment: J2SE-1.5
Import-Package: com.apress.prodmserver.bookshop.export,
  org.osgi.framework;version="1.3.0",
  org.osgi.util.tracker;version="1.3.3"


Manifest-Version: 1.0
Bundle-ManifestVersion: 2
Bundle-Name: Stock Plug-in
Bundle-SymbolicName: com.apress.prodmserver.bookshop.stock
Bundle-Version: 1.0.0
Bundle-Activator: com.apress.prodmserver.bookshop.stock.Activator
Bundle-Vendor: APRESS
```

```
Bundle-RequiredExecutionEnvironment: J2SE-1.5
Import-Package: com.apress.prodmserver.bookshop.export,
 org.osgi.framework;version="1.3.0",
 org.osgi.util.tracker;version="1.3.3"
```

Next, modify their activator classes to create a service tracker for the export service, open the tracker in the start() method, and close it in the stop() method:

```java
package com.apress.prodmserver.bookshop.ranking;
...
import org.osgi.util.tracker.ServiceTracker;

public class Activator implements BundleActivator {

    private ServiceTracker exportServiceTracker;
    ...
    public void start(BundleContext context) throws Exception {
        exportServiceTracker =
                new ServiceTracker(context, ExportService.class.getName(), null);
        exportServiceTracker.open();

        final RankingService rankingService =
                new RankingServiceImpl(exportServiceTracker);
        ...
    }

    public void stop(BundleContext context) throws Exception {
        ...
        exportServiceTracker.close();
    }
}

package com.apress.prodmserver.bookshop.stock;
...
import org.osgi.util.tracker.ServiceTracker;

public class Activator implements BundleActivator {

    private ServiceTracker exportServiceTracker;
    ...
```

```
public void start(BundleContext context) throws Exception {
    exportServiceTracker =
            new ServiceTracker(context, ExportService.class.getName(), null);
    exportServiceTracker.open();

    final StockService stockService =
            new StockServiceImpl(exportServiceTracker);
    ...
}

public void stop(BundleContext context) throws Exception {
    ...
    exportServiceTracker.close();
}
}
```

Finally, pass the service tracker to the RankingServiceImpl and StockServiceImpl classes. Every time these classes need to use an export service, make a call to the getService() method of the service tracker. In case of service unavailability, throw a RuntimeException for the caller to handle:

```
package com.apress.prodmserver.bookshop.ranking.impl;
...
import org.osgi.util.tracker.ServiceTracker;

public class RankingServiceImpl implements RankingService {

    private ServiceTracker exportServiceTracker;

    public RankingServiceImpl(ServiceTracker exportServiceTracker) {
        this.exportServiceTracker = exportServiceTracker;
    }

    public void exportRanking() throws IOException {
        ExportService exportService =
                (ExportService) exportServiceTracker.getService();
        if (exportService == null) {
            throw new RuntimeException("Export service not available");
        }
        ...
    }
}
```

```
package com.apress.prodmserver.bookshop.stock.impl;
...
import org.osgi.util.tracker.ServiceTracker;

public class StockServiceImpl implements StockService {

    private ServiceTracker exportServiceTracker;

    public StockServiceImpl(ServiceTracker exportServiceTracker) {
        this.exportServiceTracker = exportServiceTracker;
    }

    public void exportStock() throws IOException {
        ExportService exportService =
                (ExportService) exportServiceTracker.getService();
        if (exportService == null) {
            throw new RuntimeException("Export service not available");
        }
        ...
    }
}
```

Now, by using service trackers in the bundles, you no longer need to start the bundles in a specific order as before. Consider that if you start the ranking and stock bundles before the export and report implementation bundles, the timer tasks of the ranking and stock bundles will catch a RuntimeException because the export service or the report generator services will not have been available yet. However, if those bundles become ready in the next timer tasks, the ranking and stock bundles will be able to consume the services and therefore begin to work immediately.

Enterprise OSGi

The OSGi topics explored in the previous sections on bundle packaging, versioning and services are all related to OSGi's core specification. This means that irrespective of the realm in which OSGi is used—such as an embedded application or web application—each of these concepts is applicable and works in the same manner.

It's left to an OSGi implementation (or *OSGi container*, as I've called it in this chapter) to support these features, which form part of the OSGi specification—much as a Java EE application server implementation needs to support the Java EE specification. However, given OSGi's broader scope, this has created a void in supporting peripheral case scenarios belonging to the enterprise.

For this reason, the OSGi alliance, which oversees the specification's direction, created the OSGi Enterprise Expert Group (EEG). The EEG work spans a series of requests for comments (RFCs) that form part of the OSGi Release 4 (R4) version 4.2. They include the following:

RFC 66 (OSGi and web applications): Describes how enterprise web applications written to Java Servlets and JSP specifications are supported in OSGi, in addition to describing a model for web application components to access OSGi services.

RFC 98 (Transactions in OSGi): Defines a transaction model and identifies Java transaction APIs for use in OSGi environments, including embedded and constrained environments.

RFC 119 (Distributed OSGi): Defines a minimal level of function for distributed OSGi processing, including service discovery and access to and from external environments.

RFC 122 (Database access): Describes approaches for accessing JDBC resources in an OSGi environment.

RFC 124 (Blueprint Service): Describes a set of core features widely used in enterprise programming that are used outside of OSGi. These include a rich component model for declaring components within a bundle and for instantiating, configuring, assembling, and decorating such components when a bundle is started.

RFC 139 (JMX control of OSGi): Defines a Java Management Extension(JMX)-compliant model for managing the OSGi framework and critical compendium services.

RFC 142 (JNDI and OSGi integration): Describes how Java Naming and Directory Interface(JNDI) can be integrated into an OSGi environment.

Just as the OSGi implementations mentioned in this chapter's "Introducing OSGi Containers" section are said to be compliant with OSGi's R4 core specification, the SpringSource dm Server objective is to be compliant with these enterprise OSGi RFCs.

Among these RFCs, two merit particular attention: RFC 66 and RFC 124. As the dm Server integrates with Eclipse Equinox as its OSGi container and allows the deployment of OSGi-based web applications, the dm Server uses the reference implementation (RI) for RFC 66, which is known as the OSGi *web* container.

The importance of the dm Server using OSGi's web container or RFC 66 is that all OSGi web applications designed for the dm Server are guaranteed OSGi standard compatibility—just as Java web applications designed for Java EE servers are ensured standard compatibility.

At the time of this writing, the OSGi RI for RFC 66 used by the dm Server is the only implementation of its kind—unlike the OSGi core specification, which as already mentioned has several implementations (including Equinox, Felix, and Knopflerfish). It should also be mentioned that just like its OSGi core container counterpart, the OSGi web container (you can find an introduction to it at `http://blog.springsource.com/2009/05/27/introduction-to-the-osgi-web-container/`) can also be used in standalone fashion—that is, without the dm Server. In other words, the dm Server is more than just an OSGi web container, but this will become clearer as the book progresses.

In addition, the reference implementation for OSGi's RFC 124 (Blueprint service) is based on the foundations of the Spring Dynamic Modules (Spring-DM) project. Spring-DM is another building block for the dm Server and is explored fully in the next chapter.

Summary

In this chapter, you saw why you need OSGi for building dynamic and modular systems, and you learned the advantages gained by using OSGi. You had a basic introduction to the OSGi technology, the composition of OSGi bundles, and several open-source OSGi containers popular in the community.

You also learned how to develop OSGi bundles with Eclipse's OSGi support features, which provide wizards and GUIs to help you develop bundles more quickly. You can start the Equinox OSGi container either in Eclipse for testing and debugging purposes, or from the command line in a production environment. Then you can export the bundles you developed in Eclipse as JAR files and deploy them to Equinox.

The dependencies of OSGi bundles are managed by the OSGi container and resolved at runtime. OSGi is flexible enough to allow more than one version of a particular bundle running at the same time. In addition to its support for bundle versioning, OSGi supports versioning individual packages to export.

OSGi supports registering and consuming services between bundles, and it allows you to switch between different service implementations dynamically at runtime. By using OSGi services, you make your system more loosely coupled and more service-oriented. OSGi also provides a utility called a service tracker to automatically track the changes of an OSGi service by listening to service registration and unregistration events, and thus address the dynamic nature of OSGi services.

In the next chapter, you will learn about the Spring Dynamic Modules for OSGi Service Platforms—a Spring Portfolio project that combines the advantages of the Spring Framework and OSGi to help you develop OSGi-based applications.

CHAPTER 2

■ ■ ■

Developing Bundles with Spring Dynamic Modules

Spring Dynamic Modules for OSGi Service Platforms (Spring-DM or Spring-OSGi for short) is a Spring Portfolio project that allows developers to use the Spring Framework to develop applications that can run on the OSGi platform. Spring-DM also simplifies the development of OSGi bundles by using the Spring Framework's concepts and features. In addition, it provides the foundation for the Blueprint Service (RFC 124), which forms part of OSGi Release 4 (R4) version 4.2.

Most importantly, the dm Server relies on Spring-DM to simplify the development and deployment of OSGi bundles used in applications running on the server. Spring-DM brings many of the Spring framework's characteristics (such as dependency injection and XML file configuration) to the OSGi world, so instead of relying on some of OSGi's APIs to develop bundles, as you did in the last chapter, you can take advantage of the greater degree of simplicity Spring-DM offers for this process. In this chapter, you will learn how to develop bundles using Spring-DM, which is a prerequisite to learning about application development for the dm Server. This chapter covers the following topics:

- Introducing the major features and mechanisms of Spring-DM
- Setting up Spring-DM in your OSGi container
- Configuring Spring-DM for your application bundles
- Importing and exporting OSGi services with Spring-DM
- Advanced Spring-DM configurations for OSGi services

To understand the contents of this chapter, you should already be familiar with basic Spring Framework concepts and usage. If you are new to Spring, I suggest reading the first three chapters of the book *Spring Recipes.*[1]

When reading this chapter, keep in mind that it focuses on the common features and mechanisms of Spring-DM and is not a complete reference to it. Spring-DM has many advanced but relatively low-level features that are out of this chapter's scope. For a complete reference to Spring-DM, you can read the book *Spring Dynamic Modules for OSGi.*[2]

Introduction to Spring-DM

The Spring Portfolio is a series of open-source projects, including the Spring Framework project and other projects that extend and build on the principles of the Spring Framework. Spring-DM is a Spring Portfolio project that integrates the Spring Framework with OSGi to simplify the building of dynamic

---

[1] Gary Mak, *Spring Recipes: A Problem-Solution Approach* (Berkeley, CA: Apress, 2008),
[2] Daniel Rubio, *Pro Spring Dynamic Modules for OSGi Service Platforms* (Berkeley, CA: Apress, 2009)

and modular applications, in addition to serving as the foundation for OSGi's standardized Blueprint Service (RFC 124). In this section, I will introduce the major features and mechanisms of Spring-DM.

WHEN WILL SPRING-DM BECOME THE BLUEPRINT SERVICE (RFC 124)?

The estimated time line for Spring-DM becoming the reference implementation for OSGi's Blueprint Service (RFC-124) is the Spring-DM 2.0 version. Currently, Spring-DM's latest release is the 1.2 version.

For a dm Server user, however, the particular Spring-DM version used by the dm Server should be of little concern, since conceptually Spring-DM and the Blueprint Service (RFC 124) are based on the same principles.

The Major Features of Spring-DM

The development goal of Spring-DM is to extend the Spring Framework's usage scope to the OSGi platform. Spring-DM integrates Spring's simple and flexible programming model with the OSGi platform's dynamic and modular approaches, allowing developers to use Spring's programming concepts (e.g., dependency injection and aspect-oriented programming) and powerful features for enterprise support (e.g., web support, persistence support, and transaction management) in building applications that can run on the OSGi platform. The major features of Spring-DM include the following:

- Automatically discovering Spring-based bundles and instantiating a Spring application context for each bundle discovered
- Supporting the installation of a web container (e.g., Tomcat or Jetty) as a bundle and deploying WAR bundles to the installed web container automatically
- Exporting a Spring bean in the application context as an OSGi service via simple XML configurations
- Dynamically discovering and importing an OSGi service reference as a bean via simple XML configurations
- Managing OSGi's services dynamics, such as refreshing updated services and proxying service interfaces for pending services that have yet to be deployed
- Providing an integration testing framework that can automatically start the target OSGi container for running bundle integration tests

At the time of writing, the current stable release of Spring-DM is 1.1.2, while 1.2 is in its milestone release. Spring-DM requires Java 1.4 or higher versions and supports the OSGi R4 specifications. That means Spring-DM can run in any OSGi R4-compliant container, and it has been officially tested against the following container versions:

- Equinox 3.2.2
- Apache Felix 1.0.3
- Knopflerfish 2.0.4

OSGi Bundles and Spring Application Contexts

The heart of the Spring Framework is a lightweight IoC (inversion of control) container that manages POJOs (plain old Java objects) as its components, allowing developers to use dependency injection to decouple the dependencies between the components. The context of a Spring application, which is also called the *application context*, contains a number of components managed by the Spring IoC container, and these components are also called *beans*. A powerful feature of the Spring IoC container is that it can add enterprise services to its beans in a declarative manner and can integrate with many enterprise technologies.

Application Contexts of an Enterprise Application

An enterprise Spring application may contain more than one application context, organized in a hierarchical structure. For example, a Spring application with web interfaces and database persistence can define service- and persistence-layer beans in the root application context and define web-layer beans in a child application context that refers to the root application context as its parent, as illustrated in Figure 2-1. Child application contexts can access beans defined in the parent application context, but not vice versa.

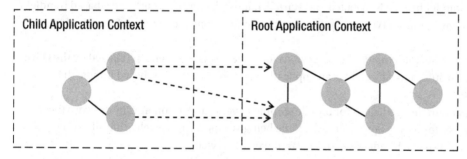

Figure 2-1. *Application contexts of an enterprise application*

Application Contexts of Bundles

In OSGi, the deployment and modularity unit is a bundle, which can be installed, uninstalled, updated, started, and stopped independently and dynamically. Like a typical Java/Java EE application, a bundle may have its internal states represented by a group of objects, some of which can be exported as OSGi services for other bundles to consume. By using the Spring IoC container to manage the objects, you can make use of dependency injection to decouple dependencies and configure the objects with Spring's simple and flexible approaches, such as via XML or annotations.

Since a bundle represents a single module of an application, it is a more fine-grained unit than a complete application. When you use Spring-DM, a properly configured bundle in the ACTIVE state will have an application context created. The application context is responsible for instantiating, managing, and wiring the objects (beans) within the bundle. The beans can optionally be exported as OSGi services so that they can be accessed between the application contexts of different bundles, as illustrated in Figure 2-2, in which the circles represent beans and the triangles represent OSGi services and references.

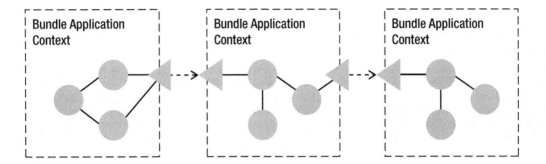

Figure 2-2. *Application contexts of bundles*

The Spring-DM Extender Bundle

Spring-DM determines whether a bundle is Spring-based and requires an application context through its *extender bundle*, which works in the following way:

1. Once the extender bundle is installed and started, it looks for any existing Spring-based bundles that are already in the ACTIVE state and in turn creates an application context for each of these bundles.

2. In the ACTIVE state, the extender bundle listens for bundle starting events published by the OSGi container and automatically creates an application context for a Spring-based bundle that is newly started.

3. The extender bundle also listens for bundle stopping events and automatically destroys the application context of the Spring-based bundle being stopped, further releasing all the resources associated with such a bundle (e.g., unregistering OSGi services).

4. When the extender bundle is stopped, it will destroy all the application contexts it previously created.

    The extender bundle recognizes that a bundle is Spring-based if either of the following is true:

    • The bundle contains a META-INF/spring directory in the classpath root, and that directory contains one or more files with the xml extension. All these XML files will be loaded as Spring bean configuration files for creating the application context.

    • The bundle's manifest file (META-INF/MANIFEST.MF) contains the Spring-Context header, which specifies the locations of one or more bean configuration files used for creating the application context.

Exporting and Importing OSGi Services

A Spring-based bundle can export its objects as OSGi services for other bundles to consume, and it can also import OSGi service references from other bundles. When using Spring-DM to manage the bundle application context, you can selectively export a local bean as an OSGi service and import an OSGi service reference as a local bean, via simple XML configurations without programming against the OSGi API. Spring-DM provides the osgi schema, which defines XML elements such as <service> and <reference> for these purposes.

Exporting a Spring Bean as an OSGi Service

A Spring bean exported as an OSGi service using the <service> element will be automatically registered to the service registry when the bundle's application context is created for the first time. The service will be unregistered automatically when the bundle is stopped, which destroys the application context.

Importing an OSGi Service Reference as a Spring Bean

Spring-DM can also look up an OSGi service from the service registry and import the service reference as a Spring bean using the <reference> element. The reference bean can be injected into other beans for their uses. Because OSGi is dynamic, however, an OSGi service may become unavailable (and therefore the service reference will become stale) at any time, even if it has already been imported by other bundles. For this reason, Spring-DM will create a proxy that forwards calls to the service reference but does not use the actual service reference as the reference bean to inject into other beans. When a call is made to a proxy whose service reference is not available at the moment, the proxy will wait (by default the timeout is 5 minutes) for the service until it can look up a satisfied service from the service registry. If it cannot find a satisfied service before the timeout expires, Spring-DM will then throw an exception to indicate that the OSGi service is unavailable.

Setting Up Spring-DM

Before you start creating bundles using Spring-DM, you must download its distribution and install its bundles to your OSGi container to complete the setup process.

Be advised that the dm Server comes pre-installed with Spring-DM, so many of the installation and configuration (e.g., logging) steps outlined next are either unnecessary or not applicable to the dm Server. However, I would recommend you attempt to do the following exercise as it will help you gain a stronger understanding of how Spring-DM works.

Downloading and Installing Spring-DM

As a Spring Portfolio project, Spring-DM can be downloaded from the official SpringSource community web site:

http://www.springsource.org/download

As noted earlier, the current stable release of Spring-DM at the time of writing is 1.1.2. Choose this version to download, and you will be directed to SourceForge (http://sourceforge.net/), an extensive open-source project repository, to download a Spring-DM distribution, as shown in Figure 2-3.

As you can see, a Spring-DM release includes two distributions that you can download. The first contains the complete Spring-DM project, including the distribution bundles, third-party libraries, documentation, source code, and sample applications, while the second contains only the distribution bundles and documentation. Of these, I recommend that you download the distribution with dependencies (`spring-osgi-1.1.2-with-dependencies.zip`) so that you can more conveniently access the third-party libraries used by Spring-DM.

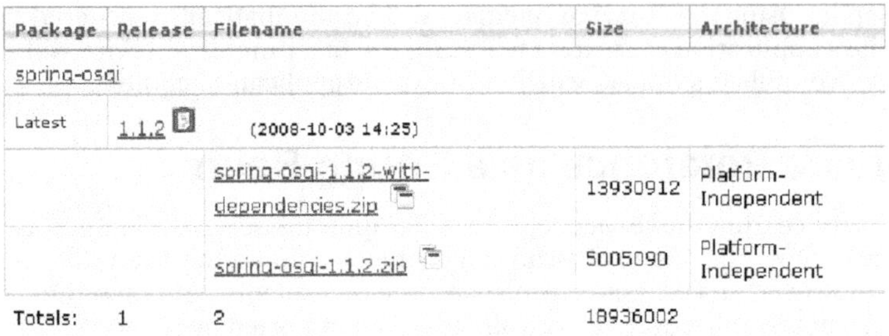

Package	Release	Filename	Size	Architecture
spring-osgi				
Latest	1.1.2	(2008-10-03 14:25)		
		spring-osgi-1.1.2-with-dependencies.zip	13930912	Platform-Independent
		spring-osgi-1.1.2.zip	5005090	Platform-Independent
Totals:	1	2	18936002	

Figure 2-3. *Downloading a Spring-DM distribution*

After downloading a Spring-DM distribution, simply extract the file to a directory of your choice (e.g., `c:\spring-osgi-1.1.2`) to complete the installation.

Installing Spring-DM Bundles to the OSGi Container

As mentioned earlier in this chapter, Spring-DM will automatically create and maintain an application context for each properly configured bundle via its extender bundle. In order to enable the extender bundle, you must install this bundle and its dependent bundles to the same OSGi container. In the `dist` directory of the Spring-DM installation you can find the required Spring-DM bundles as listed in Table 2-1.

Table 2-1. *Required Spring-DM Bundles*

Bundle	Symbolic Name	Description
spring-osgi-core↵ -1.1.2.jar	org.springframework.bundle.osgi.core	The Spring-DM core implementation bundle
spring-osgi-extender↵ -1.1.2.jar	org.springframework.bundle.osgi.extender	The Spring-DM extender bundle
spring-osgi-io↵ -1.1.2.jar	org.springframework.bundle.osgi.io	The Spring-DM I/O support library bundle

All these bundles comply with the OSGi R4 specifications, so they can be installed to any OSGi R4-compliant container, including Equinox 3.2 and above, Felix, and Knopflerfish 2. Following this book's practice, I will demonstrate how to install these bundles to Equinox. If you start Equinox directly from the command line, you can only install these bundles using the console commands install and start. However, if you are developing your bundles and start Equinox in Eclipse for testing purposes, you should import these bundles into Eclipse's workspace first. From Eclipse's File menu choose Import ➤ Plug-in Development ➤ Plug-ins and Fragments, as shown in Figure 2-4.

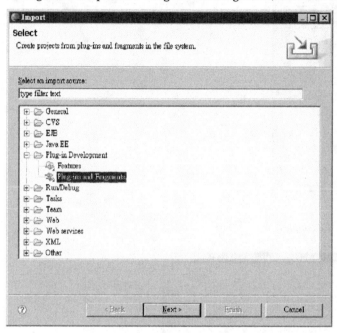

Figure 2-4. *Importing bundles to Eclipse's workspace*

In the next screen, specify the dist directory of the Spring-DM installation as the plug-in location, as shown in Figure 2-5.

Next, you can select the Spring-DM bundles listed in Table 2-1 to import into the Eclipse workspace, as shown in Figure 2-6. Note that each bundle's symbolic name, not the JAR file name, is displayed for your selection.

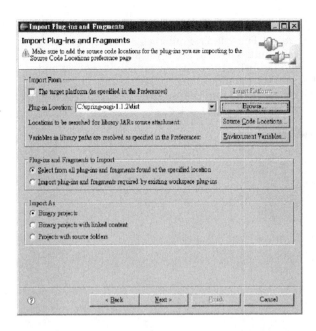

Figure 2-5. *Specifying the location of Spring-DM's bundles*

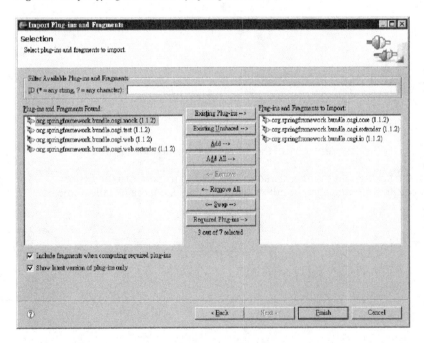

Figure 2-6. *Selecting the Spring-DM bundles to import*

These Spring-DM bundles depend on several modules of the Spring Framework as well as other third-party libraries, whose corresponding OSGi bundles can be found in the lib directory of the Spring-DM installation, as listed in Table 2-2.

Table 2-2. Spring-DM's Dependent Bundles

Bundle	Symbolic Name	Description
spring-aop-2.5.5.jar	org.springframework.bundle↩ .spring.aop	The Spring Framework AOP module
spring-beans-2.5.5.jar	org.springframework.bundle↩ .spring.beans	The Spring Framework Beans module
spring-context-2.5.5.jar	org.springframework.bundle↩ .spring.context	The Spring Framework Context module
spring-core-2.5.5.jar	org.springframework.bundle↩ .spring.core	The Spring Framework Core module
com.springsource.org↩ .aopalliance-1.0.0.jar	com.springsource.org↩ .aopalliance	The AOP Alliance library
com.springsource.edu.emory↩ .mathcs.backport-3.1.0.jar	com.springsource.edu.emory↩ .mathcs.backport	The concurrency library backport, required only for Java 1.4
com.springsource.slf4j↩ .api-1.5.0.jar	com.springsource.slf4j.api	The SLF4J API
com.springsource.slf4j↩ .log4j-1.5.0.jar	com.springsource.slf4j.log4j	The SLF4J adapter for Log4j
com.springsource.slf4j.org↩ .apache.commons.logging↩ -1.5.0.jar	com.springsource.slf4j↩ .org.apache.commons.logging	The SLF4J Apache Commons Logging wrapper
log4j.osgi-1.2.15↩ -SNAPSHOT.jar	org.springframework.osgi↩ .log4j.osgi	The Log4j implementation library

To import these bundles into Eclipse's workspace, specify the lib directory as the plug-in location, and then select the bundles to import as shown in Figure 2-7. If you are using Java 1.5 or higher versions, you needn't import the concurrency library backport because it's only required for Java 1.4.

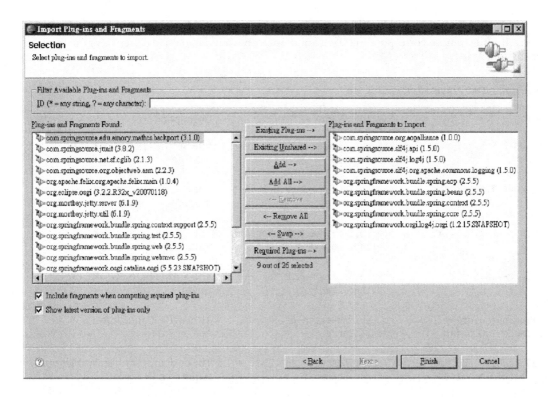

Figure 2-7. *Selecting Spring-DM's dependent bundles to import*

Internally, the Spring Framework and Spring-DM use the Apache Commons Logging API for logging purposes. Commons Logging provides a set of abstract APIs that are independent of the underlying logging implementation. Commons Logging mainly supports Apache Log4j and JDK Logging (available for JDK 1.4 and higher) as its logging implementation, and it can dynamically bind an implementation at runtime by discovering it from the classpath. However, because of the different class-loading mechanism in OSGi, this dynamic binding is too complex to work. A better substitution in an OSGi environment is to use the SLF4J (Simple Logging Facade for Java) library, which provides an abstraction approach similar to that of Commons Logging but uses static binding at deployment time.

SLF4J does not dynamically discover a logging implementation from the classpath; instead, it binds a logging implementation via a JAR file statically. As a result, it doesn't rely on the runtime environment's class-loading mechanism. To use SLF4J in OSGi, you must install the SLF4J API bundle (`com.springsource.slf4j.api-1.5.0.jar`) to the OSGi container. Then, for a particular logging implementation such as Log4j (`log4j.osgi-1.2.15-SNAPSHOT.jar`), install the corresponding SLF4J adapter bundle (`com.springsource.slf4j.log4j-1.5.0.jar`) to the OSGi container. Finally, because the Spring Framework and Spring-DM use the Commons Logging API internally, you must also install SLF4J's Commons Logging wrapper bundle (`com.springsource.slf4j.org.apache.commons.logging-1.5.0.jar`), which wraps the SLF4J API with the Commons Logging API.

Unfortunately, after importing all these bundles into Eclipse's workspace, you will see errors for the circular dependencies between the SLF4J API bundle and the SLF4J adapter bundle. First, the SLF4J adapter bundle has to import SLF4J's API package and implement this API by delegating logging requests to the logging implementation library. Second, the SLF4J API bundle has to import the SLF4J adapter bundle's package to establish a binding. As a result, these two bundles depend on each other and cause circular dependencies. However, that is the binding mechanism of SLF4J, and the error shouldn't prevent Eclipse from building the bundles. A workaround is to change the circular dependency reporting level from Error to Warning, by choosing the Window menu ➤ Preferences ➤ Java ➤ Compiler ➤ Building, as shown in Figure 2-8.

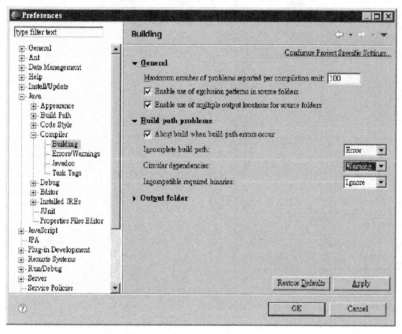

Figure 2-8. *Changing the circular dependency reporting level*

Configuring Logging for Spring-DM

Both the Spring Framework and Spring-DM write log messages to help diagnose problems. When using Log4j as the logging implementation, you have to configure it to output the log messages for you to read. In a non-OSGi environment, you can configure Log4j by creating a Log4j configuration file (log4j.properties) in the classpath root so that Log4j can detect this file automatically. But in an OSGi environment each bundle has its own classpath, so you must make sure that this file is available for each bundle that needs to configure Log4j. You may include a Log4j configuration file in each of the bundles, but that is very inefficient because the file needs to be distributed to multiple bundles and also because it's hard to maintain a consistent Log4j configuration across all your bundles.

A better solution is to use a fragment bundle, which will be attached to a host bundle by the OSGi container and loaded using the class loader of the host bundle. You can create a fragment bundle that attaches to the Log4j bundle and include a Log4j configuration file in the fragment's classpath root. Once you have done this, all bundles that need to use the Log4j bundle will have the Log4j configuration file available. In Eclipse, you can create a Fragment Project by choosing the File menu ➤ New ➤ Project, as shown in Figure 2-9.

Figure 2-9. *Creating a new Fragment Project*

Then, in the New Fragment Project dialog, enter org.springframework.osgi.log4j.config as the project name and select An OSGi Framework ➤ Standard as the target platform, as shown in Figure 2-10.

In the next dialog, you select the host bundle for this fragment. Because you are going to attach a Log4j configuration file to the Log4j bundle, select the bundle whose symbolic name is org.springframework.osgi.log4j.osgi as the host bundle, as shown in Figure 2-11.

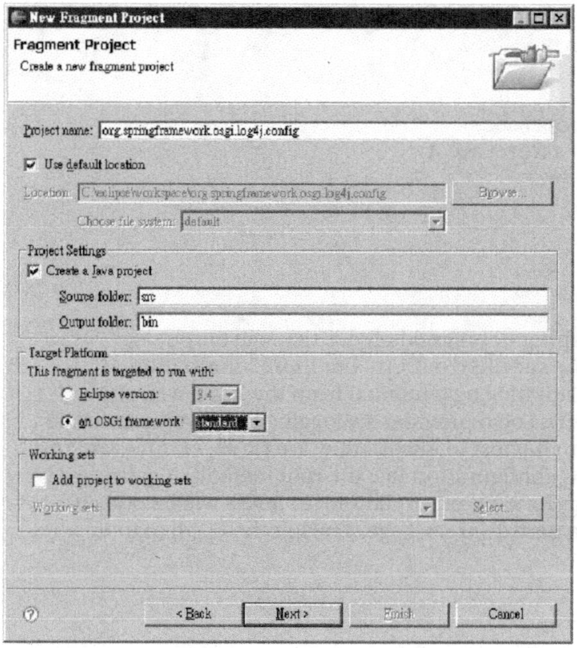

Figure 2-10. *Selecting the target fragment platform*

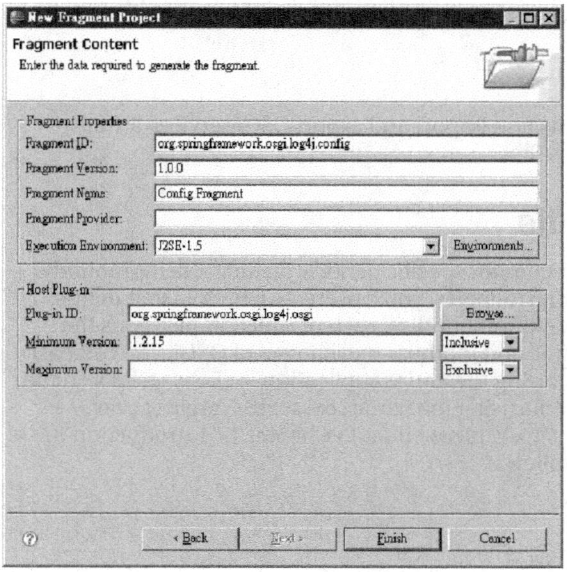

Figure 2-11. *Selecting the host bundle*

Finally in the project root of this fragment, create the default Log4j configuration file (`log4j.properties`) with the following contents:

```
### direct log messages to stdout ###
log4j.appender.stdout=org.apache.log4j.ConsoleAppender
log4j.appender.stdout.layout=org.apache.log4j.PatternLayout
log4j.appender.stdout.layout.ConversionPattern=↵
%d{yyyy-MM-dd HH:mm:ss} %5p %c{1}:%L - %m%n

### set root logger level ###
log4j.rootLogger=info, stdout
```

This Log4j configuration file defines a log appender named `stdout` that will output log messages to the console in a format controlled by the specified pattern. For more information about the logging patterns supported by Log4j, consult the Log4j manual from the Log4j web site (`http://logging.apache.org/log4j/1.2/manual.html`). Log4j provides six logging levels you can use to set the severity of your logging messages. Listed from highest to lowest, they are `fatal`, `error`, `warn`, `info`, `debug`, and `trace`. As specified in the preceding Log4j configuration file, the root (default) logging level is `info`, which means that only log messages of the `info`, `warn`, `error`, and `fatal` levels will be output by default. You can further set the logging level for a particular package. Consult the Log4j manual for details.

Creating Bundles Using Spring-DM

Once you have set up Spring-DM properly, you can start creating bundles using Spring-DM. In this section, I will use an interest calculator application that consists of two modules, the rate module and the interest module, as an example to demonstrate how to use Spring-DM to create Spring application contexts and import and export OSGi services for your bundles.

Creating the Bundle Interfaces and Classes

Before using Spring-DM to create application contexts and import and export OSGi services for the bundles, let's create the bundle interfaces and classes first.

Creating the Rate Interface Bundle

The rate module is responsible for calculating interest rates for specific periods, including daily, monthly, and annual rates. To support different rate calculation strategies, you can create a bundle that defines the rate interfaces, and also create multiple implementation bundles, each of which implements the interfaces with a single strategy. Thanks to the dynamic and modular mechanism of OSGi, you can easily switch between different strategies even without restarting the entire application. In Eclipse, let's create a plug-in project to define interfaces for the rate module using the name `com.apress.prodmserver.bank.rate`. For instructions on creating a bundle in Eclipse, please refer to Chapter 1, "Introduction to OSGi." Then create the `RateCalculator` interface as follows:

```
package com.apress.prodmserver.bank.rate;

public interface RateCalculator {

    public double getAnnualRate();
    public double getMonthlyRate();
    public double getDailyRate();
}
```

Next, this bundle should export the com.apress.prodmserver.bank.rate package for other bundles to access the interfaces. In Eclipse's manifest editing GUI, you can either add this package to the Exported Packages list in the Runtime tab or directly modify the MANIFEST.MF file's source code as follows:

```
Manifest-Version: 1.0
Bundle-ManifestVersion: 2
Bundle-Name: Rate Plug-in
Bundle-SymbolicName: com.apress.prodmserver.bank.rate
Bundle-Version: 1.0.0
Bundle-Vendor: APRESS
Bundle-RequiredExecutionEnvironment: J2SE-1.5
Export-Package: com.apress.prodmserver.bank.rate
```

Creating the Fixed-Rate Implementation Bundle

Now you must implement the RateCalculator interface with a rate calculation strategy. For simplicity's sake, let's calculate the interest rates statically from a fixed annual interest rate, which you can inject through a setter method. Create a plug-in project for this strategy and name it com.apress. prodmserver.bank.rate.fixed. Then create the following implementation class:

```
package com.apress.prodmserver.bank.rate.fixed;

import com.apress.prodmserver.bank.rate.RateCalculator;

public class FixedRateCalculator implements RateCalculator {

    private double rate;

    public void setRate(double rate) {
        this.rate = rate;
    }

    public double getAnnualRate() {
        return rate;
    }

    public double getMonthlyRate() {
        return rate / 12;
    }
```

```
    public double getDailyRate() {
        return rate / 365;
    }
}
```

Finally, this bundle should import the com.apress.prodmserver.bank.rate package so that it can access the RateCalculator interface. In Eclipse's manifest editing GUI, you can either add this package to the Imported Packages list in the Runtime tab or modify the MANIFEST.MF file's source code. However, to prevent other bundles from instantiating this implementation class directly, don't export the com.apress.prodmserver.bank.rate.fixed package. The modified MANIFEST.MF file looks like this:

```
Manifest-Version: 1.0
Bundle-ManifestVersion: 2
Bundle-Name: Fixed Plug-in
Bundle-SymbolicName: com.apress.prodmserver.bank.rate.fixed
Bundle-Version: 1.0.0
Bundle-Vendor: APRESS
Bundle-RequiredExecutionEnvironment: J2SE-1.5
Import-Package: com.apress.prodmserver.bank.rate
```

You saw in Chapter 1 that a bundle can register OSGi services to the service registry for other bundles to consume. In order for other bundles to use this rate calculator, you must instantiate the FixedRateCalculator class and register the instance to the service registry as an OSGi service. Later in this section I will show how to perform this registration by exporting a Spring bean as an OSGi service using Spring-DM.

Creating the Interest Interface Bundle

The interest module is responsible for calculating interest using the rates returned by the rate module. First let's create a plug-in project to define interfaces for this module and name it com.apress. prodmserver.bank.interest. Then define the InterestCalculator interface as follows:

```
package com.apress.prodmserver.bank.interest;

public interface InterestCalculator {

    public double calculate(double principal, double year);
}
```

This bundle needs to export the com.apress.prodmserver.bank.interest package in order for other bundles to access the interfaces. The revised MANIFEST.MF file looks like this:

```
Manifest-Version: 1.0
Bundle-ManifestVersion: 2
Bundle-Name: Interest Plug-in
Bundle-SymbolicName: com.apress.prodmserver.bank.interest
Bundle-Version: 1.0.0
Bundle-Vendor: APRESS
Bundle-RequiredExecutionEnvironment: J2SE-1.5
Export-Package: com.apress.prodmserver.bank.interest
```

Creating the Simple Interest Implementation Bundle

There are many interest calculation strategies that can be used in real-world applications, but for simplicity's sake, let's consider the following simple interest formula:

Interest = Principal × Annual Rate × Year

To implement this interest calculation strategy, first create a plug-in project with the name com.apress.prodmserver.bank.interest.simple, and then create the following implementation class:

```
package com.apress.prodmserver.bank.interest.simple;

import com.apress.prodmserver.bank.interest.InterestCalculator;
import com.apress.prodmserver.bank.rate.RateCalculator;

public class SimpleInterestCalculator implements InterestCalculator {

    private RateCalculator rateCalculator;

    public void setRateCalculator(RateCalculator rateCalculator) {
        this.rateCalculator = rateCalculator;
    }

    public double calculate(double principal, double year) {
        return principal * year * rateCalculator.getAnnualRate();
    }
}
```

This implementation requires a RateCalculator instance, which can be injected through a setter method. Finally, this bundle should import the com.apress.prodmserver.bank.interest and com.apress.prodmserver.bank.rate packages so that it can access the InterestCalculator and RateCalculator interfaces.

```
Manifest-Version: 1.0
Bundle-ManifestVersion: 2
Bundle-Name: Simple Plug-in
Bundle-SymbolicName: com.apress.prodmserver.bank.interest.simple
Bundle-Version: 1.0.0
Bundle-Vendor: APRESS
Bundle-RequiredExecutionEnvironment: J2SE-1.5
Import-Package: com.apress.prodmserver.bank.interest,
 com.apress.prodmserver.bank.rate
```

Next, you will use Spring-DM to export a Spring bean of type SimpleInterestCalculator as an OSGi service for other bundles to consume.

Configuring Bundles to Be Recognized by Spring-DM

As noted earlier in this chapter, Spring-DM provides an extender bundle that is able to create an application context and import and export OSGi services for a bundle installed in the same OSGi container. To have the extender bundle perform these tasks for your bundle, you need to create one or more bean configuration files, either in the META-INF/spring directory or in other locations specified in the `MANIFEST.MF` file's `Spring-Context` header. Spring-DM will read these bean configuration files and delegate the application context creation to the Spring Framework.

To separate OSGi-related bean configurations from other Spring bean configurations, a recommended practice is to split the application context configurations into two or more files. For example, the `module-context.xml` file contains regular Spring bean configurations that are not OSGi-aware, and the `osgi-context.xml` file contains OSGi-related bean configurations for importing and exporting OSGi services.

Configuring Spring-DM for the Fixed-Rate Implementation Bundle

Recall that the fixed-rate implementation bundle (`com.apress.prodmserver.bank.rate.fixed`) has to export its rate calculator as an OSGi service. For this purpose, first create a `module-context.xml` file, which contains only bean configurations that are not OSGi-aware, in the `META-INF/spring` directory with the following contents:

```
<beans xmlns="http://www.springframework.org/schema/beans"
    xmlns:xsi="http://www.w3.org/2001/XMLSchema-instance"
    xsi:schemaLocation="http://www.springframework.org/schema/beans
        http://www.springframework.org/schema/beans/spring-beans-2.5.xsd">

    <bean id="rateCalculator"
        class="com.apress.prodmserver.bank.rate.fixed.FixedRateCalculator">
        <property name="rate" value="0.05" />
    </bean>
</beans>
```

This bean configuration file defines a bean instance, whose identifier is `rateCalculator` and whose concrete type is `FixedRateCalculator`, in the application context of the current bundle (the fixed-rate implementation bundle). When the extender bundle reads this file and delegates the application context creation to the Spring Framework, the Spring Framework will instantiate the `FixedRateCalculator` class and put the bean instance into the application context under the identifier `rateCalculator`.

An XML file can contain elements defined in different schemas. From the first line of the preceding bean configuration file, you can see that the default XML namespace refers to the Spring Framework's beans schema, which defines Spring bean definition elements including the `<beans>` root element, the `<bean>` element for defining a bean, the `<property>` element for defining a bean property, and so on.

Next and most importantly, this bundle also has to export this same `rateCalculator` bean as an OSGi service for other bundles to consume. For this purpose, create an `osgi-context.xml` file, which contains OSGi-related bean configurations, in the `META-INF/spring` directory with the following contents:

```
<beans xmlns="http://www.springframework.org/schema/beans"
    xmlns:xsi="http://www.w3.org/2001/XMLSchema-instance"
    xmlns:osgi="http://www.springframework.org/schema/osgi"
    xsi:schemaLocation="http://www.springframework.org/schema/beans
        http://www.springframework.org/schema/beans/spring-beans-2.5.xsd
        http://www.springframework.org/schema/osgi
        http://www.springframework.org/schema/osgi/spring-osgi.xsd">
```

```
<osgi:service ref="rateCalculator"
        interface="com.apress.prodmserver.bank.rate.RateCalculator" />
</beans>
```

This bean configuration file defines an OSGi service using the `<service>` element defined in Spring-DM's XML schema, which you must remember to import in the root element. This `<service>` element will export the `rateCalculator` bean in the application context as an OSGi service under the service interface `RateCalculator`. Spring-DM will handle this element and accordingly register the `rateCalculator` bean to the service registry as an OSGi service under the `RateCalculator` interface.

Normally, the default namespace of a regular Spring bean configuration file is beans, so you can use the `<beans>`, `<bean>`, and `<property>` elements without the beans prefix. However, all Spring-DM elements such as `<service>` and `<reference>` must be used with the osgi prefix. Since the elements in an OSGi-related bean configuration file mostly belong to Spring-DM's schema, you can define osgi as the default namespace instead, in order to use these elements without the osgi prefix. But if you do that, you have to include the beans prefix for the `<beans>`, `<bean>`, and `<property>` elements in the file. You can modify the preceding bean configuration file as follows:

```
<beans:beans xmlns="http://www.springframework.org/schema/osgi"
    xmlns:xsi="http://www.w3.org/2001/XMLSchema-instance"
    xmlns:beans="http://www.springframework.org/schema/beans"
    xsi:schemaLocation="http://www.springframework.org/schema/beans
        http://www.springframework.org/schema/beans/spring-beans-2.5.xsd
        http://www.springframework.org/schema/osgi
        http://www.springframework.org/schema/osgi/spring-osgi.xsd">

    <service ref="rateCalculator"
        interface="com.apress.prodmserver.bank.rate.RateCalculator" />
</beans:beans>
```

Now the `<service>` element doesn't need the osgi prefix, because the default namespace of this XML file is osgi.

Configuring Spring-DM for the Simple Interest Implementation Bundle

Using Spring-DM, the fixed-rate implementation bundle has exported its rate calculator as an OSGi service for other bundles to consume. Similarly, you can configure Spring-DM for the simple interest implementation bundle (`com.apress.prodmserver.bank.interest.simple`), which has to export its interest calculator as an OSGi service and import a rate calculator to complete its jobs. First, create a `module-context.xml` file in the `META-INF/spring` directory with the following contents:

```
<beans xmlns="http://www.springframework.org/schema/beans"
    xmlns:xsi="http://www.w3.org/2001/XMLSchema-instance"
    xsi:schemaLocation="http://www.springframework.org/schema/beans
        http://www.springframework.org/schema/beans/spring-beans-2.5.xsd">
```

```
<bean id="interestCalculator" class=
    "com.apress.prodmserver.bank.interest.simple.SimpleInterestCalculator">
    <property name="rateCalculator" ref="rateCalculator" />
</bean>
</beans>
```

This bean configuration file defines a bean instance of type SimpleInterestCalculator in the application context of the current bundle (the simple interest implementation bundle). After instantiating the bean class, the Spring Framework will find another bean, whose name is rateCalculator, from the current application context to set the rateCalculator property via setter injection. For this bundle the rateCalculator bean should be an imported OSGi service, which should be defined in the osgi-context.xml file in the META-INF/spring directory; the file has the following contents:

```
<beans:beans xmlns="http://www.springframework.org/schema/osgi"
    xmlns:xsi="http://www.w3.org/2001/XMLSchema-instance"
    xmlns:beans="http://www.springframework.org/schema/beans"
    xsi:schemaLocation="http://www.springframework.org/schema/beans
        http://www.springframework.org/schema/beans/spring-beans-2.5.xsd
        http://www.springframework.org/schema/osgi
        http://www.springframework.org/schema/osgi/spring-osgi.xsd">

    <reference id="rateCalculator"
        interface="com.apress.prodmserver.bank.rate.RateCalculator" />

    <service ref="interestCalculator"
        interface="com.apress.prodmserver.bank.interest.InterestCalculator" />
</beans:beans>
```

This bean configuration file first defines a service reference named rateCalculator, using the <reference> element defined in Spring-DM's XML schema. Spring-DM will handle this element and accordingly look up the service registry for an OSGi service registered under the RateCalculator interface. Also notice that you exported the interestCalculator bean as an OSGi service under the InterestCalculator interface.

Deploying the Bundles to the OSGi Container

The bundles you have developed up to this point should work properly. You can deploy these bundles to the Equinox container, which has Spring-DM set up, and then use the ss command to check the bundle status (your order may be different):

```
osgi> ss

Framework is launched.

id   State      Bundle
0    ACTIVE     org.eclipse.osgi_3.4.2.R34x_v20080826-1230
1    ACTIVE     org.springframework.bundle.osgi.core_1.1.2
2    ACTIVE     org.springframework.bundle.osgi.extender_1.1.2
3    ACTIVE     org.springframework.bundle.osgi.io_1.1.2
4    ACTIVE     org.springframework.bundle.spring.aop_2.5.5
```

```
5    ACTIVE      org.springframework.bundle.spring.beans_2.5.5
6    ACTIVE      org.springframework.bundle.spring.context_2.5.5
7    ACTIVE      org.springframework.bundle.spring.core_2.5.5
8    ACTIVE      com.springsource.org.aopalliance_1.0.0
9    ACTIVE      com.springsource.slf4j.api_1.5.0
10   ACTIVE      com.springsource.slf4j.log4j_1.5.0
11   ACTIVE      com.springsource.slf4j.org.apache.commons.logging_1.5.0
12   ACTIVE      org.springframework.osgi.log4j.osgi_1.2.15.SNAPSHOT
                 Fragments=13
13   RESOLVED    org.springframework.osgi.log4j.config_1.0.0
                 Master=12
14   ACTIVE      com.apress.prodmserver.bank.rate_1.0.0
15   ACTIVE      com.apress.prodmserver.bank.rate.fixed_1.0.0
16   ACTIVE      com.apress.prodmserver.bank.interest_1.0.0
17   ACTIVE      com.apress.prodmserver.bank.interest.simple_1.0.0
```

To verify that the OSGi services are exported properly, you can use the services command to display the details of all registered OSGi services (your service and bundle identifiers may be different):

```
osgi> services
...
{com.apress.prodmserver.bank.rate.RateCalculator}=
   {org.springframework.osgi.bean.name=rateCalculator,
    Bundle-SymbolicName=com.apress.prodmserver.bank.rate.fixed,
    Bundle-Version=1.0.0, service.id=27}
  Registered by bundle:
    initial@reference:file:workspace/com.apress.prodmserver.bank.rate.fixed/ [15]
  Bundles using service:
    initial@reference:file:workspace/com.apress.prodmserver.bank.interest.simple/
    [17]

{com.apress.prodmserver.bank.interest.InterestCalculator}=
   {org.springframework.osgi.bean.name=interestCalculator,
    Bundle-SymbolicName=com.apress.prodmserver.bank.interest.simple,
    Bundle-Version=1.0.0, service.id=28}
  Registered by bundle:
    initial@reference:file:workspace/com.apress.prodmserver.bank.interest.simple/
    [17]
  No bundles using service.
```

In the first block of output you can see that the fixed-rate implementation bundle has registered an OSGi service under the RateCalculator interface, and this service is being used by the simple interest implementation bundle. In the second output block, you can see that the simple interest implementation bundle has registered an OSGi service under the InterestCalculator interface, and at this moment no bundle is using the service.

Creating the Client Bundle

In order to test the bundle classes and OSGi services, let's create a client bundle and name it com.apress. prodmserver.bank.client. In this bundle create the following class, which uses the interest calculator exported from the simple interest implementation bundle:

```java
package com.apress.prodmserver.bank.client;

import com.apress.prodmserver.bank.interest.InterestCalculator;

public class Client {

    private InterestCalculator interestCalculator;

    public void setInterestCalculator(InterestCalculator interestCalculator) {
        this.interestCalculator = interestCalculator;
    }

    public void printInterestTable() {
        double principal = 1000;
        double[] years = new double[] { 0.5, 1, 2, 5, 10 };
        System.out.println("Principal\tYear\tInterest");
        for (double year : years) {
            double interest = interestCalculator.calculate(principal, year);
            System.out.println(principal + "\t" + year + "\t" + interest);
        }
    }
}
```

This is a simple Java class that requires an InterestCalculator instance to be injected via setter injection. Then the printInterestTable() method makes use of this interest calculator to print a table listing interest on a principal of $1,000 for periods of half a year, 1, 2, 5, and 10 years respectively.

Also remember that this bundle has to import the com.apress.prodmserver.bank.interest package in the MANIFEST.MF file so that it can access the InterestCalculator interface. The MANIFEST.MF file's source code looks like this:

```
Manifest-Version: 1.0
Bundle-ManifestVersion: 2
Bundle-Name: Client Plug-in
Bundle-SymbolicName: com.apress.prodmserver.bank.client
Bundle-Version: 1.0.0
Bundle-Vendor: APRESS
Bundle-RequiredExecutionEnvironment: J2SE-1.5
Import-Package: com.apress.prodmserver.bank.interest
```

Next, create a module-context.xml file in the META-INF/spring directory with the following contents:

```xml
<beans xmlns="http://www.springframework.org/schema/beans"
    xmlns:xsi="http://www.w3.org/2001/XMLSchema-instance"
    xsi:schemaLocation="http://www.springframework.org/schema/beans
```

```
            http://www.springframework.org/schema/beans/spring-beans-2.5.xsd">

    <bean id="client"
        class="com.apress.prodmserver.bank.client.Client"
        init-method="printInterestTable">
        <property name="interestCalculator" ref="interestCalculator" />
    </bean>
</beans>
```

This bean configuration file defines a client bean instance in the application context with a reference to the interestCalculator bean, which is a service reference that will be defined in the next bean configuration file. Notice that the client bean also has an initialization method defined through the init-method attribute. This method will be called automatically when the application context initializes the bean.

For OSGi configurations, create an osgi-context.xml file in the META-INF/spring directory to define a service reference named interestCalculator, which will be injected into the client bean:

```
<beans:beans xmlns="http://www.springframework.org/schema/osgi"
    xmlns:xsi="http://www.w3.org/2001/XMLSchema-instance"
    xmlns:beans="http://www.springframework.org/schema/beans"
    xsi:schemaLocation="http://www.springframework.org/schema/beans
        http://www.springframework.org/schema/beans/spring-beans-2.5.xsd
        http://www.springframework.org/schema/osgi
        http://www.springframework.org/schema/osgi/spring-osgi.xsd">

    <reference id="interestCalculator"
        interface="com.apress.prodmserver.bank.interest.InterestCalculator" />
</beans:beans>
```

Finally, you can install this bundle to the OSGi container. When the bundle is started, the extender bundle will create an application context for it, and the context will in turn create the client bean instance and call its initialization method. If everything is correct, you will see the interest table printed to the console as follows:

```
Principal   Year    Interest
1000.0      0.5     25.0
1000.0      1.0     50.0
1000.0      2.0     100.0
1000.0      5.0     250.0
1000.0      10.0    500.0
```

Advanced Spring-DM Configurations for OSGi Services

In this section, I will introduce some advanced Spring-DM configurations for OSGi services so that you can better deal with the dynamics of OSGi services.

79

The Cardinality of OSGi Service References

Spring-DM supports setting the *cardinality* of a service reference bean so that you can decide whether a matching OSGi service is required at the time the bean is created. A reference bean with the cardinality 1..1 is a *mandatory* reference, whose matching service must be available at creation time. A reference bean with the cardinality 0..1 is an *optional* reference, whose matching service is not required at creation time.

Because OSGi is dynamic, an OSGi service may be registered and unregistered at any time. Therefore, a service reference bean created by Spring-DM is in fact a proxy that forwards calls to the backing service reference. The application context of a mandatory service reference bean cannot be created until a matching service is available. By contrast, an optional service reference bean will be created immediately, regardless of whether there is a matching service at creation time.

The <reference> element defined in the osgi schema supports the cardinality attribute. If this attribute isn't set, its default value is 1..1 (that is, a service reference bean is mandatory by default). Recall that in the osgi-context.xml file for the simple interest implementation bundle (com.apress.prodmserver.bank.interest.simple) you have a reference to an OSGi service under the RateCalculator interface:

```
<reference id="rateCalculator"
    interface="com.apress.prodmserver.bank.rate.RateCalculator" />
```

Since you haven't set the cardinality attribute, this service reference is mandatory. It has the same effect as setting the cardinality attribute to 1..1 explicitly:

```
<reference id="rateCalculator"
    interface="com.apress.prodmserver.bank.rate.RateCalculator"
    cardinality="1..1" />
```

When the simple interest implementation bundle's application context is being created, if no service under the RateCalculator interface is available, then the creation will be blocked until a matching service is available. If you set the cardinality attribute to 0..1, the reference is optional, and the reference bean will be created immediately even if no service under the RateCalculator interface is available:

```
<reference id="rateCalculator"
    interface="com.apress.prodmserver.bank.rate.RateCalculator"
    cardinality="0..1" />
```

When a call is made on a reference bean whose backing service isn't available, no matter whether it is mandatory or optional, the reference bean will wait (by default 5 minutes) for the service until it can look up a resolved service from the service registry. If no resolved service can be looked up before the timeout expires, Spring-DM will throw a ServiceUnavailableException to indicate that the OSGi service is unavailable. You can also customize the timeout value by setting the <reference> element's timeout attribute (in milliseconds), as shown in the following configuration:

```
<reference id="rateCalculator"
    interface="com.apress.prodmserver.bank.rate.RateCalculator"
    cardinality="0..1" timeout="60000" />
```

Constraining OSGi Service Lookups

In some cases, an OSGi container may have more than one OSGi service registered under the same interface, so you may have to specify criteria other than the service interface to look up a service. To demonstrate this situation, let's consider another interest implementation bundle for the following compound interest formula:

$$\text{Interest} = \text{Principal} \times ((1 + \text{Monthly Rate})^{\text{Year} \times 12} - 1)$$

To implement this interest calculation strategy, first create a plug-in project with the name com.apress.prodmserver.bank.interest.compound, and then create the following class:

```
package com.apress.prodmserver.bank.interest.compound;

import com.apress.prodmserver.bank.interest.InterestCalculator;
import com.apress.prodmserver.bank.rate.RateCalculator;

public class CompoundInterestCalculator implements InterestCalculator {

    private RateCalculator rateCalculator;

    public void setRateCalculator(RateCalculator rateCalculator) {
        this.rateCalculator = rateCalculator;
    }

    public double calculate(double principal, double year) {
        return principal
                * (Math.pow(1 + rateCalculator.getMonthlyRate(), year * 12) - 1);
    }
}
```

In MANIFEST.MF, this bundle should import the com.apress.prodmserver.bank.interest and com.apress.prodmserver.bank.rate packages so that it can access the InterestCalculator and RateCalculator interfaces:

```
Manifest-Version: 1.0
Bundle-ManifestVersion: 2
Bundle-Name: Compound Plug-in
Bundle-SymbolicName: com.apress.prodmserver.bank.interest.compound
Bundle-Version: 1.0.0
Bundle-Vendor: APRESS
Bundle-RequiredExecutionEnvironment: J2SE-1.5
Import-Package: com.apress.prodmserver.bank.interest,
 com.apress.prodmserver.bank.rate
```

Next, create the module-context.xml file in the META-INF/spring directory to define a bean of type CompoundInterestCalculator as follows:

```
<beans xmlns="http://www.springframework.org/schema/beans"
    xmlns:xsi="http://www.w3.org/2001/XMLSchema-instance"
    xsi:schemaLocation="http://www.springframework.org/schema/beans
        http://www.springframework.org/schema/beans/spring-beans-2.5.xsd">
```

```
    <bean id="interestCalculator" class=
        "com.apress.prodmserver.bank.interest.compound.CompoundInterestCalculator">
        <property name="rateCalculator" ref="rateCalculator" />
    </bean>
</beans>
```

Finally, create the osgi-context.xml file in META-INF/spring to import a service under the RateCalculator interface, and export an OSGi service under the InterestCalculator interface as follows.

```
<beans:beans xmlns="http://www.springframework.org/schema/osgi"
    xmlns:xsi="http://www.w3.org/2001/XMLSchema-instance"
    xmlns:beans="http://www.springframework.org/schema/beans"
    xsi:schemaLocation="http://www.springframework.org/schema/beans
        http://www.springframework.org/schema/beans/spring-beans-2.5.xsd
        http://www.springframework.org/schema/osgi
        http://www.springframework.org/schema/osgi/spring-osgi.xsd">

    <reference id="rateCalculator"
        interface="com.apress.prodmserver.bank.rate.RateCalculator" />

    <service ref="interestCalculator"
        interface="com.apress.prodmserver.bank.interest.InterestCalculator" />
</beans:beans>
```

Now if you install and start this bundle in the OSGi container, there will be two services registered under the InterestCalculator interface, one registered by the simple interest bundle and the other by the compound interest bundle. When the client bundle looks up a service under the InterestCalculator interface, the OSGi container will return the one with the lowest service ID (i.e., the service registered first).

Specifying a Ranking for an OSGi Service

OSGi allows you to specify a service ranking for an OSGi service so that the OSGi container can decide which service to return when there is more than one service matching the lookup criteria. An OSGi service with a higher ranking will have higher priority. The <service> element in the osgi schema supports the ranking attribute for specifying the service ranking. For instance, you can assign the ranking 1 to the simple interest bundle's InterestCalculator service as follows:

```
<service ref="interestCalculator"
    interface="com.apress.prodmserver.bank.interest.InterestCalculator"
    ranking="1" />
```

Then, you can assign the ranking 2 to the compound interest bundle's InterestCalculator service as follows:

```
<service ref="interestCalculator"
    interface="com.apress.prodmserver.bank.interest.InterestCalculator"
    ranking="2" />
```

If both services are registered to the service registry and a bundle (the client bundle) looks up a service under the InterestCalculator interface, the OSGi container will return the service with the highest service ranking (the compound interest bundle's InterestCalculator service in this case).

Specifying Properties for an OSGi Service

OSGi allows you to specify a set of service properties for an OSGi service so that they can be included in lookup criteria. The <service> element in the osgi schema supports embedding a <service-properties> element with multiple <entry> elements in the beans schema to specify service properties. For instance, you can set a service property strategy with the value simple for the simple interest bundle's InterestCalculator service as follows:

```
<service ref="interestCalculator"
    interface="com.apress.prodmserver.bank.interest.InterestCalculator">
    <service-properties>
        <beans:entry key="strategy" value="simple" />
    </service-properties>
</service>
```

Also, you can set the service property strategy with the value compound for the compound interest bundle's InterestCalculator service as follows:

```
<service ref="interestCalculator"
    interface="com.apress.prodmserver.bank.interest.InterestCalculator">
    <service-properties>
        <beans:entry key="strategy" value="compound" />
    </service-properties>
</service>
```

On the other hand, the <reference> element supports the filter attribute for specifying an OSGi filter expression to constrain the service lookup. For example, in the client bundle you can specify the following filter in the reference's filter attribute to look up a service with the strategy property set to simple:

```
<reference id="interestCalculator"
    interface="com.apress.prodmserver.bank.interest.InterestCalculator"
    filter="(strategy=simple)" />
```

You can also specify the following filter in the filter attribute to look up a service whose strategy property is set to compound:

```
<reference id="interestCalculator"
    interface="com.apress.prodmserver.bank.interest.InterestCalculator"
    filter="(strategy=compound)" />
```

Summary

In this chapter, you first had an introduction to Spring-DM's major features and mechanisms. Spring-DM is a Spring Portfolio project that integrates the Spring Framework with OSGi to simplify building dynamic and modular applications. Spring-DM provides the extender bundle for discovering Spring-based bundles and managing the application contexts of the bundles. Spring-DM also supports importing and exporting OSGi services via simple XML configurations.

Once you have downloaded Spring-DM, you need to install its core bundles, including the extender bundle, and their dependent bundles to the target OSGi container. Spring-DM internally uses Commons Logging to write log messages. In an OSGi environment, it would be better to bridge Commons Logging to SLF4J and use Log4j as the logging implementation library. To maintain a consistent Log4j configuration across all your bundles, you can create a fragment bundle that attaches to the Log4j bundle and then include a Log4j configuration file in its classpath root.

With Spring-DM set up, you developed a complete and modular OSGi-based application by using Spring-DM to manage the application contexts of its bundles and import and export OSGi services between the bundles.

Finally, you saw some advanced Spring-DM configurations for OSGi services to better deal with the dynamics of OSGi services. You can set the cardinality of a service reference bean to specify whether a matching OSGi service is required at the bean creation time. When there is more than one OSGi service registered under the same interface, you can specify a service ranking for each service so that a service with a higher ranking will have higher priority. You can also specify a set of service properties for an OSGi service so that they can be included in lookup criteria.

The first two chapters have familiarized you with the prerequisites for using OSGi and Spring-DM, which are the core implementation technologies of the dm Server. In the next chapter you will find an overview of the dm Server's components, solutions, features, and architecture.

CHAPTER 3

■ ■ ■

Introduction to the dm Server

The dm Server is a new-generation Java application server delivered by SpringSource, the company that wrote the Spring Framework. The dm Server is an OSGi-based Java server designed to run enterprise Java applications and Spring-powered applications with a new degree of flexibility and reliability. In general, the dm Server brings the advantages of OSGi to Java EE application development, packaging, and deployment. This chapter introduces the following topics:

- The dm Server and its core components
- Why you need the dm Server in Java EE development and deployment
- The highlights of the dm Server
- The overall architecture of the dm Server

When reading this chapter, keep in mind that its purpose is to introduce the dm Server to provide a general understanding of it. In subsequent chapters, you will learn in detail about its installation, administration, configuration, development, and deployment.

What Is the dm Server?

The dm Server is a modular OSGi-based Java application server designed for developing, packaging, deploying, running, and tracing enterprise Java applications. The dm Server is built on several essential Java platform technologies, and it integrates and extends these technologies to provide a complete and integrated solution. The core components of the dm Server include the following:

- OSGi R4 version 4.1 as the core technology, including OSGi enterprise RFCs belonging to OSGi R4 version 4.2.
- Eclipse Equinox as the OSGi container
- Spring Framework as the application framework
- Spring Dynamic Modules to add Spring support to OSGi-based applications
- OSGi web container

Eclipse Equinox

Introduced in Chapter 1, Equinox (http://www.eclipse.org/equinox/) is an Eclipse project that provides the reference implementation (RI) of the OSGi R4 core framework specification. In addition to the OSGi framework implementation, Equinox provides various services and infrastructures for running OSGi-based systems on the OSGi platform. Note that Equinox is used internally by the Eclipse IDE to manage its plug-ins. In fact, each Eclipse plug-in is an OSGi bundle with additional Eclipse-specific code.

The dm Server integrates Equinox as the OSGi container to provide OSGi functionality for the server and run bundles deployed on the server.

The Spring Framework

The Spring Framework (http://www.springframework.org/) is a comprehensive Java/Java EE application framework designed by SpringSource. Spring addresses many aspects of enterprise application development, such as database persistence, transaction management, web development, testing, and enterprise service integration, to help you build high-quality and high-performance Java/Java EE applications more efficiently.

The Spring Framework's architecture is divided into modules, as illustrated in Figure 3-1. The modules are organized in a hierarchical fashion, with the upper modules depending on the lower modules. The Spring Framework allows great flexibility in assembling its modules, so your applications can build on different module subsets in different usage scenarios, according to their requirements and implementation technologies.

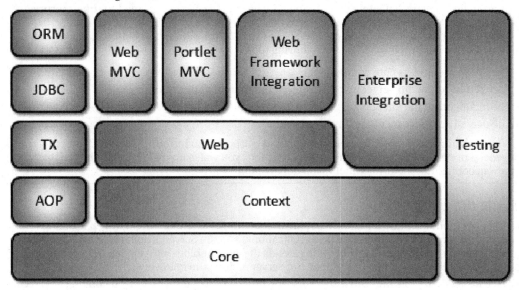

Figure 3-1. *The Spring Framework's architecture*

The Spring Framework's core is a lightweight IoC container that is able to manage the components (also called beans) that make up an application. Spring's power lies in its ability to decouple dependencies between components, using dependency injection, and to add enterprise services to its managed components in a declarative manner using AOP (aspect-oriented programming).

The dm Server uses the Spring Framework modules in the form of bundles for its operation. In addition, this approach also allows you to use Spring's features to develop applications that run on the server.

Spring Dynamic Modules

Spring Dynamic Modules for OSGi Service Platforms (http://www.springsource.org/osgi), or Spring-DM for short, is a Spring Portfolio project that integrates the Spring Framework with OSGi to simplify the building of dynamic and modular Spring-based Java applications.

Spring-DM comes with an extender bundle that can automatically discover Spring-based bundles and manage a Spring application context for each of these bundles. It can also export a bean in the application context as an OSGi service and import an OSGi service reference as a bean via simple XML configurations.

The dm Server preinstalls the Spring-DM extender bundle and other Spring-DM bundles to add Spring and Spring-DM capabilities to bundles running on the server. It should also be noted that Spring-DM provides the foundations for the Blueprint Service (RFC 124), which forms part of OSGi R4 version 4.2.

OSGi Web Container

An OSGi web container (RFC 66) is included with the dm Server to support Java web applications. Similar to a Java EE web container like Apache Tomcat (`http://tomcat.apache.org/`), an OSGi web container provides an implementation to run Java Servlet and JavaServer Pages (JSP) components with OSGi features. The OSGi web container supports the Servlet 2.5 and JSP 2.1 specifications.

Unlike a Java EE web container, which supports Web Archives (WARs) as the deployment format, an OSGi web container supports web bundles as the deployment format. The web bundle format will be described in the upcoming section "Deployment Formats for Web Applications," as well as future chapters that contain web bundle code samples.

The dm Server preinstalls an OSGi web container in the form of bundles, so it can run web applications deployed on it.

WHAT ABOUT THE TC SERVER?

In addition to the dm Server, SpringSource also offers another server: the tc Server. It is an enterprise version of Apache Tomcat with special features such as high-concurrency connection pools (an enhancement compared to Tomcat's traditional DBCP), better application management, and advanced server diagnostics.

However, the tc Server is based on Apache Tomcat, which is not an OSGi web container; therefore they are substantially different. The tc Server is OSGi-agnostic and is intended for Tomcat users who need additional operational management and diagnostics capabilities, as well as organizations using Spring with legacy Java EE servers that are considering moving off such servers. By contrast, the dm Server is for those organizations looking to take advantage of OSGi technology in enterprise Java applications.

Why Do You Need the dm Server?

In this section I will first discuss some common problems in traditional Java EE application development and deployment and then introduce the dm Server's solutions to these problems. As a Java EE application developer, you may have become resigned to these problems, but as you will see, you can avoid them altogether with the dm Server.

Dependency Management

A Java EE application usually depends on a group of libraries, which are supplied in the form of JAR files. A Java EE application server typically has a shared class loader to load shared application classes that are visible to every application deployed on the server. On the other hand, each application has a private class loader, which refers to the shared class loader as its parent and is used to load application classes that are private to the current application. Such classes are not visible to any other application and are located in either the WEB-INF/classes or WEB-INF/lib directory of an application's web archive (WAR) structure.

Therefore you can choose to load an application's library in two ways: either with the application server's shared class loader, by deploying the library JAR file in a specific directory of the application server (e.g., the lib top-level directory in Tomcat 6.x); or with the application's private class loader, by including the library JAR file in the application's deployment archive (e.g., in the WEB-INF/lib directory of a web application). Now let's consider a scenario in which your application server has deployed four applications, which depend on two different versions of the same library, as illustrated in Figure 3-2.

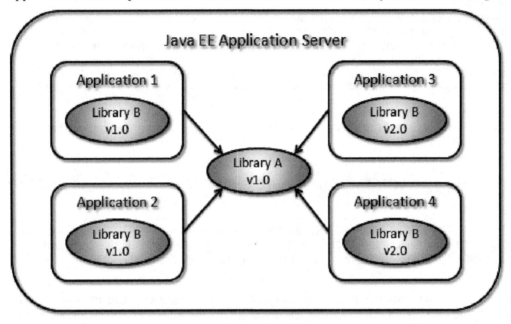

Figure 3-2. *Dependency management in a traditional Java EE application server*

As you can see, all these applications depend on the same version (1.0) of Library A, so you can load this library with the shared class loader to avoid repeating the library JAR file in every application (for instance, a relational database driver used by every application). However, Applications 1 and 2 depend on Library B version 1.0, while Applications 3 and 4 depend on Library B version 2.0. Suppose these versions of Library B are not compatible. In this case, you can only load Library B with each application's private class loader, because the shared class loader cannot load different versions of Library B at the same time. Even if it could, there is no mechanism by which your applications can specify the library version to use. As a result, you have to repeat different versions of the Library B JAR file in these applications, and it will be hard to manage and reuse these versions as more and more applications depend on different versions of Library B.

The dm Server incorporates OSGi as its core technology to enhance dependency and version management for applications. The dm Server allows you to deploy different versions of a library at the same time in the form of bundles. Then your applications can specify which version of the bundle to import. The dm Server can help solve the problem in the preceding scenario with OSGi, as illustrated in Figure 3-3.

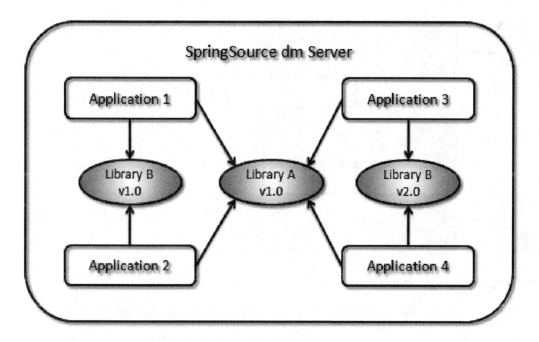

Figure 3-3. *Dependency management in the SpringSource dm Server*

The previous scenario pertains to dependency management in the context of web applications; however, this is a particular case that illustrates OSGi's more general-purpose role for the Java platform.

Java's standard dependency management strategy is done through JARs and the classpath variable. In other words, dependency management is fulfilled among JARs declared in the classpath variable. The limitation with this approach is its lack of versioning information, which in turn makes it difficult to create modular applications (e.g mixing and matching parts while avoiding clashes).

Relying on OSGi, however, enhances dependency management and makes modular application design easier. Because OSGi equips JARs with versioning information and supersedes the use of the classpath variable to manage dependencies, it is possible to have multiple versions of a JAR coexist in Java's run-time.

Deployment Granularity

An enterprise Java application is usually designed to consist of multiple modules, an example of which is shown in Figure 3-4.

In the traditional development process, you first develop each module of your application and then package all these modules into a single archive file (WAR or EAR). Last, you deploy this archive file to the application server for it to run your application. However, if you later update a single module of your application, you have to repackage, redeploy, and restart the entire application, including all other modules that have not been updated. In other words, although your application is designed to be modular in the development phase, when it's deployed to the application server, the modules fall into a single archive whose module boundaries have been lost.

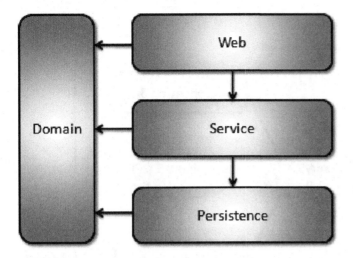

Figure 3-4. Sample modules in a Java EE application

By leveraging OSGi, the dm Server allows you to deploy and manage each module of your application in isolation in the form of a bundle so that you can update a module without affecting other running modules. This can minimize system update effort and risk, and it can reduce system down time.

Modularity and Encapsulation

In object-oriented design, a module is the encapsulation of a functional unit. A well-designed module should expose only the interfaces, not the implementation details, to other modules to reduce module coupling. However, in traditional Java applications, a module is free to access the interfaces exposed by other modules, as well as their implementation classes. At runtime, a module can also access the internal objects of other modules, as shown in Figure 3-5, in which the circles represent internal objects.

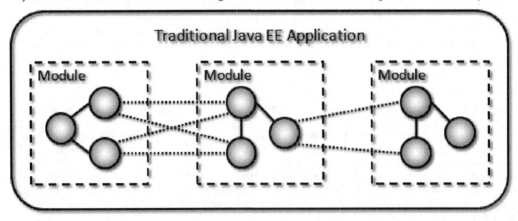

Figure 3-5. Module encapsulation in traditional Java EE applications

When you implement each module as an OSGi bundle to run on the dm Server, you can hide a bundle's implementation classes by not exporting their packages. Also, a bundle can contain objects to represent its internal states, which are not accessible to other bundles. If you would like to expose certain objects for other bundles to access, you can register them as OSGi services for the other bundles to consume at runtime, as shown in Figure 3-6, in which the triangles represent OSGi services and references.

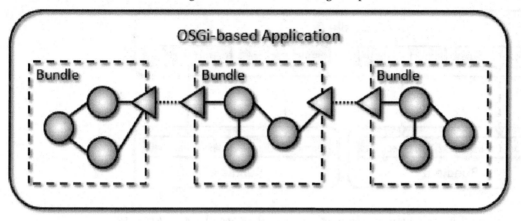

Figure 3-6. *Module encapsulation in the dm Server*

Introducing the dm Server's Features

As an OSGi-based Java application server, the dm Server offers a wide range of features that cover developing, packaging, deploying, running, and tracing OSGi-based enterprise applications. In this section, I will focus on the dm Server's highlights to give you a quick introduction showing how you can benefit from the technology.

Deployment Formats for Web Applications

An enterprise may have a number of web applications developed and deployed in the WAR format. To ease converting these applications to take advantage of OSGi, the dm Server operates on an OSGi web container that is capable of running web bundles. A web bundle is an "umbrella" term used to describe three deployment formats for Java web applications that can be run on the dm Server, in accordance with OSGi's R4 version 4.2 RFC 66 specification. The dm Server via its OSGi web container supports the following deployment formats ordered in what can be considered a migration path:

Standard WAR: Deploy a standard Java EE WAR file on the dm Server for the first step.

Shared Libraries WAR: Remove library JAR files from the WAR file (i.e., WEB-INF/lib) and install the libraries as OSGi bundles.

Shared Services WAR: Separate the services that the WAR file depends on to form a new bundle and register the services as OSGi services.

Support for such a migration path allows organizations to move toward OSGi applications at their own pace. With the dm Server capable of running web bundles, this support includes the standard Java EE WAR format, Shared Library WAR, and Shared Services WAR. The migration path for a web bundle from a standard WAR file to a Shared Services WAR capable of taking full advantage of OSGi is shown in Figure 3-7.

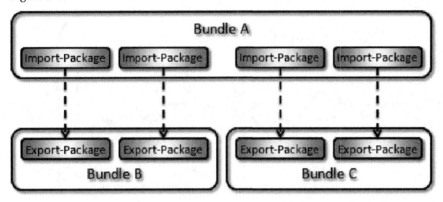

Figure 3-7. Migration path for web bundles from a standard WAR to a shared services WAR

Enhanced Dependency Management

A large-scale application framework usually organizes its classes into a number of packages. If a bundle needs to use such a framework, it will typically import most or all of the packages one by one using the standard OSGi manifest header Import-Package, as illustrated in Figure 3-8. As a result, this header will contain a long list of packages to import, and the list will be hard to read and maintain.

Note that the dm Server's manifest header Import-Bundle is similar to the standard OSGi manifest header Require-Bundle in that both can import all packages of the specified bundles. However, the packages will be processed in different ways. The dm Server will translate each Import-Bundle header entry into multiple Import-Package entries at deployment time, while the OSGi container will interpret the Require-Bundle entries directly. As specified in the OSGi specifications, the Import-Package and Require-Bundle manifest headers have different import semantics (for example, the Require-Bundle header will merge fragments of the same package exported by multiple bundles). Another reason the dm Server introduces the Import-Bundle header is that as the server evolves, it may need to support more directives for the Import-Bundle header (e.g., the import-scope directive).

Sometimes an application framework such as the Spring Framework consists of multiple modules, each of which is made available in the form of a bundle. If you have many bundles that are related, you can consider defining a *library* in the dm Server to include all its bundles.

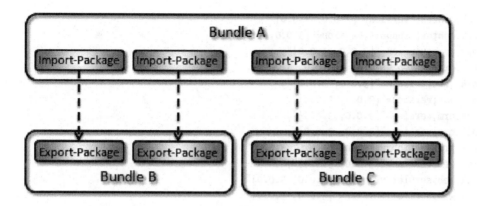

Figure 3-8. *Importing individual packages*

The dm Server can help solve this kind of problem by introducing the manifest header Import-Bundle, which will automatically import all packages exported by the bundle whose symbolic name is specified in the header, as illustrated in Figure 3-9.

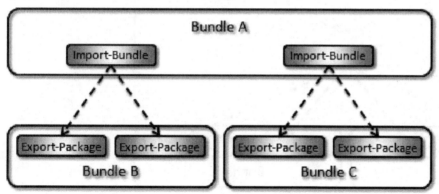

Figure 3-9. *Importing all packages of a bundle*

A dm Server library is simply a text file that points toward a group of bundles installed in a dm Server instance. The structure of a dm Server library file—which has a libd extension—is the following:

```
Library-SymbolicName: org.springframework.spring
Library-Version: 3.0.0
Library-Name: Spring Framework
Import-Bundle:
 org.springframework.aop;version="[3.0.0, 3.0.0]",
 org.springframework.asm;version="[3.0.0, 3.0.0]",
 org.springframework.aspects;version="[3.0.0, 3.0.0]",
 org.springframework.beans;version="[3.0.0, 3.0.0]",
```

```
org.springframework.context;version="[3.0.0, 3.0.0]",
org.springframework.context.support;version="[3.0.0, 3.0.0]",
org.springframework.core;version="[3.0.0, 3.0.0]",
org.springframework.expression;version="[3.0.0, 3.0.0]",
org.springframework.jdbc;version="[3.0.0, 3.0.0]",
org.springframework.jms;version="[3.0.0, 3.0.0]",
org.springframework.orm;version="[3.0.0, 3.0.0]",
org.springframework.oxm;version="[3.0.0, 3.0.0]",
org.springframework.transaction;version="[3.0.0, 3.0.0]",
org.springframework.web;version="[3.0.0, 3.0.0]",
org.springframework.web.servlet;version="[3.0.0, 3.0.0]",
org.springframework.web.portlet;version="[3.0.0, 3.0.0]",
com.springsource.org.aopalliance;version="[1.0.0, 1.0.0]"
```

This listing represents the Spring framework library, which defines a series of bundles that make up the bulk of the Spring framework. When a bundle has to use the group of bundles, it can simply use the dm Server's manifest header Import-Library to automatically import all packages exported by all bundles defined in a library, as illustrated in Figure 3-10.

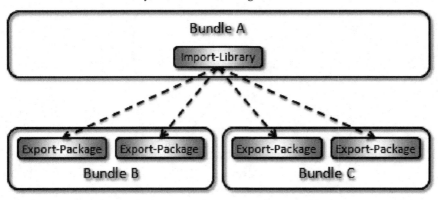

Figure 3-10. *Importing a library that includes multiple bundles*

In addition to these special headers—Import-Bundle and Import-Library—that enable enhanced dependency management, the dm Server also supports the special directive sharing:=clone. As its names implies, this directive allows the dm Server to generate a bundle clone for certain scenarios.

The first scenario the sharing:=clone directive is designed to address is the use of bundles with static state. Although OSGi and the dm Server's foundations permit the sharing of a single bundle among multiple applications, sharing bundles with static state works best by cloning such bundles.

Take the case of the Log4J logging framework, which relies on static variables to store its configuration values. If such a framework's bundle is deployed on the dm Server, even though the bundle can be reused by multiple applications, there can only be a single copy of the bundle and hence the Log4J framework classes will only have one configuration value set.

Therefore, by cloning a bundle that has static state, the dm Server guarantees that any bundle importing a bundle with these semantics will get its own copy (clone). For example, if bundle A uses a declaration in the following form:

```
Import-Bundle: org.apache.log4j;bundle-version="1.5.0";sharing:=clone
```

it ensures that bundle A will get its own Log4J copy, as illustrated in Figure 3-11.

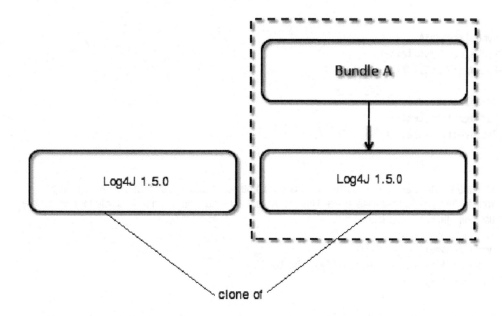

Figure 3-11. *Cloning of Log4J bundle*

In this figure, a clone of the Log4J bundle is created and scoped to be visible only to bundle A.

The second scenario the sharing:=clone directive is designed to solve is *pinning*. Pinning is a problem that is often encountered when a bundle relies on OSGi's standard uses directive, which is used to avoid run-time class cast exceptions. The uses directive is an extensive topic in itself, and the accompanying sidebar provides further explanation of its use. The discussion that follows explains how dm Server's cloning functionality solves certain scenarios for bundles relying on the uses directive.

WHAT IS THE PURPOSE OF OSGI'S *USES* DIRECTIVE ? A CLOSER LOOK

The uses directive is OSGi's mechanism to avoid run-time class cast exceptions. Since OSGi bundles possess their own classloader, it is vital that prior to entering Java's run-time each bundle have its dependencies resolved to avoid such exceptions.

Initially the uses directive may appear redundant with the basic behavior of the Import-Package and Export-Package headers. Take for example a scenario in which bundle A and bundle Z have the following MANIFEST.MF files:

```
-------
Bundle-SymbolicName:A
Export-Package: first.letter
Import-Package: last.letter
-------
Bundle-SymbolicName:Z
Export-Package:last.letter
Import-Package:first.letter
-------
```

If bundle A and bundle Z are installed, the process should be successful, given that the package imported by bundle A is exported by bundle Z, and vice versa. This is a typical approach, but it's also possible to have bundle A's manifest use something like the following:

```
Bundle-SymbolicName:A
Export-Package: first.letter;uses:="last.letter"
Import-Package: last.letter
```

This last MANIFEST.MF file would be used if somewhere inside the first.letter package there was a dependency on some class or type contained in the last.letter package. In such cases, the uses directive safeguards any other bundle relying on the first.letter package to throw a run-time class cast exception. Take a look at the following application bundle MANIFEST.MF file, which illustrates this further:

```
Bundle-SymbolicName:TNT
Import-Package:first.letter
```

Since the creator of the TNT bundle would be unaware that somewhere inside the `first.letter` package there is a dependency on the `last.letter` package, a run-time class exception would occur. It's the `uses` directive accompanying the `Export-Package` header of bundle A which guarantees that the `last.letter` package is pinned to the `first.letter` package, thus avoiding any unsuspecting run-time class cast exception.

For the same reason, a new application bundle attempting to use the `first.letter` package in conjunction with a new version of `last.letter` package would fail, since the first version of the `last.letter` package would already be pinned to the `first.letter` package to begin with.

An application bundle can define dependencies on any number of bundles it requires. However, if one of these bundles relies on the uses directive to point toward any of the same dependencies, a pinning problem can arise. Figure 3-12 illustrates a typical uses directive with a potential pinning problem.

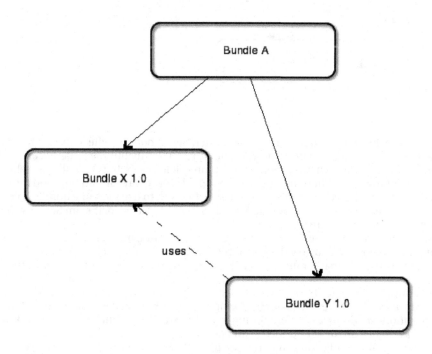

Figure 3-12. OSGi uses *directive with potential pinning problem*

Here you can see that bundle A has dependencies on bundle X and bundle Y. However, notice how bundle Y relies on the uses directive to associate itself with bundle X. Under most circumstances the uses directive can go unnoticed. But take a look at Figure 3-13, which introduces bundle B; it also makes us of bundle X and bundle Y.

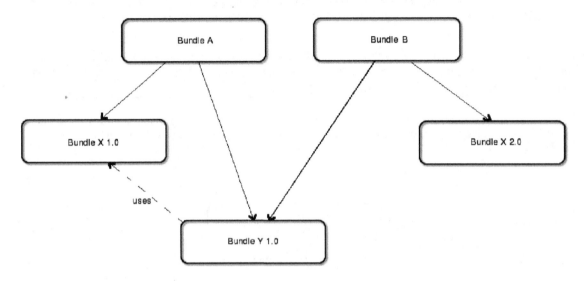

Figure 3-13. *OSGi uses directive pinning conflict*

In this last figure, bundle B is defined with dependencies to both bundle X and bundle Y. But a version upgrade is also performed on bundle X. Though apparently bundle B has access to its dependencies—including bundle X's new version—resolution will fail since bundle Y already relies on the uses directive to point toward a different bundle X version. The only way for bundle A and bundle B to fulfill their dependencies in the same OSGi environment is for both to use the same bundle X version, given that bundle Y is pinned to a particular bundle X version. For this scenario, the dm Server supports the use of cloning as illustrated in Figure 3-14.

This illustrates how a new clone for bundle Y is created, allowing multiple bundle X versions to be used, even though bundle Y makes use of the uses directive to pin bundle X and avoid run-time class cast exceptions. See the earlier sidebar for further details about why bundles often rely on the uses directive.

A more elaborate scenario for the dm Server's cloning functionality is best explained by the Spring framework. Since the dm Server relies on the Spring framework version 3.0 for its operation, any attempt to run applications requiring a different Spring framework version would encounter collisions, given the framework's reliance on the uses directive and pinning.

By supporting cloning, applications that require different Spring framework versions can run on the dm Server without conflict. In this scenario, an application requiring a different Spring framework version would get its own copy (clone), without raising collisions with the default Spring framework version used by the dm Server. Cloning in the dm Server is fully addressed in Chapter 8.

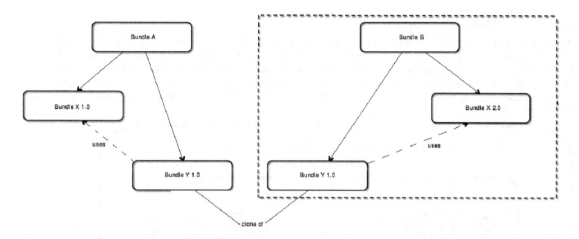

Figure 3-14. *OSGi uses directive with dm Server cloning*

The Enterprise Bundle Repository

A Java application usually has to rely on several JARs to implement its functionality. Each JAR therefore must be converted into a valid OSGi bundle, which has the bundle information specified in the MANIFEST.MF file, before it can be deployed and run on the dm Server. Although conversion tasks of this type are not complicated, they are redundant and add to the cost of using OSGi.

To save developers the trouble of converting JAR files into bundles, SpringSource hosts a public enterprise bundle repository that includes converted OSGi bundles for popular Java libraries. The dm Server distribution already includes common bundles (e.g., Java Extension APIs, the Spring Framework, and AspectJ) that will be installed along with the dm Server. If you need other bundles that are not preinstalled, you can simply download the bundles from the public repository and copy them to the dm Server's local repository to have them installed. The URL of the SpringSource public repository is

```
http://www.springsource.com/repository/
```

In addition to OSGi bundles for common JARs, the repository also includes dm Server library definitions for common application frameworks (e.g., the Spring Framework and the Hibernate-based JPA implementation). Each of these libraries can be imported as a whole to have all its constituent bundles imported automatically.

If you can't locate a particular OSGi-converted JAR needed by your application in the SpringSource public Repository, you can also rely on the Bundlor tool. Bundlor automates the creation of OSGi manifest directives for JARs and can be executed from a variety of environments that include Ant, Maven, Eclipse and an operating system's command line. You can download Bundlor from the following URL:

```
http://www.springsource.org/bundlor/
```

Chapter 8 presents a series of Bundlor examples.

Application Boundary Support

In a standard OSGi environment the deployment and management unit is a bundle, and there's no concept of an application. As a result, a bundle is not aware of the application it belongs to or of other bundles in the same application. All bundles in the OSGi container share the entire OSGi service registry. However, the lack of application boundary support may cause trouble in some cases. Suppose you are going to deploy two applications to the OSGi container, each of which consists of two bundles, as shown in Figure 3-15.

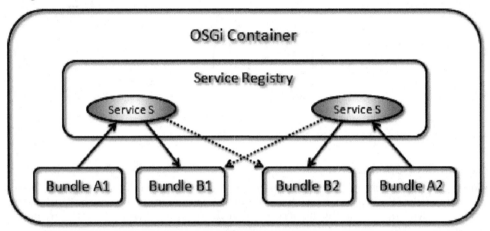

Figure 3-15. *Bundles without application boundaries*

Suppose you have deployed two applications: Application 1 consists of Bundles A1 and B1. and Application 2 consists of Bundles A2 and B2. Bundles A1 and A2 register an OSGi service under Interface S for B1 and B2 to consume respectively, as represented by the solid lines. However, in a standard OSGi environment, there's no concept of an application, so there is no guarantee that the OSGi services will be consumed in the way you expect. The result may be that B1 consumes the service registered by A2, while B2 consumes the service registered by A1, as represented by the dotted lines. A possible solution is to assign appropriate service properties (e.g., the application name) to the OSGi services and look up the services with a filter specified. However, this will add complexity to the bundles.

The dm Server provides a solution by supporting the concept of an application that consists of a set of bundles. An application is deployed to the dm Server in the Platform Archive (PAR) format. A PAR file contains multiple bundle JAR files and a `MANIFEST.MF` file. It can group the bundles into a single deployment unit so that they can be deployed, refreshed, and undeployed as a whole, while each of the bundles can be redeployed and refreshed independently. An application defines a boundary for its bundles so that OSGi services registered by bundles in an application will be isolated from those registered by other applications, as shown in Figure 3-16.

The use of PAR files and application boundary support also sets a precedent for other dm Server functionality, such as the special OSGi dm Server directive `import-scope:=application`. Just as the dm Server's `Import-Bundle` and `Import-Library` manifest headers serve to simplify the use of OSGi's standard `Import-Package` and `Export-Package` headers, the intent behind the dm Server directive `import-scope:=application` is similar.

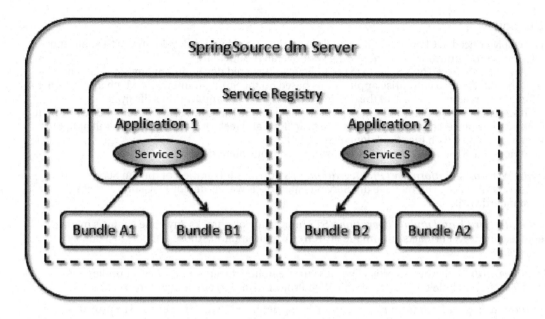

Figure 3-16. *Bundles with application boundaries supported by the dm Server*

Let's assume you have one particular package or bundle that is required by multiple bundles in your application. Take for example a JPA implementation bundle—such as EclipseLink, OpenJPA or Hibernate—which would typically be used in an application's domain and persistence bundles.

Although using something like the `Import-Bundle` or `Import-Library` manifest header in each of the application's bundles certainly simplifies the entire import process, it also makes each bundle dependant on a particular JPA implementation, with a change in JPA implementation requiring changes to multiple bundles. Which is what the `import-scope:=application` directive tries to alleviate.

If a single application bundle uses a statement like the following:

```
Import-Bundle:org.eclipse.persistence;version="1.0.0";import-scope:=application
```

that is sufficient to make the bundle—`org.eclipse.persistence`—visible to all other application bundles belonging to a PAR file. In this manner, you don't have to manage multiple import statements in various bundles, but instead rely on a single statement and let the dm Server propagate visibility to all the other application bundles belonging to a PAR file.

Besides the concept of a PAR file for defining an application's boundaries, the dm Server also supports the concept of a *plan*. In the dm Server, a plan is a logical group of artifacts (bundles or configuration elements) located in a server's local repository for defining an application with the same semantics as a PAR file.

The main difference between a PAR and plan file is that the former requires its parts to be contained in the same file structure, whereas the latter simply points toward artifacts already installed in the dm Server's local repository. A plan is similar to the dm Server's library concept; it's simply a text file with an association of parts.

Tool Support

As you probably noticed in Chapter 2, having tools like Eclipse to aid you in developing OSGi applications can be an important contribution to increasing your overall productivity.

The SpringSource Tools Suite (STS) is an Eclipse-powered development environment aimed at organizations that develop enterprise applications based on the Spring framework, which also includes a series of tools to streamline the use of the dm Server throughout an application's life cycle.

It should be noted that even though STS is a standalone Integrated Development Environment (IDE), because it is powered by Eclipse it has a similar "look and feel," which should be familiar to most users who have worked with the standalone Eclipse IDE.

Among the STS features related to the dm Server you will find:

Eclipse Web Tools Platform (WTP) integration: STS provides integration of the dm Server with Eclipse's WTP, letting you manage dm Server instances, as well as deploy OSGi bundles, PARs and standard WARs.

Automatic refresh and update operations: STS integration also tracks any code changes made to deployed dm Server artifacts, automatically refreshing or updating those artifacts in a dm Server instance.

Project wizards: STS provides project wizards to streamline the creation of OSGi bundles and PAR files. They include the WTP Dynamic Web Project wizard to create standard WARs.

Manifest editing and validation: For bundles being deployed to the dm Server, STS provides content assist, hyperlinking and validation for MANIFEST.MF files to make the task of managing OSGi metadata as easy as possible. Common problems can be automatically resolved by using integrated Quick Fixes, such as downloading a missing dependency or correcting a version range).

Classpath management: STS can detect OSGi dependency metadata from a bundle's MANIFEST.MF file and create a classpath container with correct visibility rules. Such dependencies can be resolved against a dm Server's local repository.

Enterprise Bundle Repository access: STS integrates with the SpringSource Enterprise Bundle Repository, providing integrated access to publicly available OSGi bundles and libraries, making it easier to download and install third-party dependency bundles.

Finally, it is worth mentioning that STS is available at no cost and free for all development purposes, even though licensed under a commercial license (unlike the Eclipse IDE).

Versatile Management and Deployment

While working directly with the dm Server from a development environment like STS is important, support for interacting with the dm Server in production environments is just as important.

The dm Server provides an administration shell that provides command-line access to its administrative functionalities, which include:

- Installing, uninstalling, starting, stopping, updating and refreshing artifacts.
- Querying artifact dependency graphs and services.
- Diagnosing dependency resolution problems.

Besides being available through the administrative shell, these same dm Server functionalities are supported in SpringSource's Application Management Suite (AMS). AMS is an enterprise application management solution designed to manage and monitor Spring-powered applications, as well as manage servers like dm Server, tc Server and even standard Apache Tomcat and Apache web server instances, providing a single console with dashboards to check the health of applications, including performance, uptime, service-level agreements, and overall trends.

Adapting to more stringent demands, the dm Server is also capable of being run as a cluster composed as a series of nodes (instances). This allows certain nodes to fulfill the function of shared repositories, thereby centralizing the location and management of artifacts available to other dm Server instances, where other nodes function as client dm Server nodes communicating with repository nodes.

Finally, the dm Server is also available for deployment on some of the more novel cloud computing environments, like Amazon's Elastic Cloud (EC2). SpringSource makes available an AMI (Amazon Machine Instance), which includes the dm Server and can be used to scale your dm Server deployments to EC2's architecture.

First Failure Data Capture (FFDC)

With most Java EE application servers, when a server failure occurs, developers have to reproduce the failure in order for the application server's service team to diagnose the error and create a fix. In some cases a server failure occurs randomly and is therefore very difficult to reproduce.

The dm Server enhances its error diagnostic capability by introducing the first failure data capture (FFDC) feature. When a server failure occurs for the first time, FFDC will capture a snapshot of all necessary information in a service dump file. Developers and administrators can simply send this dump file to the dm Server's service team to diagnose the error, without having reproducing it first.

Introducing the dm Server's Architecture

The dm Server has a layered and modular architecture as shown in Figure 3-17. Its core is the SpringSource Dynamic Module Kernel (dm Kernel or DMK), an OSGi-based kernel that builds on Equinox to take full advantage of the modularity and versioning capabilities of OSGi. The dm Kernel provides core functionality for the dm Server and also extends the OSGi capabilities for dependency provisioning and management. The dm Kernel installs bundles in its repository on demand to minimize memory usage.

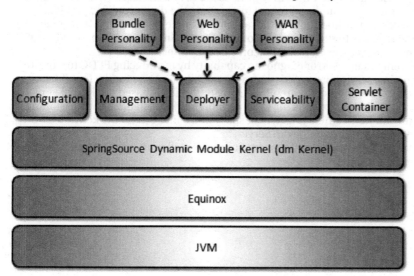

Figure 3-17. The dm Server's overall architecture

On top of the dm Kernel there is a layer of subsystems that extend the kernel's core functionality and implement various features of the dm Server. The dm Server's architecture is designed to be modular to allow great flexibility in developing and deploying subsystems. The dm Server's subsystems include configuration, management, deployer, serviceability, and the OSGi web container.

Summary

In this chapter, you first had an introduction to the dm Server and its core components, which include OSGi, Eclipse Equinox, Spring Framework, Spring Dynamic Modules, and the OSGi web container. The dm Server integrates and extends these technologies to provide a complete and integrated solution.

You also saw the dm Server's solutions to several common problems in traditional Java EE application development and deployment. First, the dm Server allows you to deploy different versions of a Java library at the same time in the form of bundles. Second, it allows you to deploy each module of your application in isolation in the form of a bundle so that you can update a module without affecting other running modules. Last, it allows you to hide the implementation classes and internal objects of a module with the package-sharing mechanism and service registry of OSGi.

The dm Server offers a wide range of enterprise features. First, it supports a clear migration path for developers to migrate existing web applications in the WAR format to OSGi web bundles gradually. Next, it supports the `Import-Bundle` and `Import-Library` headers to import all packages exported by a bundle and all bundles in a library, in addition to solving the OSGi problem of pinning by supporting the cloning of bundles. SpringSource also hosts an enterprise bundle repository that includes OSGi bundles and dm Server library definitions for popular Java libraries for you to install into the dm Server. It also supports the Bundlor tool for automating the creation of OSGi manifest directives for JARs.

Also, the dm Server supports the concept of an application, consisting of a set of artifacts (bundles and configuration files) in either the Platform Archive (PAR) or plan format. Formats which facilitate provisions like the `import-scope:=application` directive, that grant a bundle visibility to all other bundles belonging to an application.

The dm Server is also tightly integrated with the SpringSource Tools Suite (STS), allowing for a more streamlined development process. In addition to tool integration, the dm Server also provides management interfaces from a command-line shell, as well as SpringSource Application Management Suite (AMS). Besides having the capacity to run as a cluster of servers, the dm Server is supported as an AMI (Amazon Machine Instance), so it can work with Amazon's EC2 architecture.

Finally, the dm Server enhances its error diagnostic capability by introducing FFDC to capture all necessary server information in a service dump file when a server failure occurs for the first time.

The dm Server has a layered and modular architecture, with the OSGi-based dm Kernel at its core. The dm Kernel builds on Equinox and extends the OSGi capabilities for dependency provisioning and management. On top of the dm Kernel there is a layer of subsystems that extend the kernel's core functionality and implement various features of the dm Server.

In the next chapter, you will get started with the dm Server's installation, administration, configuration, and deployment.

Getting Started with the dm Server

In the previous chapter, you had an overview of the components, features, and architecture of the dm Server. In this chapter, you will learn about the dm Server's general concepts and get started working with it. You will install and run the dm Server on your local machine, and then you will deploy applications and install their dependencies to its provisioning repository. This chapter covers the following topics:

- Downloading and installing the dm Server
- Introducing the dm Server's installation directory
- Starting and stopping the dm Server
- Starting the dm Server with different starting options
- Using the dm Server's web-based administration console
- Deploying applications to the dm Server
- Configuration files for the dm Server
- Managing the dm Server's provisioning repository

Installing the dm Server

The first step in getting started with the dm Server is to install it on your local machine. Prior to installing the dm Server, you should have a Java Development Kit (JDK) installed. Note that the dm Server requires Java SE 6 or higher versions.

Downloading the dm Server

Like any other Spring product, the dm Server can be downloaded from the official SpringSource web site:

`http://www.springsource.org/dmserver`

From this site you can download the latest release of the dm Server, which is 2.0.x at the time of writing. Throughout this book I will use the dm Server release 2.0.0 so that features introduced in this book are also applicable to other 2.0.x releases. There are two versions of the dm Server you can download:

The community version: This allows you to use the dm Server for free, but it includes no support or service level guarantees.

The enterprise version: This integrates with other SpringSource enterprise products as an integrated solution. It includes commercial support from SpringSource and has been QA tested.

For learning purposes you may choose to download the free community version, which is distributed as a single ZIP file (e.g., `springsource-dm-server-2.0.0.RELEASE.zip` for the dm Server release 2.0.0).

Setting Up the dm Server

The dm Server's community installation is very simple. Just extract the downloaded ZIP file into a directory of your choice, for example, `c:\springsource-dm-server-2.0.0.RELEASE` on a Windows platform or `/opt/springsource-dm-server-2.0.0.RELEASE` on a Unix/Linux platform, to complete the installation.

After the file extraction, there is one more step before you can use the server. You must create a `SERVER_HOME` environment variable that indicates the dm Server's installation directory. For example, on a Windows platform you can set this variable in the Environment Variables dialog, which you bring up by selecting the Start menu ➤ Settings ➤ Control Panel ➤ System ➤ the Advanced tab ➤ the Environment Variables button. Then you can create a new system variable as shown in Figure 4-1.

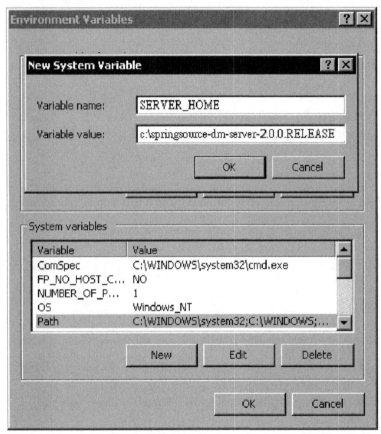

Figure 4-1. *Creating the SERVER_HOME environment variable on a Windows platform*

If you installed the dm Server on a Unix/Linux platform, you can export the SERVER_HOME environment variable with the following command:

```
export SERVER_HOME=/opt/springsource-dm-server-2.0.0.RELEASE/
```

Exploring the dm Server's Installation Directory

After you have installed the dm Server on your local machine, its installation directory should contain the subdirectories listed in Table 4-1.

Table 4-1. Subdirectories in the dm Server's Installation Directory

Directory	What It Contains
bin	Scripts for starting and stopping the dm Server.
boot	Provisioning library (JAR) for booting the dm Server.
config	Configuration files for configuring the dm Server itself and components of the dm Server, such as the Tomcat Servlet container and the Equinox OSGi container.
docs	Documentation, including a user guide and a programmer guide for the dm Server.
lib	Standard library JAR files used by the dm Server.
pickup	Applications that will be hot-deployed.
repository	The provisioning repository that contains OSGi bundles and library definitions used by the dm Server.
resources	Licenses that apply to the many components that make up the dm Server.
serviceability	Log files, trace files, and service dumps generated by the dm Server.
work	Working files such as copies of deployed applications, serialized session files, and temporary files for the dm Server. This directory in the dm Server serves the same purpose as the work directory in a standard Apache Tomcat web container. However, note that the dm Server operates with a standard OSGi (RFC-66) web container, which although similar to a standard Apache Tomcat web container is different.

Running the dm Server

Once you have the dm Server installed on your local machine, you can run it to validate that the installation was successful.

Starting and Stopping the dm Server

To start the dm Server, simply run the startup script located in the `bin` subdirectory of the dm Server's installation directory. On a Windows platform this is `startup.bat`; on a Unix/Linux platform it is `startup.sh`. If the dm Server has been installed successfully, you will see the following output:

```
<SPKB0001I> Server starting.
<SPOF0001I> OSGi telnet console available on port 2401.
<SPKE0000I> Boot subsystems installed.
<SPKE0001I> Base subsystems installed.
<SPPM0000I> Installing profile 'web'.
<SPPM0001I> Installed profile 'web'.
<SPSC0001I> Creating HTTP/1.1 connector with scheme http on port 8080.
<SPSC0001I> Creating HTTP/1.1 connector with scheme https on port 8443.
<SPSC0001I> Creating AJP/1.3 connector with scheme http on port 8009.
<SPSC0000I> Starting ServletContainer.
<SPPM0002I> Server open for business with profile 'web'.
<SPDE0048I> Processing 'INITIAL' event for file
            'server.admin.splash-2.0.0.RELEASE.war'.
<SPSC1000I> Creating web application '/'.
<SPSC1001I> Starting web application '/'.
<SPDE0010I> Deployment of 'com.springsource.server.servlet.splash' version '0'
            completed.
<SPDE0048I> Processing 'INITIAL' event for file
            'server.admin.web-2.0.0.RELEASE.jar'.
<SPSC1000I> Creating web application '/admin'.
<SPSC1001I> Starting web application '/admin'.
<SPDE0010I> Deployment of 'com.springsource.server.servlet.admin' version
            '2.0.0.RELEASE' completed.
```

Now if you open `http://localhost:8080/` in your web browser, you should see the dm Server splash page, illustrated in Figure 4-2.

To stop the dm Server, simply run `shutdown.bat` on a Windows platform or `shutdown.sh` on a Unix/Linux platform.

Figure 4-2. The splash page of the dm Server

Starting Options for the dm Server

The dm Server's startup scripts support several options that allow you to start it for specific purposes.

Clean Starting

You can clean-start the dm Server with the `-clean` command-line argument. For example, on a Windows platform you can run the following command:

```
startup.bat -clean
```

When you specify clean-starting, the dm Server will first remove the following files before it starts up and redeploys all applications:

- All working files in the work directory
- All log files in the serviceability/logs directory
- All trace files in the serviceability/trace directory
- All service dumps in the serviceability/dump directory

Starting in the Debug Mode

By starting the dm Server in the debug mode, you can remotely debug applications running on the server, using the command prompt or a Java IDE such as Eclipse. To start the dm Server in the debug mode, use the -debug argument. For example, on a Windows platform you can run the following command:

```
startup.bat -debug
```

By default, the dm Server's debug agent listens on port 8000, which is the default remote debug port used by Eclipse. If you would like to choose another debug port number, you can specify it after the -debug argument:

```
startup.bat -debug 8001
```

Now in Eclipse you can attach to a remote dm Server process via a socket for debugging purposes. Choose Debug Configurations from Eclipse's Run menu to bring up the Debug dialog and create a Remote Java Application configuration. Then choose the project you are going to debug and specify the host name and port number, as shown in Figure 4-3.

You can assign an arbitrary name (e.g., SpringSource dm Server) to this configuration and click the Debug button. Now you can set breakpoints in the project and debug it in a similar way to a local running Java application.

In some cases, you might wish to debug an application to diagnose problems that occur at startup. For this purpose you need to prevent the dm Server from starting up until a debugger has attached to its debug agent. You can start the dm Server in the debug mode and suspend the JVM until a debugger has attached, using the following command:

```
startup.bat -debug -suspend
```

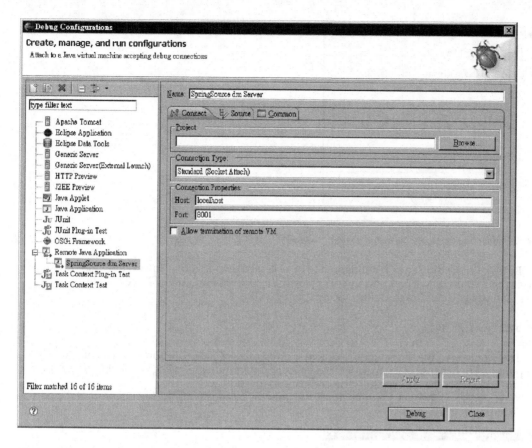

Figure 4-3. *Attaching to a remote Java process for debugging purposes*

Starting with JMX Enabled

JMX (Java Management Extensions) is a standard technology for managing and monitoring system resources such as applications, objects, devices, and networks. Those resources are represented by objects called MBeans (managed beans). You can connect to a JMX-enabled resource locally or remotely using a JMX console, such as JConsole (supplied with JDK) and MC4J (an open-source JMX console).

Assuming you opt for dm server's default JMX settings, if you start JConsole on a Windows platform (by running either jconsole.exe from the bin directory of the JDK installation or the utility jconsole.bat script inside the dm server's bin directory)—or Jconsole on a Unix/Linux platform(by running either jconsole.sh from the bin directory of the JDK installation or the utility jconsole.sh script inside the dm server's bin directory) you will see that a local Java process with the name com.springsource.server.kernel.bootstrap.Bootstrap has JMX enabled, as shown in Figure 4-4. You can then connect to this local process to manage and monitor the dm Server's JMX-enabled resources.

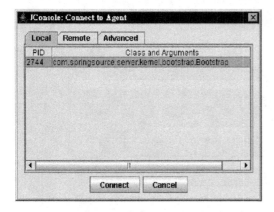

Figure 4-4. *Connecting to a local dm Server process with JMX*

By default, the dm Server is configured to be accessed on port 9875. However, it's also possible to override this default JMX access port by specifying the ñjmxremote argument. For example, on a Windows platform you can run the following command:

```
startup.bat -jmxport 9009
```

This would start the dm server's JMX access point on port 9009. The port is often changed for security purposes or because of a particular JMX console configuration. If using such JMX port settings, you need to ensure that the JMX console also connects to this port.

You can also connect to a remote dm Server process by specifying the host name and the port number, as shown in Figure 4-5.

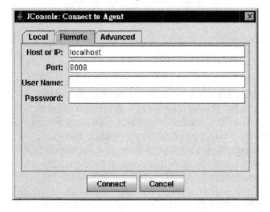

Figure 4-5. *Connecting to a remote dm Server process with JMX*

By default, the dm Server has authentication and SSL disabled for remote JMX access so that everyone can connect to the dm Server process using a JMX client. In a production environment, I strongly recommend that you enable authentication and SSL by modifying the dm Server's JMX configuration files located in the dm Server's config/management directory. For details on these properties, please refer to the "Monitoring and Management Using JMX" guide at the following URL:

`http://java.sun.com/j2se/1.5.0/docs/guide/management/agent.html`

Once connected to the dm Server process using JConsole, you can monitor its memory consumption, thread use, and class loading, and monitor and manage its MBeans, as shown in Figures 4-6 through 4-9, respectively. For details on JConsole usage, please refer to the "Using JConsole" guide at the following URL:

`http://java.sun.com/j2se/1.5.0/docs/guide/management/jconsole.html`

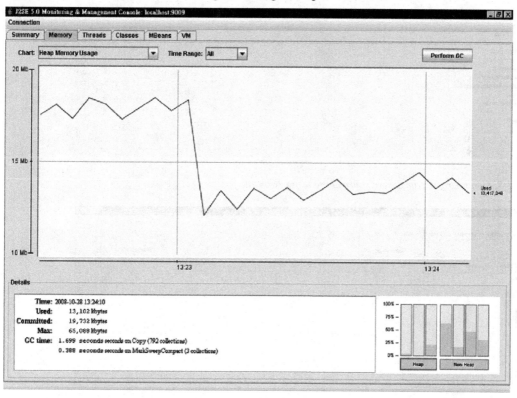

Figure 4-6. *Monitoring the dm Server's memory consumption using JConsole*

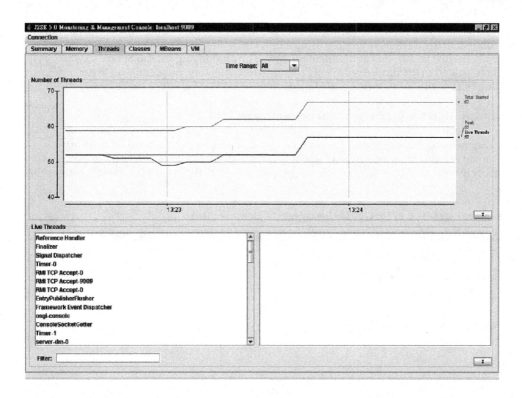

Figure 4-7. Monitoring the dm Server's thread use using JConsole

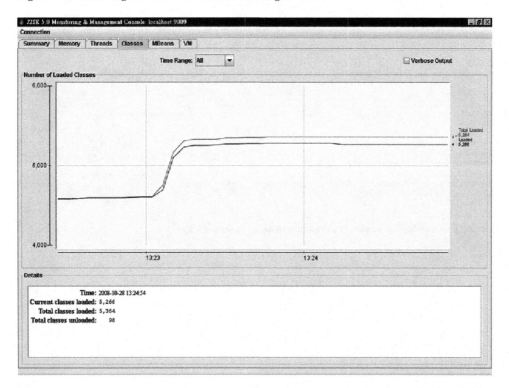

Figure 4-8. *Monitoring the dm Server's class loading using JConsole*

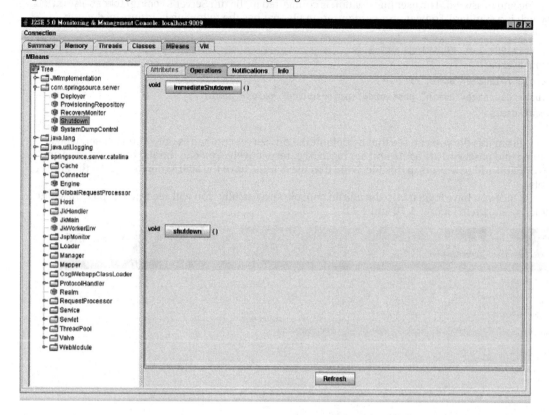

Figure 4-9. *Monitoring and managing the dm Server's MBeans using JConsole*

As you can see, the dm Server exposes several MBeans, such as Deployer and Shutdown, under the com.springsource.server category to enable you to monitor and manage its resources via JMX. On the other hand, its embedded Tomcat Servlet container (Catalina) also exposes MBeans under the springsource.server.catalina category.

Using the Administration Console

The dm Server provides a web-based administration console, which allows server users to administrate the server from a web browser. Once the dm Server has started, you can access this admin console either by clicking the Admin Console link on the splash page or by directly opening the following URL:

http://localhost:8080/admin

The admin console has HTTP basic authentication enabled, so you must log into it with a valid username and password. The user information is configured in the dm Server's config/tomcat-users.xml file, which is a standard Tomcat user configuration file that has the following contents by default:

```xml
<?xml version='1.0' encoding='utf-8'?>
<tomcat-users>
    <role rolename="admin"/>
    <user username="admin" password="springsource" roles="admin"/>
</tomcat-users>
```

From this file you can see that by default the dm Server configures only a single user, whose username and password are admin and springsource, respectively. You can modify this username and password and add new users in this file. Note that users must have the admin role to log into the admin console.

Once you have logged into the admin console successfully, you will see that the page has four sections, as shown in Figures 4-10 and 4-11.

Figure 4-10. *The Admin Console and Deployed Applications sections of the admin console*

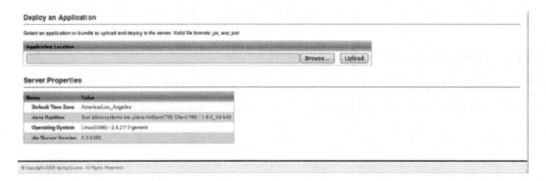

Figure 4-11. *The Deploy an Application and Server Properties section of the admin console*

116

As you can see, these four sections compose the admin console's main page. They are intended for the following uses:

Admin Console: This section displays operation results and messages.

Deployed Applications: This section displays a list of installed applications and the modules they comprise.

Deploy an Application: This section allows you to upload an application archive file, which will be deployed automatically to the dm Server.

Server Properties: This section displays the dm Server's properties and configurations.

From the Deployed Applications section, you can see that the dm Server has predeployed the following three applications:

`com.springsource.server.servlet.splash`: This is the Splash application deployed at the context root (/) for rendering the splash page.

`com.springsource.server.servlet.admin.plan`: This is the Admin application deployed at the /admin context path to provide functionality for the admin console.

`com.springsource.server.repository.hosted`: This application manages remote repositories.

Deploying Applications to the dm Server

The dm Server supports deploying application archive files in the following formats:

Bundle JAR: You can deploy a standard OSGi bundle packaged in a JAR file to the dm Server.

Web bundles: You can deploy a web bundle packaged as a standard Java EE WAR file, a Shared Libraries WAR file, or a Shared Services WAR file to the dm Server.

PAR: You can package multiple bundles of an application in a PAR file and deploy it to the dm Server.

To deploy an application in any of these formats you have several options. One is through the admin console presented earlier, whereby you select an application archive via your web browser, and upon submission it is deployed to the dm Server.

Another option is through the multiple dm Server directories used to load application archives. One of these locations is the pickup directory, located under the dm Server's home, where once you place an application archive it is automatically deployed.

In addition to this location, the dm Server also has a series of subdirectories, located under the repository directory, that can also be used to deploy application archives. Unlike in the pickup directory, however, application archives placed within the repository directory are not automatically deployed, requiring the dm Server to be restarted in order for deployment to take place. The particular structure and purpose of the subdirectories inside the repository directory is explained in the "Managing the Provision Repository" section later in the chapter.

To get started with application deployment, you can download a sample application from the dm Server's download page (http://www.springsource.org/dmserver). As a starting point, you should try the Formtags sample application (formtags-1.4.0.RELEASE.zip) because it requires neither installation of additional dependencies nor database setup. You can download the file from http://dist.springsource.com/release/SAMPL/formtags-1.4.0.RELEASE.zip. Next, deploy it to the dm Server following the instructions you will find in this section.

Deploying Applications through the Admin Console

The admin console allows you to deploy an application to a remote dm Server instance through the web. If you upload an application archive file from your local file system in the Deploy an Application section, it will be deployed automatically to the dm Server. For example, you can upload and deploy the formtags-par-1.4.0.RELEASE.par file that is available in the dist directory. When the operation is complete, you will see the success message in the Admin Console section, and the application will be added to the list in the Deployed Applications section, as shown in Figure 4-12.

As you can see from the Deployed Applications section, the PAR file contains a web module deployed to the formtags-par context path. You can now access the application with the following URL:

```
http://localhost:8080/formtags-par/
```

Admin Console

Result of the last operation: 'Application deployed'.

Deployed Applications

Name	Version	Origin	Date	Undeploy
com.springsource.server.servlet.admin	2.0.0.D-69	Hot Deployed	May 19, 2009 6:25:40 PM PDT	undeploy
⊕ Associated Modules:				
com.springsource.server.servlet.admin	(type: Web)	/admin		
com.springsource.server.servlet.splash	2.0.0.D-69	Hot Deployed	May 19, 2009 6:25:42 PM PDT	undeploy
⊕ Associated Modules:				
com.springsource.server.servlet.splash	(type: Web)	/		
com.springsource.server.repository.hosted	2.0.0.D-52	Hot Deployed	May 19, 2009 6:25:43 PM PDT	undeploy
⊕ Associated Modules:				
com.springsource.server.repository.hosted.web		(type: Web)	/com.springsource.server.repository	
com.springsource.server.repository.hosted-synthetic.context		(type: Bundle)	No personality identifier	
com.springsource.server.repository.hosted.core		(type: Bundle)	No personality identifier	
formtags-par	1.4.0.RELEASE	Admin Console	May 19, 2009 7:28:00 PM PDT	undeploy
⊕ Associated Modules:				
org.springframework.showcase.formtags.web_par		(type: Web)	formtags-par	
formtags-par-synthetic.context		(type: Bundle)	No personality identifier	
org.springframework.showcase.formtags.domain_par		(type: Bundle)	No personality identifier	
org.springframework.showcase.formtags.service_par		(type: Bundle)	No personality identifier	

Figure 4-12. *Deploying an application successfully in the admin console*

To undeploy the application from the admin console, simply click the application's Undeploy link in the Deployed Applications section. When the operation is complete, the admin console will display the success message in the Admin Console section and remove the application from the list in the Deployed Applications section, as shown in Figure 4-13.

Result of the last operation: '*Application undeployed*'.

Deployed Applications

Name	Version	Origin	Date	Undeploy
com.springsource.server.servlet.admin	2.0.0.D-69	Hot Deployed	May 19, 2009 6:25:40 PM PDT	undeploy
⊕ Associated Modules:				
com.springsource.server.servlet.admin	(type: Web)	/admin		
com.springsource.server.servlet.splash	2.0.0.D-69	Hot Deployed	May 19, 2009 6:25:42 PM PDT	undeploy
⊕ Associated Modules:				
com.springsource.server.servlet.splash	(type: Web)	/		
com.springsource.server.repository.hosted	2.0.0.D-52	Hot Deployed	May 19, 2009 6:25:43 PM PDT	undeploy
⊕ Associated Modules:				
com.springsource.server.repository.hosted.web	(type: Web)	/com.springsource.server.repository		
com.springsource.server.repository.hosted-synthetic.context	(type: Bundle)	No personality identifier		
com.springsource.server.repository.hosted.core	(type: Bundle)	No personality identifier		

Figure 4-13. Undeploying an application successfully in the admin console

Hot-Deploying Applications

If you can directly access the dm Server's file system, you can choose the hot deployment method to save the trouble of logging into the admin console. To hot-deploy an application, simply copy its archive file to the pickup directory of the dm Server home. For example, let's hot-deploy the formtags-par-1.4.0. RELEASE.par file to the dm Server. If the dm Server is running, you will notice the following messages output to its console:

```
[2009-05-19 17:45:23.781] fs-watcher          <SPDE0048I> Processing 'CREATED'
event for file 'formtags-par-1.4.0.RELEASE.par'.
[2009-05-19 17:45:24.937] fs-watcher          <SPSC1000I> Creating web
application '/formtags-par'.
[2009-05-19 17:45:25.078] async-delivery-thread-1  <SPSC1001I> Starting web
application '/formtags-par'.
[2009-05-19 17:45:25.546] fs-watcher          <SPDE0010I> Deployment of
'formtags-par' version '1.4.0.RELEASE' completed.
```

To hot-undeploy the application, simply delete its archive file from the pickup directory of the dm Server home. If the dm Server is running, you will notice the following messages from its console output:

```
[2009-05-19 17:50:12.906] fs-watcher          <SPDE0048I> Processing 'DELETED'
event for file 'formtags-par-1.4.0.RELEASE.par'.
[2009-05-19 17:50:12.921] fs-watcher          <SPSC1002I> Removing web
application '/formtags-par'.
[2009-05-19 17:50:13.046] fs-watcher          <SPDE0012I> Undeployment of
'formtags-par' version '1.4.0.RELEASE' completed.
```

The default hot-deployment directory—pickup—including the allotted time to deploy an application before giving up (default timeout) can be overridden in the kernel.properties file located under the dm Server's config directory. The relevant section of this file is the following:

```
######################
# Deployer Configuration
######################
deployer.timeout=300
deployer.pickupDirectory=pickup
```

As you can observe, the pickup directory is specified relative to the dm Server's home directory. In addition, you can also modify the default 6 minute (300 second) waiting period before the dm Server times out on deploying an application.

Besides this configuration file, the dm Server also relies on other configuration files that share a similar syntax, all of which are described in the next section.

Configuration Files

The kernel.properties configuration file partially described in the previous section is one of the many configuration files located in the dm Server's config directory. Table 4-2 illustrates all the configuration files located in the config directory of the dm Server.

Table 4-2. SpringSource dm server configuration files

Configuration File	Usage
config/hostedRepository.properties	Used for defining remotely accessible repositories on a dm Server. Of use on multiple-node dm Server architectures.
config/kernel.properties	Contains various dm Server properties, including Deployment configuration (Deployment directory and timeouts), IO configuration (Work directory), OSGi shell configuration (Access and port) and Profile Configuration (Subsystems).
config/repository.properties	Configures the repositories from which the dm Server will attempt to resolve application dependencies.
config/serviceability.config	Configures the location and parameters for dm Server's diagnostic output (logs, trace, and dump files).
config/tomcat-server.xml	Configures dm Server's embedded Apache Tomcat instance.
config/tomcat-users.xml	Configures users, passwords, and roles for the dm Server (syntax/parameters based on Apache Tomcat).
config/management/jmxremote.access	Configures JMX access for the dm Server.
config/management/jmxremote.password	Contains JMX access password for the dm Server.
config/management/keystore	Keystore for dm Server's JMX access.

Note: It is recommended to disable OSGi console telnet access—in `kernel.properties`—*for production environments, since it has no security provisions (such as username/password). JMX is the preferred access method for production environments—see files under* `config/management/` *for configuring JMX—whereas OSGi console telnet access is intended for development environments.*

Each of these last configuration files is described in detail in pertinent sections of the book (such as the `kernel.properties` file in the previous section on hot-deployment and the `repository.properties` file in the upcoming section on the provision repository).

Managing the Provisioning Repository

In OSGi, application dependencies are provided in the form of bundles. To centralize the bundles required by all applications deployed on it, the dm Server provides a *provisioning repository* to store these bundles. Bundles in the provisioning repository are shared between all applications on the dm Server. The versioning capability of OSGi allows multiple versions of a bundle to be installed in the same repository.

In some cases you must import multiple bundles of an application framework in order to use it. It would be very cumbersome to import these bundles one by one and repeat such imports for each application. The dm Server allows you to define a *library* that includes multiple bundles, so you can simply import a single library into your application. Library definitions are also stored in the provisioning repository.

Introducing the Repository Structure

By default, the provisioning repository is located in the `repository` directory of the dm Server home. It consists of three top-level directories, as listed in Table 4-3.

Table 4-3. Top-level Directories of the Provisioning Repository

Directory	Description
bundles	This contains bundles installed in the provisioning repository.
libraries	This contains library definitions installed in the provisioning repository, each of which refers to bundles installed in the same repository.
installed	This is internally used by the dm Server at runtime and should not contain user bundles or library definitions.

As you can see, the installed directory is intended for the dm Server's internal use, not for server users to store bundles and library definitions. The bundles and libraries directories contain the subdirectories listed in Tables 4-4 and 4-5, respectively.

Table 4-4. *Subdirectories of the Bundles Directory*

Directory	What It Contains
ext	Bundles supplied with the dm Server's installation
subsystems	Bundles that implement the dm Server's subsystems
usr	Bundles installed by the dm Server's users

Table 4-5. *Subdirectories of the Libraries Directory*

Directory	What It Contains
ext	Library definitions supplied with the dm Server's installation
usr	Library definitions installed by the dm Server's users

From these tables you can see that dm Server users should only install bundles and library definitions to the bundles/usr and libraries/usr directories, respectively.

Installing Bundles and Libraries to the Repository

To provide dependencies required by applications on the dm Server, you have to install these bundles or library definitions to the provisioning repository so that the applications can access them at runtime. This installation is simply a matter of copying the corresponding file to the appropriate directory.

At runtime, the dm Server will automatically detect changes to its provisioning repository so that you needn't restart the dm Server after installing a new bundle or library definition. When the dm Server deploys an application, it dynamically loads the application's required dependencies from the provisioning repository. If you have missed a dependency for an application, you can simply install it to the repository and then redeploy the application. The redeployment will cause the new dependency to be loaded without restarting the dm Server. However, if an indirect dependency that's required by a direct application dependency is missed, you must restart the dm Server after installing it, because the dm Server will not reload direct dependencies automatically.

Finding Bundles and Libraries from the SpringSource Enterprise Bundle Repository

A Java application usually depends on multiple Java libraries, which are available in the form of JAR files. However, before you can install these library JAR files to the dm Server's provisioning repository, they must be converted into OSGi bundles. To save developers the trouble of converting JAR files into bundles, SpringSource hosts an enterprise bundle repository that includes converted OSGi bundles for popular Java libraries. In addition to OSGi bundles for common libraries, the repository includes library definitions for common application frameworks. The URL of this repository is

`http://www.springsource.com/repository/`

The main page of this repository is shown in Figure 4-14. The repository supports basic search (by keyword), advanced search (by keyword and version range), and package search (by Java package, e.g. `org.foo`) for both bundles and library definitions. It also allows you to browse bundles and library definitions with their names indexed alphabetically.

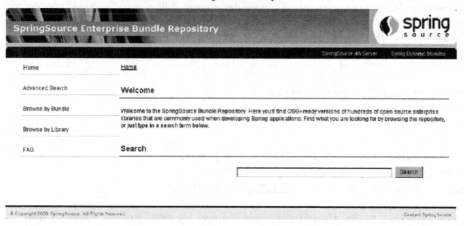

Figure 4-14. *The main page of the SpringSource enterprise bundle repository*

As an example, let's find and download Spring Web Flow 2.0.3, which is available in the repository as a library that consists of three bundles. First, you can download the Spring Web Flow library definition:

- `org.springframework.webflow-library-2.0.3.RELEASE.libd`

Then download the JAR files for the three bundles that the Spring Web Flow 2.0.3 library comprises:

- `org.springframework.binding-2.0.3.RELEASE.jar`
- `org.springframework.js-2.0.3.RELEASE.jar`
- `org.springframework.webflow-2.0.3.RELEASE.jar`

If the extension of any file you have downloaded is zip, you have to manually change it to jar. Because other indirectly required dependencies (the Spring Framework bundles, Apache Commons Logging, and Java Servlet API) are preinstalled in the dm Server's provisioning repository, you needn't download and install them.

Besides this web interface that allows you to download bundles and libraries, the SpringSource enterprise Bundle Repository can also be accessed directly by tools such as Maven,[1] Ivy,[2] and the SpringSource Tools Suite (STS). Access to the SpringSource enterprise Bundle Repository via STS is described in Chapter 5.

Installing Bundles

The provisioning repository allows you to install standard OSGi bundles, which can include the dm Server's manifest headers in the MANIFEST.MF file. To install a bundle to the repository, simply copy the bundle JAR file to the repository/bundles/usr directory of the dm Server home. For example, you can copy the three downloaded Spring Web Flow JAR files to this directory to have them installed.

Installing Libraries

The provisioning repository also allows you to install library definitions. A library definition is specific to the dm Server and is very similar to a MANIFEST.MF file in that they both contain multiple manifest headers, but a library definition has the libd extension. The Spring Web Flow library definition (org.springframework.webflow-library-2.0.3.RELEASE.libd) you have downloaded includes the following contents:

```
Library-SymbolicName: org.springframework.webflow
Library-Name: Spring Web Flow
Library-Version: 2.0.3.RELEASE
Import-Bundle:
 org.springframework.binding;version="[2.0.3.RELEASE, 2.0.3.RELEASE]",
 org.springframework.js;version="[2.0.3.RELEASE, 2.0.3.RELEASE]",
 org.springframework.webflow;version="[2.0.3.RELEASE, 2.0.3.RELEASE]"
```

Like a bundle's MANIFEST.MF file, a library definition requires a symbolic name, a version, and a readable name. A library definition imports multiple bundles that it includes using the Import-Bundle header.

To install a library into the repository, you must first install all its included bundles to the repository. Then simply copy the library definition file to the repository/libraries/usr directory of the dm Server home. For example, you can copy the downloaded Spring Web Flow library definition to this last directory to have it installed.

---

[1] See "How do I configure a Maven build to work with the repository?" at http://www.springsource.com/repository/app/faq#q8.

[2] See "How do I configure Ivy to work with the repository?" at http://www.springsource.com/repository/app/faq#q7.

Configuring the Provisioning Repository

The dm Server's provisioning repository can be configured in the repository.properties file located in the config directory of the dm Server's home. In this file, you can configure the provisioning repository's search paths. The default configuration is the following:

```
bundles-subsystems.type=external
bundles-subsystems.searchPattern=repository/bundles/subsystems/{subsystem}/{component}

bundles-ext.type=external
bundles-ext.searchPattern=repository/bundles/ext/{bundle}

bundles-usr.type=external
bundles-usr.searchPattern=repository/bundles/usr/{bundle}

libraries-ext.type=external
libraries-ext.searchPattern=repository/libraries/ext/{library}

libraries-usr.type=external
libraries-usr.searchPattern=repository/libraries/usr/{library}

chain=bundles-subsystems, bundles-ext,bundles-usr,libraries-ext,libraries-usr
```

As you can see, there are various declarations inside the repository.propteries file. Each of these statements represents a repository by name, which is also assigned a type and searchPattern value. Since the biggest variation in these statements lies in the searchPattern value, I will describe it first.

The searchPattern value represents a directory relative to the dm Server's home. If you look closely, you will note these last patterns all point toward the default directories described in Tables 4-3, 4-4 and 4-5. In addition, each pattern also ends with a name inside braces (e.g., {bundle} and {library}) which is used to represent a wildcard.

This wildcard notation is equivalent to * , except that it offers better readability. For example, the path repository/bundles/usr/{bundle} is equivalent to repository/bundles/usr/*. The searchPattern value also supports the use of ** to match directories of variable depth.

In addition to supporting wildcards, the searchPattern value also supports system properties in the form of ${property}, which are particularly helpful for defining repository locations that are not relative to dm Server's home (e.g. an Apache Maven or Apache Ivy repository). For example:

- ${user.home}/.m2/repository/{org}/{name}/{version}/{bundle}.jar
- ${user.home}/.m2/repository/**/*.jar
- ${user.home}/.ivy2/cache/{org}/{name}/{version}/{bundle}.jar
- ${user.home}/.ivy2/cache/**/*.jar

These last searchPattern values would allow the dm Server to search for application dependencies directly in an Apache Maven or Apache Ivy repository.

The ${user.home} syntax represents a system property—interpreted as the user's home directory that started the dm Server—where the remaining syntax are directories relying on wildcard values. Note that the first and last pair are equivalent searchPattern values, with the first value in each pair relying on {} wildcard syntax and the second on **/* instead.

Caution If using an Apache Ivy or Apache Maven repository, you must ensure that its contents are OSGi bundles (for example, that JARs are equipped with an OSGi-compliant MANIFEST.MF file). Verify your download source to ensure that your local Apache Ivy or Apache Maven repository is obtaining OSGi-compliant JARs. See the earlier footnotes on setting up Apache Ivy or Apache Maven to use the SpringSource enterprise Bundle repository, which is a repository that consists of OSGi-compliant bundles.

Besides the searchPattern value, a repository also has a type value. The repositories by default are all configured as external types. However, in addition to the external type, a repository can also be configured as a remote or watched type. Table 4-6 enumerates the different dm Server repository types.

Table 4-6. *SpringSource dm Server repository types*

Repository Type	Description
external	Defines a local system directory using a search pattern in which to locate application dependencies.
remote	Defines a remote dm server repository (node) in which to locate application dependencies.
watched	Defines a local system directory in which to locate application dependencies; this directory is also watched for new or removed artifacts, eliminating the need to restart the dm Server to reflect changes to a repository.

As you can probably infer from this last table, the majority of scenarios in which the dm Server is used can be solved using external repositories. But under certain circumstances, remote and watched repositories also provide advantages.

A remote repository is designed to accommodate the use of multiple dm Server instances as a cluster. With this approach, certain dm Server nodes can fulfill their function as repository nodes, therefore centralizing the location and management of artifacts, while other nodes can function as client dm Server nodes communicating with repository nodes. The configuration of remote repositories is a little more complicated than with the other types, as explained next.

Assuming you've decided to use a remote repository, you need to configure both the dm server that functions as a repository node and the one that functions as the client node. The client or consumer node needs to be configured in a dm Server's repository.properties file—just like a remote repository—as follows:

```
remote-server-repo.type=remote
remote-server-repo.uri= backend.mycorp.org:8080/↵
                com.springsource.server.repository/hosted-repo
remote.server-repo.indexRefreshInterval=30
```

Note the similar assignment of a repository name —remote-server-repo—as well as the change in type value to remote. However, notice that we also used a uri parameter with a value of backend.mycorp.org:8080/com.springsource.server.repositoryhosted-repo instead of a searchPattern value.

What this uri parameter tells the dm Server is to fetch application dependencies from a server running at the cited address, which will be where the dm server provisioning node will be running. The remaining indexRefreshInterval parameter tells the client dm server node how often to refresh its index from the dm provisioning node.

Let's turn our attention to the provisioning node that will host the actual repository—running at backend.mycorp.org:8080. You will need to modify the dm Server's hostedRepository.properties configuration file as illustrated next:

```
hosted-repo.type=external
hosted-repo.searchPattern=repository/hosted/*
```

This syntax and repository definition are sure to be familiar, since they're identical to those used in standalone dm Servers that define external repositories. The biggest difference is that this definition is being made in the special hostedRepository.properties configuration file, which tells the dm Server provisioning instance to expose the repository for remote access.

Further note that repository's name is hosted.repo, thus coinciding with the last part of the access address used by the client dm Server instance. The remaining address is backend.mycorp.org:8080/com.springsource.server.repository/. The dm Server provisioning instance should be set up to run at the address backend.mycorp.org:8080, with the com.springsource.server.repository access path being fulfilled by the repository application deployed by default on every dm Server (as illustrated earlier, in Figure 4-10), which is charged with managing remote repositories.

The purpose of a watched repository, on the other hand, is simpler. Since the dm Server is not capable of reloading direct dependencies automatically unless it is restarted, a watched repository constantly polls a directory so that changes can be detected without requiring a restart. The syntax used to declare a watched repository is the following:

```
watched-repo.type=watched
watched-repo.watchDirectory=repository/watched
watched-repo.watchInterval=3
```

Note the similar assignment of a repository name (watched-repo)—as well as the change in type value to watched. Further notice the use of watchDirectory, which points to the directory that is to be polled, and the watchInterval, which defines the polling interval. Generally speaking, a watched repository would be of greater use in a development environment, given the greater degree of change compared to production environment.

Finally, no matter what repository type you opt to use, if you look back at the default values in the repository.properties file, you will note the last statement starting with chain. This statement contains numerous values separated by commas, where each one represents a repository name. The purpose of the chain element is to define a precedence among the different repositories. For example, having the bundles-subsystems name before bundles-ext tells the dm Server to first attempt to fulfill dependencies by searching in the bundles-subsystems repository, followed by bundles-ext. If the contents of the bundles-ext repository cannot fulfill a dependency, the dm Server will fall back to search in the bundles-usr repository, and so on until all defined repositories are tried.

Summary

In this chapter, you learned about the dm Server's installation, which is simply a download and extraction process. You saw an overview of the contents in each subdirectory of the dm Server's installation directory.

The dm Server provides separate scripts for starting and stopping it on both Windows and Unix/Linux platforms. In addition, you can start the dm Server with different starting options, such as clean starting, starting in the debug mode, and starting with JMX access enabled, by specifying command-line arguments when running the startup scripts.

The dm Server provides a web-based admin console for server users to administrate the server from a web browser. The admin console's functionality is provided by the Admin application preinstalled on the dm Server.

The dm Server allows you to deploy application archive files in the bundle JAR, WAR, and PAR formats. You can either deploy an application archive file in the admin console or copy it to the pickup directory for hot deployment.

The dm Server also has a series of configuration files that allow you to override its default values, ranging from its OSGi environment, embedded Apache Tomcat, diagnostic file placement, repository locations and kernel parameters.

The dm Server provides a centralized provisioning repository to store bundles and library definitions required by all applications deployed on it. The provisioning repository is located in the repository directory and has several subdirectories. Installing a bundle or a library definition to the provisioning repository is simply a matter of copying the corresponding file to the appropriate directory.

SpringSource also hosts an enterprise bundle repository that includes OSGi bundles for popular Java libraries and library definitions for common application frameworks. In addition, you also learned that dm Server provisioning repositories can be custom configured, in addition to being supported in three different types: external, remote, and watched.

In the next chapter, you will learn how to develop modular and OSGi-based enterprise applications to run on the dm Server.

CHAPTER 5

■■■

Developing Applications for the dm Server

In the previous chapters, you had an overview of the dm Server's general concepts and got started with its installation, administration, configuration, and deployment. In this chapter, you will learn about application development for the dm Server. You will see how to take full advantage of the dm Server's powerful features to build modular and OSGi-based enterprise Java applications. This chapter covers the following topics:

- Installing and configuring the dm Server Tools in Eclipse
- Introducing the architecture of dm Server applications
- Creating platform archive files for bundles
- Developing OSGi bundles for the dm Server
- Developing web modules for the dm Server
- Deploying applications in the dm Server Tools
- Exporting applications using the dm Server Tools

To make use of this chapter, you need a basic knowledge of Java EE topics including Java Persistence API (JPA), transaction management, web application development, and Spring's support for these features. If you are new to these topics, I suggest that you read Chapters 8-10 of the book *Spring Recipes: A Problem-Solution Approach* (Apress, 2008).

Installing and Configuring dm Server Tools

As outlined in Chapter 3, SpringSource provides a set of tools for the dm Server that facilitate executing applications directly in a development environment.

This set of dm Server Tools—which forms part of the broader SpringSource Tools Suite (STS)—is available in either of two forms: as a plug-in that can be installed on a standard version of the Eclipse IDE, or in STS itself, which is based on the Eclipse platform. Both alternatives provide you with the same functionality.

The easiest route is to download STS—especially if you plan to develop primarily Spring-based applications—not only because it's simpler to install, but also because the environment is streamlined (for example, with various defaults) to create Spring applications.

If, on the other hand, you prefer to keep using the standalone Eclipse IDE for Java development—as was done in Chapter 1 and Chapter 2 to explore OSGi and Spring-DM, respectively—you can also install the dm Server Tools plug-in on your Eclipse IDE.

Both setup alternatives are described next.

Using dm Server Tools with Eclipse

The latest version of the dm Server Tools requires Eclipse 3.4 (Ganymede), with the corresponding version of Web Tools Platform (WTP). If you completed the exercises in Chapter 1 or Chapter 2, then your already have Eclipse 3.4 (Ganymede) and WTP installed. If on the other hand, you still don't have an Eclipse IDE installed on your workstation, you can simply install the Eclipse IDE for Java EE Developers package, which includes WTP and other Java EE development tools. The latest Eclipse packages can be downloaded from the Eclipse downloads web site:

`http://www.eclipse.org/downloads/`

Once you have an Eclipse IDE with WTP, you can proceed to installing the dm Server Tools plug-in. The dm Server Tools plug-in is built on the Eclipse WTP and can therefore be installed as a plug-in of this kind. The dm Server Tools plug-in can be installed in Eclipse's update manager using either of the following methods:

Online installation: Add the SpringSource update site in Eclipse's update manager and install the dm Server Tools plug-in online.

Archive installation: Download the SpringSource archive update site. Then add it in Eclipse's update manager as an archive site and install the dm Server Tools plug-in offline.

If your workstation has an Internet connection, I recommend that you install the dm Server Tools plug-in online from the SpringSource update site, because this will install all dependent plug-ins automatically. To perform this type of installation, choose Software Updates from Eclipse's Help menu and then open the Available Software tab. You can add the SpringSource update sites by clicking the Add Site button, and enter the following URLs (one at a time):

`http://www.springsource.org/update/e3.4`
`http://www.springsource.org/milestone/e3.4`

■ **Note** There are two recommended update sites because of the plug-in release schedule, targeting dm Server version 2.0. At the time of this writing, the main update site—http://www.springsource.org/update/e3.4—contains plug-ins only for dm Server version 1.0. Therefore, updates are also performed on the milestone update site, which contains plug-ins targeting dm Server version 2.0.

Once you enter both URLs, the Eclipse update screen will present you with two SpringSource Update Site for Eclipse 3.4 options. Choose the top-level box for the milestone update site, as illustrated in Figure 5-1. By choosing the top-level box, you automatically select all SpringSource-related Eclipse plug-ins download, including the dm Server Tools plug-in. Next, click the Install button to begin the installation.

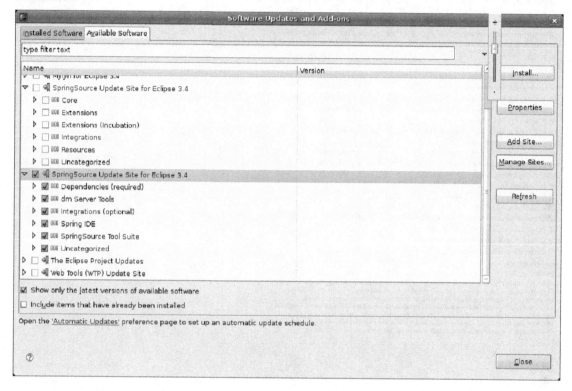

Figure 5-1. *Selecting all plug-ins under the SpringSource update site to install*

In the next screen, you will see the list of selected plug-ins and their versions, as shown in Figure 5-2.

Make sure the dm Server Tools plug-in reflects a `2.1.x` version. If it doesn't, verify the update site URL. By clicking the Next button, you will start the download and installation process for the dm Server plug-in and related SpringSource plug-ins.

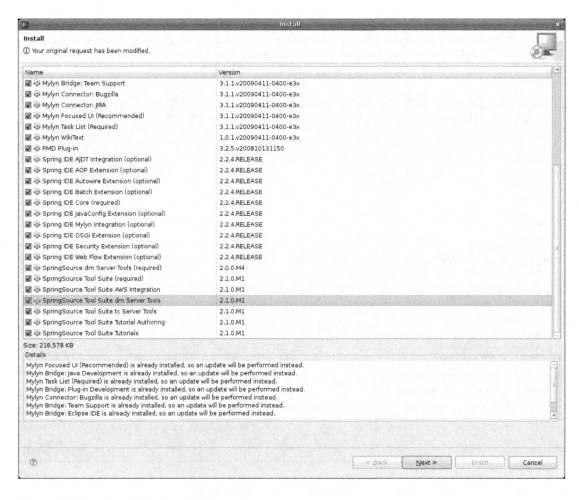

Figure 5-2. *The selected plug-ins and their versions*

Using dm Server Tools with STS

The biggest advantage to using dm Server Tools with STS is that it already comes preinstalled. The latest STS can be downloaded from the SpringSource download web site:

`http://www.springsource.com/products/sts`

Bear in mind that STS is a large download (~400MB), since it contains not only an Eclipse-based IDE but also copies of both the dm and tc Servers.

Once you have downloaded STS and unzipped the file on your workstation, descend into the `sts-2.x.x` directory. In this top-level directory, you will find an executable named `eclipse` that will start STS. Figure 5-3 illustrates the STS main screen.

Figure 5-3. *The STS main screen*

As you can see by the executable's name and the appearance of its main screen in Figure 5-3, STS is based on the Eclipse platform and as such has the same look and feel as the standard Eclipse IDE.

Thanks to this commonality, the steps outlined in the remainder of the chapter (including, for example, details like menu names and tasks) are applicable to both an Eclipse IDE equipped with the dm Server Tools plug-in and STS itself. In addition, any reference to Eclipse IDE, Eclipse, or IDE for the remainder of this chapter can be interpreted as referring to STS if that was your tool of choice. Screens illustrated may also look different from yours because of the different "skins" used by a standalone Eclipse IDE and STS.

Configuring a dm Server Instance

Eclipse allows you to define instances of well-known server types, such as Tomcat and JBoss, for publishing and testing your applications. Using dm Server Tools, you can define a dm Server instance in Eclipse as well.

First, bring up Eclipse's Servers view if it is not already visible. You can do that by choosing TRA Show View ➤ Servers from Eclipse's Window menu. To define a new dm Server instance, right-click in the view and then select New ➤ Server from the pop-up menu. This will bring up a New Server dialog as shown in Figure 5-4.

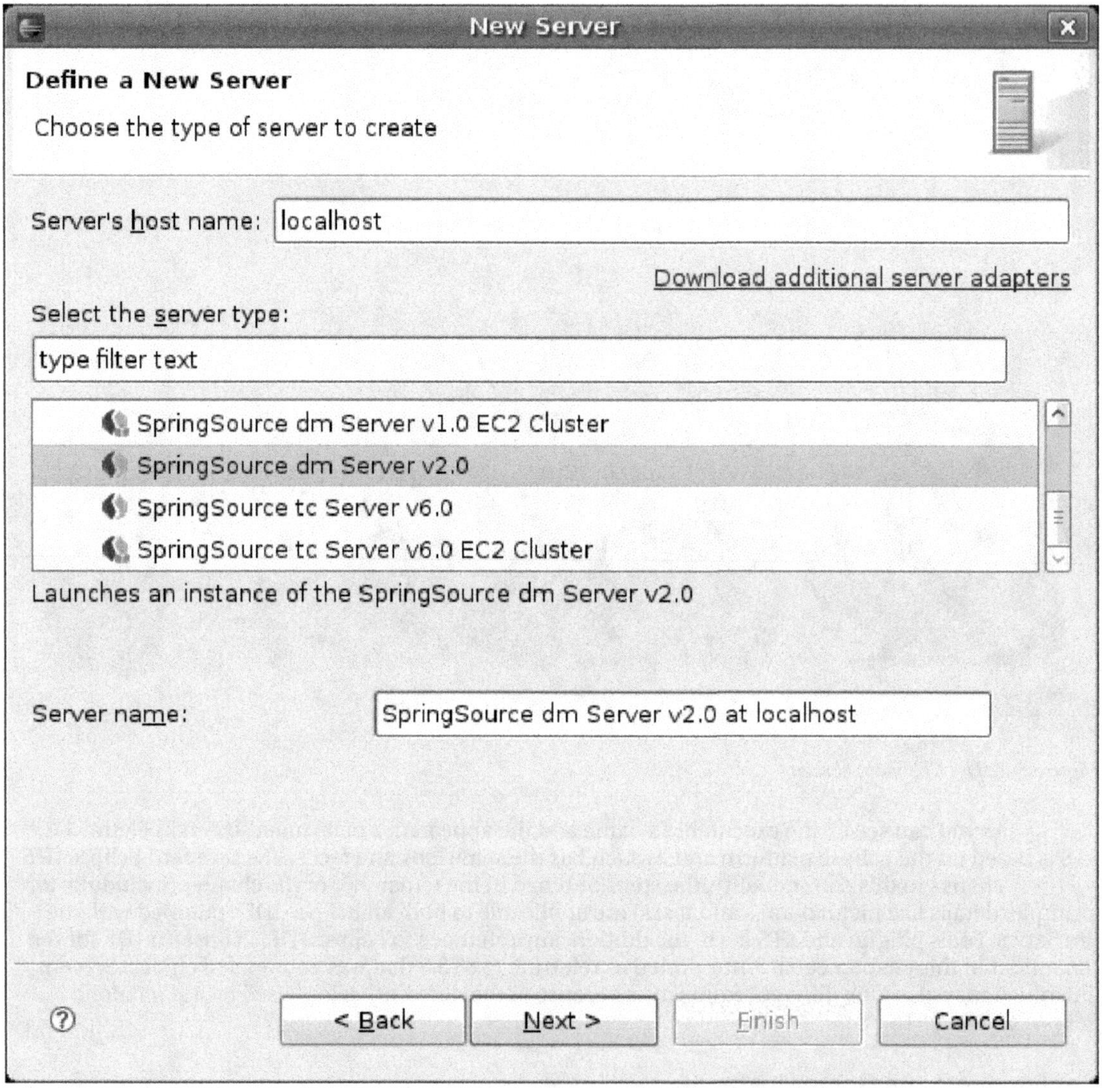

Figure 5-4. Defining a new dm Server instance

In the pop-up dialog, select SpringSource dm Server v2.0 under the SpringSource category, and a SpringSource dm Server configuration dialog will appear. Here you can specify details about the dm Server including its installation directory, as shown in Figure 5-5.

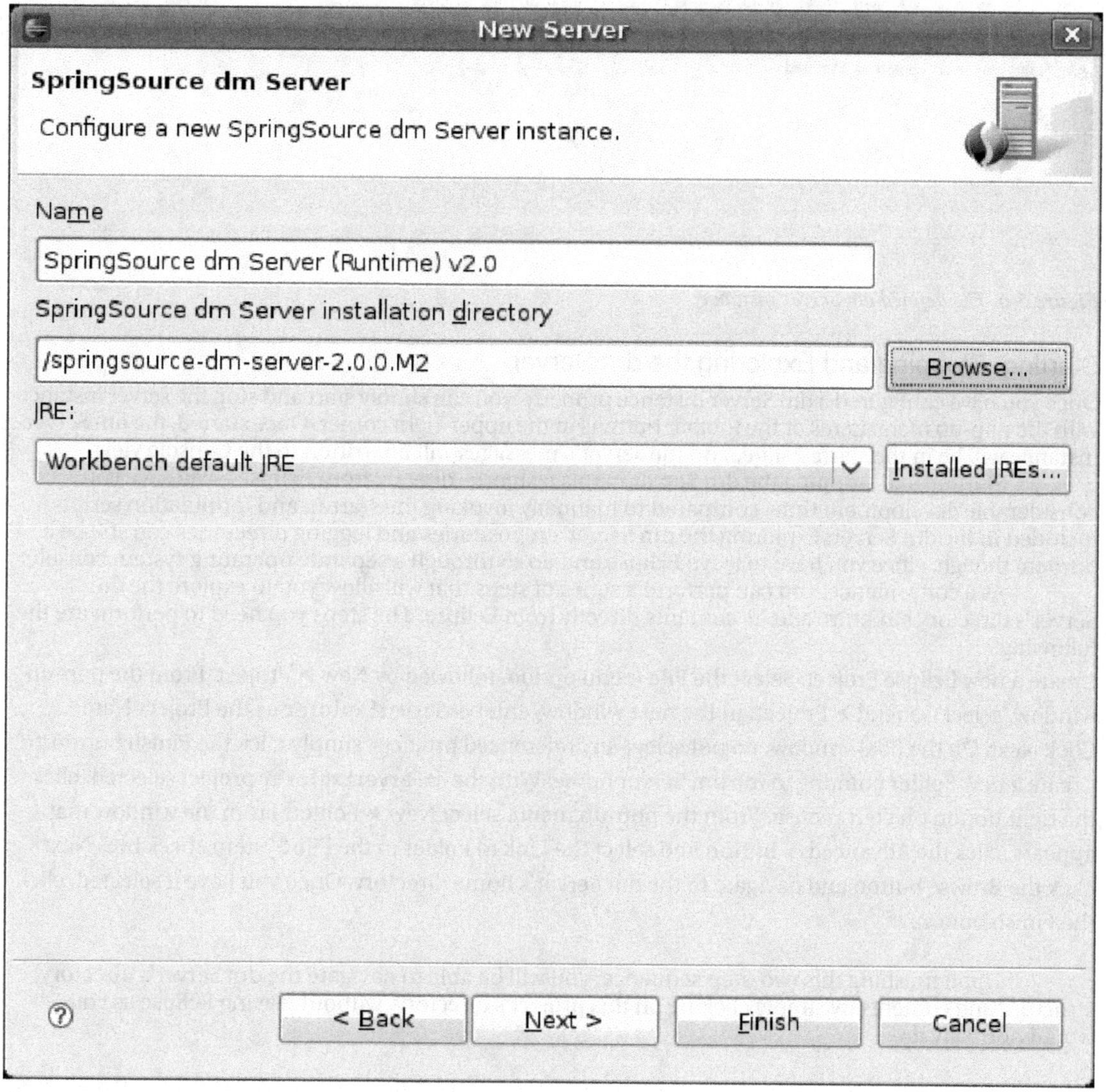

Figure 5-5. Specifying details about the dm Server

Finally, a SpringSource dm Server instance will be available in the Servers view for you to change its state and publish your applications, as shown in Figure 5-6.

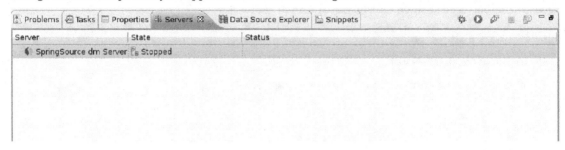

Figure 5-6. *The defined dm Server instance*

Starting, Stopping and Exploring the dm Server

Once you have configured a dm Server instance properly, you can simply start and stop the server instance with the pop-up menu items or the toolbar buttons in the upper-right corner. Once started, the dm Server instance will be in the started state, and the server's messages will be written to the Console view.

Starting and stopping the dm Server in this fashion—directly from Eclipse—will save you considerable development time, compared to manually invoking the startup and termination scripts included in the dm Server. Exploring the dm Server's repositories and logging directories can still be a burden, though, since you have to leave Eclipse and do so through a separate operating system console.

As a convenience, you can perform a series of steps that will allow you to explore the dm Server's directory structure and its contents directly from Eclipse. The steps you need to perform are the following:

1. Create a new Eclipse Project: Select the File menu option, followed by New ➤ Project. From the pop-up window, select General ➤ Project. In the next window, enter dmServerExplorer as the Project Name. Click Next. On the final window, do not select any referenced projects, simply click the Finish button.

2. Create a new Folder pointing to the dm Server home: With the dmServerExplorer project selected, click the right button on your mouse. From the pop-up menu, select New ➤ Folder. From the window that appears, click the Advanced>> button and select the Link to Folder in the File System check box. Next, click the Browse button and navigate to the dm Server's home directory. Once you have it selected, click the Finish button.

Upon finishing this two-step sequence, you will be able to navigate the dm Server's directory structure and contents by simply clicking on this project's directory, without leaving Eclipse as you would normally do.

Application Architecture for the dm Server

The dm Server is a modular and OSGi-based server designed for developing, deploying, and running enterprise Java applications. A typical enterprise Java application usually consists of multiple modules, which can be divided either horizontally by application layers (e.g. presentation layer, service layer, and persistence layer) or vertically by system functions. On a traditional Java EE application server, all these modules are packaged into a single archive file (e.g. a WAR file) before they are deployed to the server. However, to take advantage of the OSGi technology on the dm Server, you should package each module of your application into a bundle.

A typical Java EE web application can generally be divided into the following bundles by application layers:

Infrastructure: This bundle contains infrastructure items including data sources and message destinations.

Domain: This bundle contains the domain model that represents the business domain's concepts. A domain model usually consists of a group of domain classes that each layer of the application has to deal with.

Repository: This bundle contains data access objects (DAOs) of the persistence layer that encapsulate the data access logic. In most cases the repository bundle needs to use infrastructures provided by the infrastructure bundle.

Service: This bundle contains service components of the service layer that implement the business logic and act as a facade. The service bundle uses DAOs provided by the repository bundle for persistence.

Web: This bundle contains web components of the presentation layer that generate and handle web-based user interfaces. The web bundle uses service components provided by the service layer.

This partitioning scheme may seem excessive compared to the more monolithic Java EE approach, but it's done in this form to take advantage of the modularity and dynamic features offered by OSGi. These include the ability to combine an application's parts of different versions (e.g. 1.0, 2.0, and 3.0) and the ability to switch implementation details (e.g. Hibernate vs. EclipseLink vs. JDBC vs. OpenJPA) more easily. In addition, management and maintenance of an application are also simplified, since each bundle is a standalone unit that can be refactored and redeployed without disturbing the whole of an application.

This entire partitioning scheme will become clearer as you move along in the example. Figure 5-7 illustrates how the preceding bundles fit into the general bundle architecture and dependencies of an enterprise application.

In this chapter, I will use a vehicle registration system with database persistence and web interfaces as the sample application to demonstrate application development for the dm Server. This application will make use of the following technologies:

JPA: The application will use JPA to persist Java objects into the Derby database with EclipseLink as the JPA engine.

Spring Framework: The application will use the Spring Framework's JPA and data access support features, along with its transaction management facilities, to simplify implementation.

Spring MVC: The application will use Spring MVC as the web application framework to develop web interfaces.

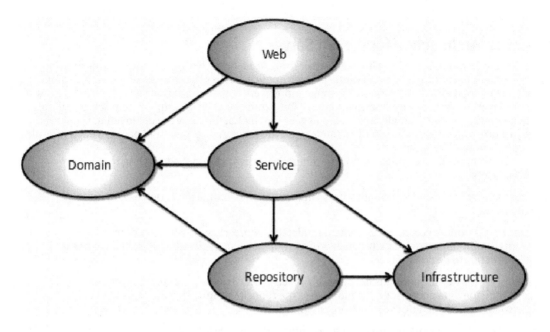

Figure 5-7. *The general bundle architecture and dependencies of an enterprise application*

With the implementation technologies identified, the specific bundles that make up the sample application are listed in Table 5-1.

Table 5-1. *Bundles That Make Up the Sample Application*

Bundle	Description
infrastructure.derby	Defines a data source for the Derby database and exports it as an OSGi service.
domain	Defines the domain model and exports the package for other bundles to access the domain classes.
repository	Defines the repository interfaces and exports the package for other bundles to access and implement the interfaces.
repository.jpa	Provides JPA-based repository implementations and exports them as OSGi services.
service	Defines the service component interfaces and exports the package for other bundles to access. Also provides implementations for the interfaces and exports them as OSGi services.
web	Contains web components and configurations for Spring MVC.

As this table illustrates, in addition to the general bundle architecture presented in Figure 5-7—which displays five bundles—this sample application also includes a sixth bundle, named repository.jpa. The repository bundle is cast into two bundles, repository and repository.jpa , because of modularity concerns. Separating the repository bundle into an interface bundle and an implementation bundle makes it easier to switch implementation strategies. For example, you may choose to implement the repository bundle using Hibernate, EclipseLink, or OpenJPA as the persistence engine.

However, if another bundle relies on making a persistence operation, and you only have an implementation bundle, this would tie the relying bundle to the particularities of one persistence engine. That would make it difficult to change to a different persistence engine, since one application module already relies on a certain persistence engine.

On the other hand, if you split the repository bundle in two—separating the interface from the implementation—this allows all relying bundles to operate directly on the interface implementation bundle (repository) and be decoupled from the implementation bundle, repository.jpa. Thus, a bundle requiring a persistence operation is designed without a particular persistence technology; it simply communicates with the interface bundle, repository, which in turn can be linked to a bundle using JPA, JDBC, JDO or any other persistence implementation.

In principle, this is similar to the object-oriented programming best practice of using separate interface and implementation classes, except in this case it applies to OSGi bundles.

Figure 5-8 illustrates the final bundle architecture and dependencies (including package dependencies and service dependencies) of the sample application.

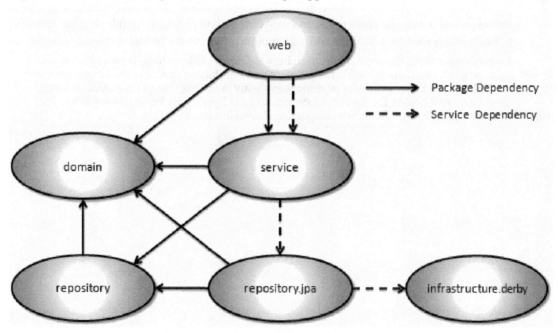

Figure 5-8. *The specific bundle architecture and dependencies of the sample application*

Creating Platform Archives with Bundles

An enterprise application usually consists of multiple modules, each of which in OSGi is encapsulated in a bundle. Even though OSGi and its bundle architecture bring a wealth of benefits to enterprise Java applications, OSGi doesn't address certain concerns that have long been solved by platforms that also target the enterprise application market, like Java EE. One of these issues is what constitutes an application and how it is deployed. The dm Server address this issue by supporting a mechanism in which to group bundles that make up an application.

To group all bundles of your application in a single deployment unit so that they can be deployed, refreshed, and undeployed as a whole, you should package the bundles in a *Platform Archive* (PAR) file and deploy the PAR file rather than each bundle in isolation to the dm Server. The PAR format has the following characteristics:

- Although all bundles of a PAR file are deployed, refreshed, and undeployed as a single deployment unit, each of them can be redeployed and refreshed independently.

- A PAR file provides a boundary for the application so that OSGi services exported by bundles in a PAR file will be isolated from those exported by other applications.

The dm Server Tools support creating PAR projects that can be deployed and run directly on the dm Server instance defined in Eclipse. When creating a PAR project for an application, you can consider two approaches:

- Create each of the bundle projects first and then create a PAR project to include all of the projects.

- Create a PAR project first and then add each bundle project to the PAR project after creation.

I highly recommend the second approach because, unlike Eclipse plug-in projects, the dm Server bundle projects can't access each other's classes and interfaces if they don't belong to the same PAR project, unless you configure project references explicitly in Eclipse's project properties dialog.

To create a PAR project for the vehicle system, from Eclipse's New Project dialog select PAR Project under the SpringSource dm Server category, as shown in Figure 5-9.

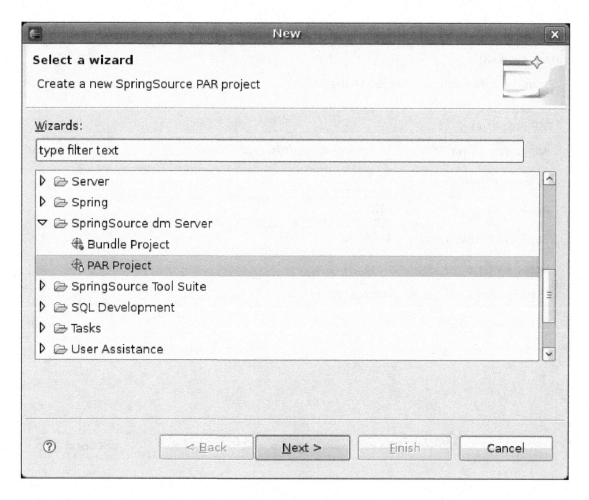

Figure 5-9. *Creating a PAR project for the dm Server*

In the next screen, enter `com.apress.prodmserver.vehicle` as the project name, which will also be used as the symbolic name by default. Next you can modify the application properties that will appear in the generated `MANIFEST.MF` file. Remember to select SpringSource dm Server (Runtime) v2.0 as the target runtime, as shown in Figure 5-10.

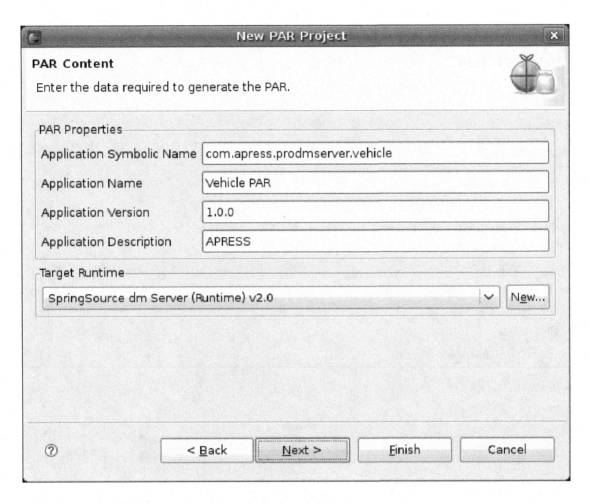

Figure 5-10. *Setting the application properties and target runtime*

You can open the META-INF/MANIFEST.MF file and view its source code in the MANIFEST.MF tab as follows:

```
Manifest-Version: 1.0
Application-SymbolicName: com.apress.prodmserver.vehicle
Application-Version: 1.0.0
Application-Description: APRESS
Application-Name: Vehicle PAR
```

Note that in the Dependencies tab of the MANIFEST.MF editor you can add and remove bundles belonging to this PAR project if they are in the same Eclipse workspace. You will do this shortly, once you create the first application bundle.

Developing OSGi Bundles for the dm Server

You've already developed a few OSGi bundles in both Chapter 1 and Chapter 2 that exposed you to OSGi Equinox and Spring-DM. The dm Server is built on the Equinox OSGi container to provide an execution environment for bundles, as well as on Spring-DM to manage bundle application contexts, so any OSGi-compliant bundles and Spring-DM-based bundles can be deployed to and run on the dm Server.

In this sense, you should be more than comfortable developing OSGi bundles that target the dm Server. However, as outlined in Chapter 3, the dm Server offers a series of features that make OSGi bundle development easier and are worth mentioning at the outset of this, your first dm Server application.

To enhance dependency management, the dm Server allows its bundles to use two additional manifest headers besides the standard Import-Package header, as listed in Table 5-2.

Table 5-2. Additional Manifest Headers Supported by the dm Server

Manifest Header	Descriptor
Import-Bundle	Automatically imports all packages exported by the bundle.
Import-Library	Automatically imports all packages exported by all bundles defined in the library.

The Import-Bundle and Import-Library headers are actually aliases for the Import-Package header. At deployment time, the dm Server will automatically translate the entries in these headers into a number of Import-Package header entries.

Now that you're aware of these special OSGi headers, let's start by creating the first application bundle.

Creating the Application Infrastructure Bundle

Almost every enterprise application stores its information in a database and thus has a need to access it. The infrastructure bundle will fulfill the role of accessing the database on behalf of other bundles (modules) belonging to the application.

However, prior to creating the infrastructure bundle, I will describe how to set up the actual database that will be accessed by our bundle.

Setting Up the Application Database

A standard Java/Java EE application uses JDBC (Java Database Connectivity) to connect to a relational database, so you can choose any JDBC-compliant database engine for your vehicle system. For its low memory consumption and easy configuration, I'll choose Apache Derby as the database engine.

Derby is an open-source relational database engine distributed under the Apache License and implemented in pure Java. You can download a Derby binary distribution (e.g. version 10.5.1.1) from the Derby web site (http://db.apache.org/derby/) and extract the file to a directory of your choice (e.g. c:\db-derby-10.5.1.1-bin) to complete the installation.

Apache Derby can run in either the embedded or the client/server mode. For testing purposes, the client/server mode is more appropriate because it allows you to inspect and edit data with any visual database tools that support JDBC; for example, the Eclipse IDE has such a database tool built-in.

To start the Derby server, execute the startNetworkServer script located in the bin directory of the Derby installation for your target platform (on a Windows platform it is startNetworkServer.bat). By default, the Derby server listens on port 1527 and disables authentication, so you are free to provide any values for the connecting username and password.

Now you can use any database tools that support JDBC to connect to the database. Here I will continue to use the Eclipse IDE for this purpose. The first step in connecting is to create a new database driver definition to be used for connecting to the Derby server. From Eclipse's Window menu, choose Preferences ➤ Data Management ➤ Connectivity ➤ Driver Definitions ➤ Add. Once you click Add, you will see a window as shown in Figure 5-11.

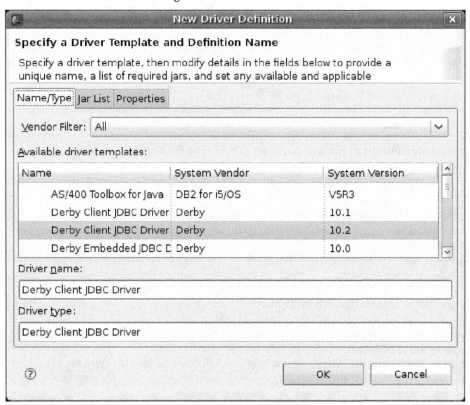

Figure 5-11. *Creating a new database driver definition*

In this dialog, select Derby as the vendor filter and pick up the latest version of the Derby Client JDBC Driver. Then, in the Jar List tab, select the derbyclient.jar file located in the lib directory of the Derby installation as the driver JAR file.

Now you can create a data source for the database. From Eclipse's Window menu choose Show View ➤ Data Source Explorer to open the Data Source Explorer view. Then, in the Databases category, right-click to create a new connection of the Derby type and set its name to Vehicle, as shown in Figure 5-12.

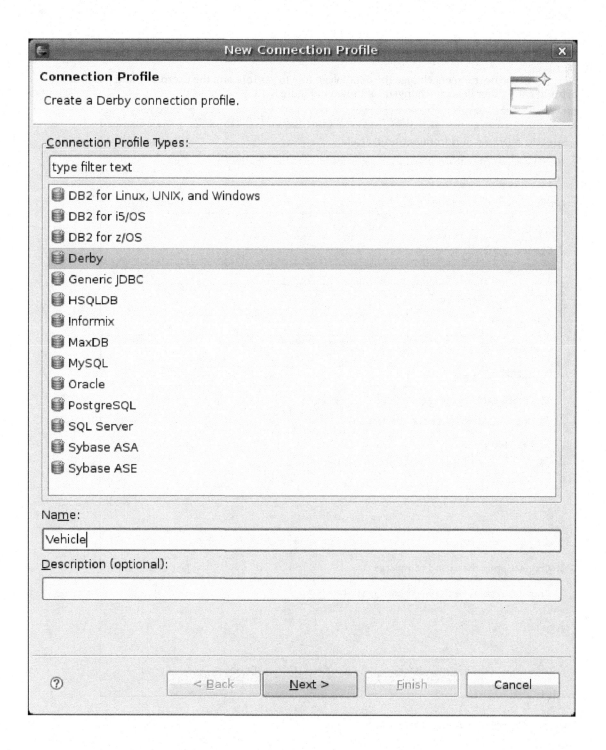

Figure 5-12. *Creating a new Derby database connection*

In the next screen, change the database name to vehicle and the username and password to app and leave other fields unchanged, as shown in Figure 5-13.

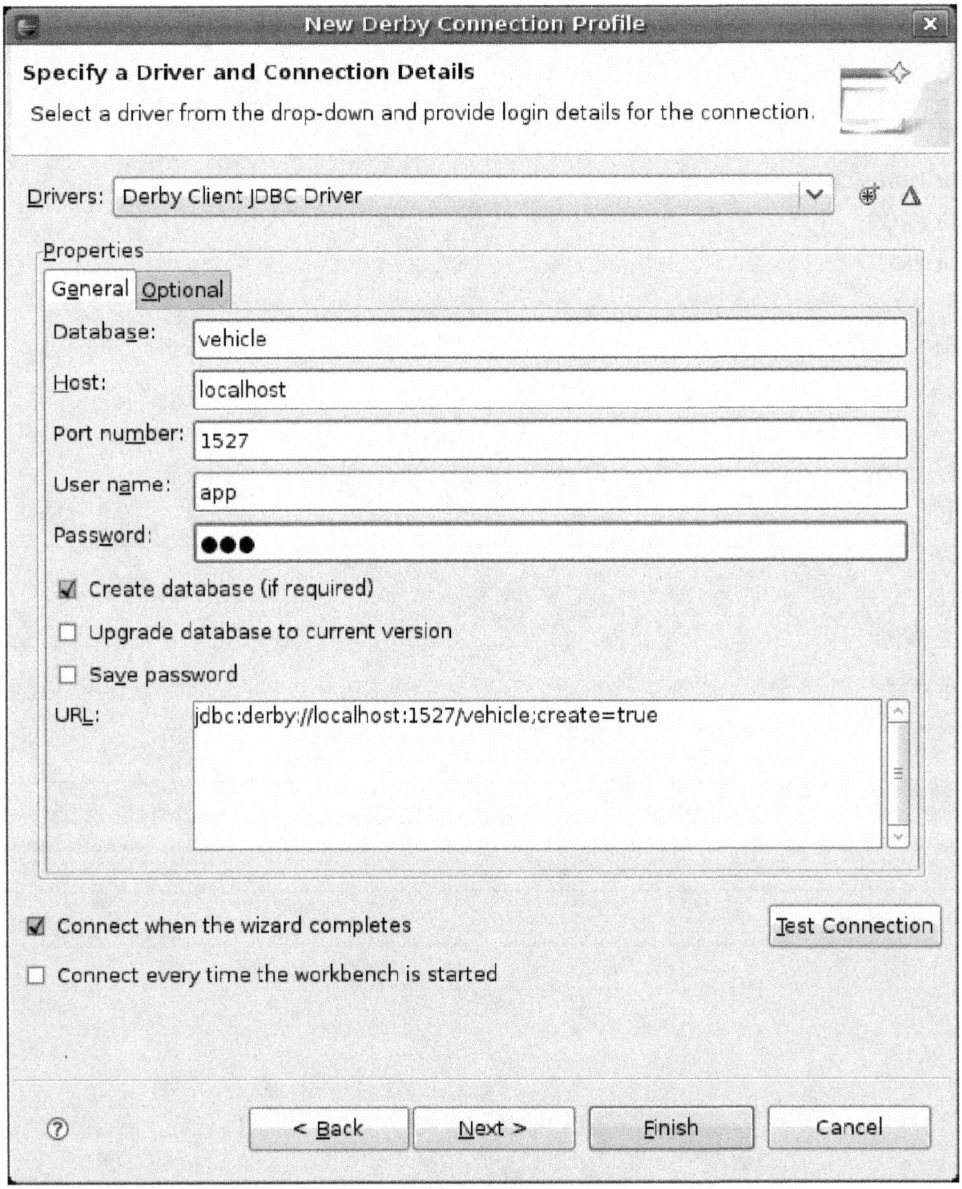

Figure 5-13. *Specifying the database connection details*

The first time you connect to this database, the database instance vehicle will be created automatically if it did not exist before, because the connection URL includes create=true at the end. If you use app as the username to connect to this database, the subsequent tables will be created in the APP schema (the same as the connecting username).

Defining a Data Source in the Infrastructure Bundle

With the database set up, you can define a data source in the infrastructure bundle to be exported as an OSGi service, which can later be used by other application bundles to access the database. First, you create a project for the infrastructure bundle. In Eclipse, you can create a bundle project that supports the dm Server-specific configurations and can run directly on the dm Server instance defined in Eclipse. From the New Project dialog, select Bundle Project under the SpringSource dm Server category as shown in Figure 5-14.

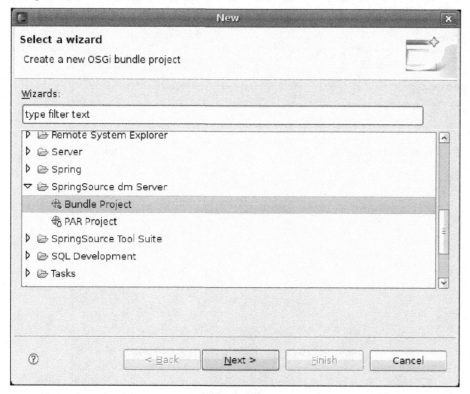

Figure 5-14. *Creating a bundle project for the dm Server*

Because this infrastructure bundle will define a data source for the database running on Derby, enter com.apress.prodmserver.vehicle.infrastructure.derby in the project name. In the next screen, you can modify the bundle properties that will appear in the generated MANIFEST.MF file. You must also select SpringSource dm Server (Runtime) v2.0 as the target runtime, as shown in Figure 5-15.

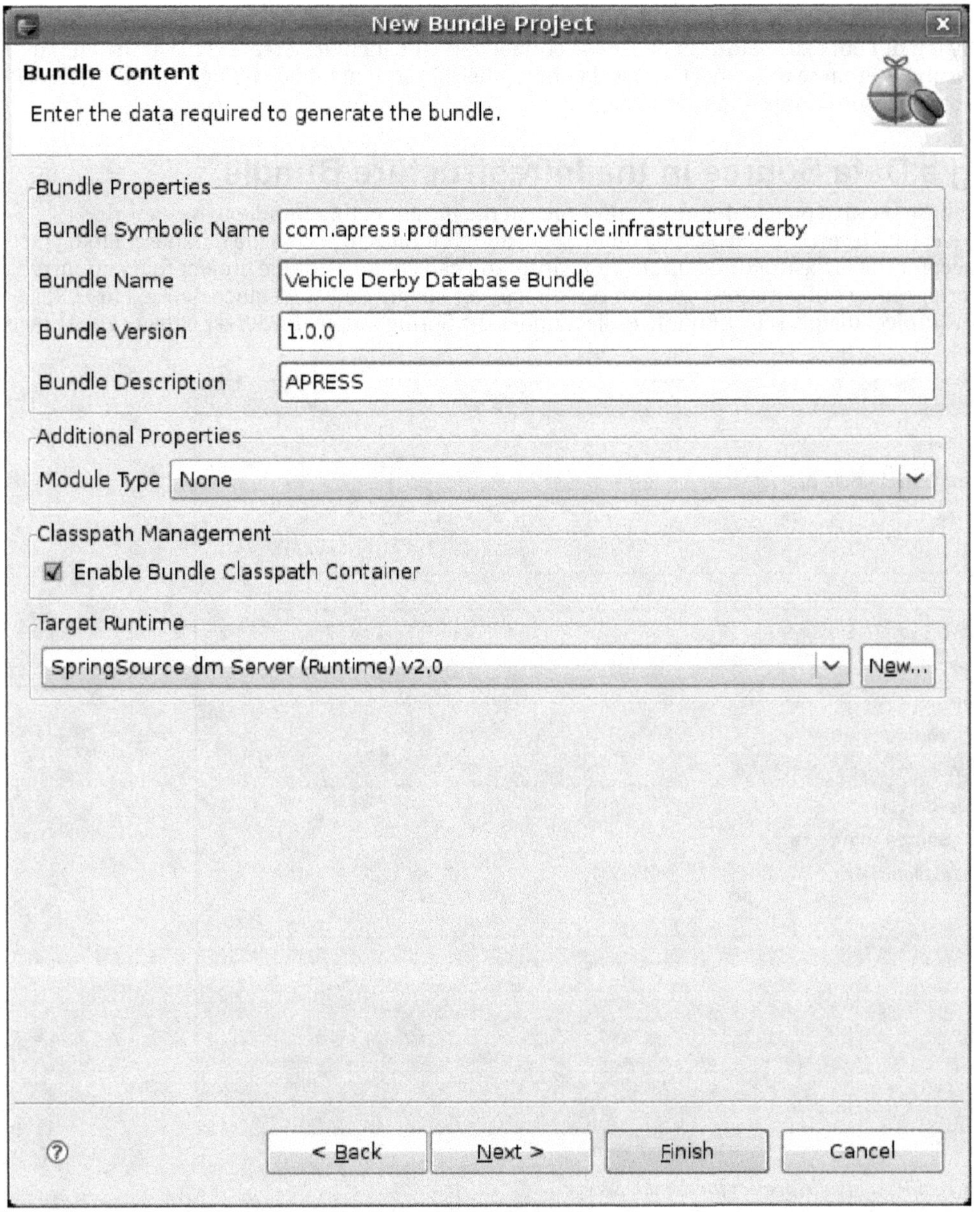

Figure 5-15. *Setting the bundle properties and target runtime*

Now that you've defined the infrastructure bundle project, it is a convenient time to associate it with the vehicle PAR project created previously. Open the PAR project's MANIFEST.MF file and add the infrastructure bundle in the Dependencies tab, as shown in Figure 5-16.

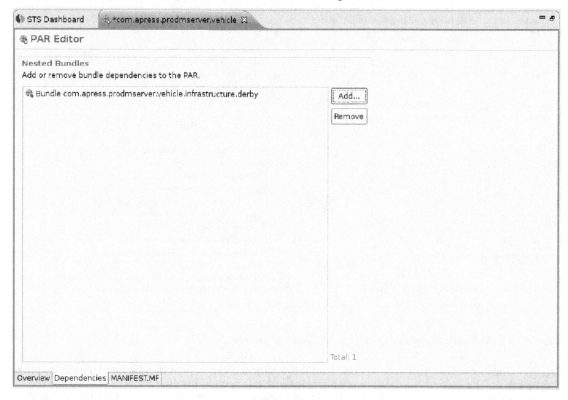

Figure 5-16. *Adding the infrastructure bundle to the PAR project*

Next, and in order to define the data source in the infrastructure bundle, remember that a bundle often requires the presence of certain dependencies in order to operate. In this case, you will also you have to download several required bundles from the SpringSource Enterprise Bundle Repository and install them to the dm Server's local repository.

Fortunately, the dm Server Tools simplify these tasks by providing a Bundle Repository Browser for the dm Server instance defined in Eclipse. You can open this browser by double-clicking the dm Server entry in the Servers view and selecting the Repository tab, as shown in Figure 5-17.

The right side of this browser displays all installed bundles and libraries of the local dm Server repository, while the left side allows you to search for bundles and libraries from the SpringSource Enterprise Bundle Repository. This browser caches the bundle and library repository index locally, so I strongly recommend that you update the index by clicking the Update Local Bundle and Library Repository Index hyperlink before performing a search, in case the index is not up to date.

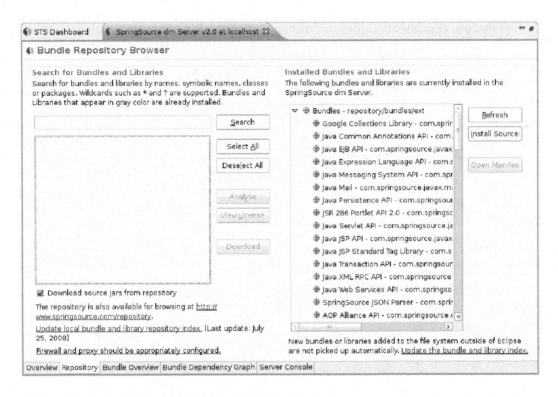

Figure 5-17. The Bundle Repository Browser for the local dm Server

The first bundle you need to download is the Apache Derby Client bundle for connecting to the Derby server. The second is a data source provider with connection pooling support to enhance the performance of database access. I recommend using the data source from Apache Commons DBCP (Database Connection Pool), which depends on Apache Commons Pool internally. All required bundles (of the current versions at the time of writing) that you need to download for the infrastructure bundle are listed in Table 5-3.

Table 5-3. Bundles Needed for the Infrastructure Bundle

Bundle Name	Bundle Symbolic Name*	Current Version
Apache Derby Client	`com.springsource.org.apache.derby.client`	`10.4.1000003.648739`
Apache Commons Database Connection Pool	`com.springsource.org.apache.commons.dbcp`	`1.2.2.osgi`
Apache Commons Pool	`com.springsource.org.apache.commons.pool`	`1.4.0`

Entering the Bundle Symbolic Name in the Search for Bundles and Libraries search box of the bundle repository browser is the easiest method of downloading.

After downloading the required bundles to the dm Server's repository, you have to import the Derby Client bundle (`com.springsource.org.apache.derby.client`) and the Commons DBCP bundle (`com.springsource.org.apache.commons.dbcp`) to your infrastructure bundle. These two bundles are needed because the packages they export will be used directly for defining a data source. However, you don't need to import the Commons Pool bundle, because it's used by the Commons DBCP bundle, not directly by your infrastructure bundle. Open the infrastructure bundle's `MANIFEST.MF` file and select the Dependencies tab, and then add the two bundles to the Import Bundle list.

As the infrastructure bundle will export the data source as an OSGi service under the `javax.sql.DataSource` interface, the `javax.sql` package—which forms part of the Java Runtime Environment (JRE)—also needs to be imported. Figure 5-18 illustrates the imports required by the infrastructure bundle.

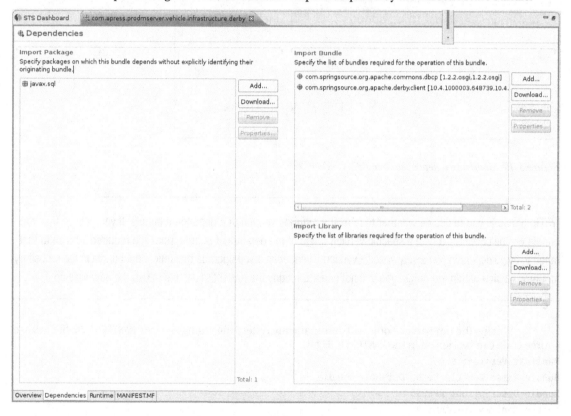

Figure 5-18. *Importing bundles for the infrastructure bundle*

To avoid depending on a very specific version of Derby (e.g. `10.4.1000003.648739`), you may consider relaxing the required version of the dependent Derby Client bundle to the range between `10.4.1000000` (inclusive) and `10.4.2000000` (exclusive). You can modify a dependent bundle's version by changing the bundle's properties with the Properties button, as shown in Figure 5-19.

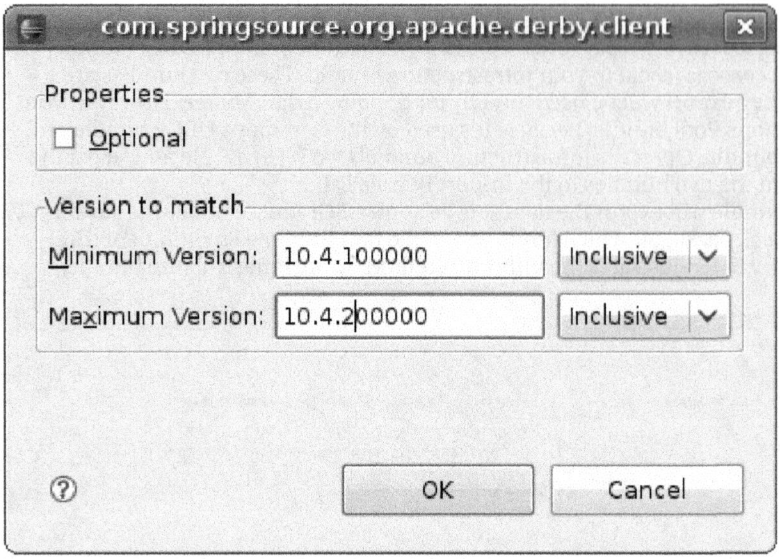

Figure 5-19. *Modifying a dependent bundle's version*

■ **Tip** It's up to you to decide whether to relax the required version of a dependent bundle. If you believe that your bundle will be compatible with a specific version range of the dependent bundle, relax the required version to that range to avoid depending on a very specific version. Then, even if you upgrade the dependent bundle in the repository to a new version within the range, you will not need to modify the MANIFEST.MF file to use the new version.

Finally, the dm Server Tools will automatically reflect the changes in the MANIFEST.MF file, whose source code can be viewed in the MANIFEST.MF tab:

```
Manifest-Version: 1.0
Bundle-Name: Vehicle Derby Database Bundle
Bundle-Description: APRESS
Bundle-ManifestVersion: 2
Bundle-SymbolicName: com.apress.prodmserver.vehicle.infrastructure.derby
Bundle-Version: 1.0.0
Import-Bundle: ↵
 com.springsource.org.apache.commons.dbcp;version="[1.2.2.osgi,1.2.2.osgi]",
 com.springsource.org.apache.derby.client;version=8
"[10.4.1000000,10.4.2000000)";import-scope:=application
Import-Package: javax.sql
```

Now you can define a data source in Spring and export it as an OSGi service using Spring-DM. Following the best practices of Spring-DM, you should separate regular Spring bean configurations (e.g. in `module-context.xml`) from OSGi-related bean configurations (e.g. in `osgi-context.xml`). First, create the `module-context.xml` file for regular bean configurations in the `META-INF/spring` directory with the following contents:

```
<beans xmlns="http://www.springframework.org/schema/beans"
    xmlns:xsi="http://www.w3.org/2001/XMLSchema-instance"
    xsi:schemaLocation="http://www.springframework.org/schema/beans
        http://www.springframework.org/schema/beans/spring-beans-2.5.xsd">

    <bean id="dataSource" class="org.apache.commons.dbcp.BasicDataSource">
        <property name="driverClassName"
            value="org.apache.derby.jdbc.ClientDriver" />
        <property name="url"
            value="jdbc:derby://localhost:1527/vehicle;create=true" />
        <property name="username" value="app" />
        <property name="password" value="app" />
    </bean>
</beans>
```

This bean configuration file simply defines a data source for the vehicle database running on Apache Derby at localhost, using the `BasicDataSource` class provided by Commons DBCP, which supports connection pooling.

Then, create the `osgi-context.xml` file in the `META-INF/spring` directory with the following OSGi-related bean configurations, which exports the data source as an OSGi service under the `javax.sql.DataSource` interface:

```
<beans:beans xmlns="http://www.springframework.org/schema/osgi"
    xmlns:xsi="http://www.w3.org/2001/XMLSchema-instance"
    xmlns:beans="http://www.springframework.org/schema/beans"
    xsi:schemaLocation="http://www.springframework.org/schema/beans
        http://www.springframework.org/schema/beans/spring-beans-2.5.xsd
        http://www.springframework.org/schema/osgi
        http://www.springframework.org/schema/osgi/spring-osgi.xsd">

    <service ref="dataSource" interface="javax.sql.DataSource" />
</beans:beans>
```

By exporting the data source as an OSGi service, you enable other bundles in the application to access the database via an OSGi service.

If you're familiar with Java EE application development, this process is fairly similar to how applications access data sources via JNDI or Spring dependency injection (Spring-DI). The data source is configured on a standard Java EE application as a *resource*, and other parts of an application that require access to the data source simply use a pointer (JNDI or Spring-DI) to access it.

In this OSGi based application, the data source is configured in its own bundle—in this case the infrastructure bundle—as a *service*, and any other application bundle requiring access to the data source simply uses a pointer (OSGi service) to access it.

Having finished the infrastructure bundle that will give the application access to a database, let's move on to the next bundle, which will handle the application's domain model.

Creating the Domain Model Bundle

The domain model bundle will contain the classes that describe the objects that will be persisted the database. In identical fashion to the earlier infrastructure bundle, create a bundle project under the SpringSource dm Server category with the name com.apress.prodmserver.vehicle.domain. And just as with the infrastructure bundle, associate this bundle with the PAR project using the Dependencies tab.

Once the domain bundle has been added as a dependency for the PAR project, it's also necessary to take care of the dependencies needed by the domain model. Since you will annotate the domain classes with JPA annotations for the sake of persistence, this bundle must import the JPA bundle to access the JPA annotations. So from the Dependencies tab of the model bundle, add the Java Persistence bundle com.springsource.javax.persistence version 1.0.0 as a dependency.

■ **Note** Since the Java Persistence bundle com.springsource.javax.persistence comes preinstalled with the dm Server, there is no need to download it as with the previous dependencies for the infrastructure bundle.

Now that you've taken care of dependencies, let's explore the code that will be included in the model bundle for the vehicle system.

In the vehicle system, each vehicle has either the ACTIVE, PROHIBITED, or DESTROYED status, which can be declared using the following enumeration:

```
package com.apress.prodmserver.vehicle.domain;

public enum Status {
    ACTIVE, PROHIBITED, DESTROYED;
}
```

The core domain class of the vehicle system is Vehicle, which has an identifier and five other properties: vehicle ID number, color, number of wheels, number of seats, and status:

```
package com.apress.prodmserver.vehicle.domain;

import javax.persistence.Column;
import javax.persistence.Entity;
import javax.persistence.GeneratedValue;
```

```java
import javax.persistence.GenerationType;
import javax.persistence.Id;
import javax.persistence.Table;

@Entity
@Table(name = "VEHICLE")
public class Vehicle {

    @Id
    @GeneratedValue(strategy = GenerationType.IDENTITY)
    @Column(name = "ID")
    private Long id;

    @Column(name = "VEHICLE_NO", length = 20, nullable = false, unique = true)
    private String vehicleNo;

    @Column(name = "COLOR", length = 20)
    private String color;

    @Column(name = "WHEEL")
    private int wheel;

    @Column(name = "SEAT")
    private int seat;

    @Column(name = "STATUS", length = 10, nullable = false)
    private Status status;

    // Getters and Setters
    ...
}
```

The domain class Vehicle and its properties have been annotated with JPA annotations so that objects of this type can be persisted into the database by the JPA engine. The objects will be persisted into the VEHICLE table as specified in the @Table annotation, while other properties will be persisted into corresponding columns as specified in the @Column annotations. The identifier of the Long type will be generated automatically using the table identity column when the object is persisted.

Once you assign these last classes to the domain model bundle, you will also need to export the com.apress.prodmserver.vehicle.domain package for other bundles to access the domain classes. This is done from the Runtime tab of the bundle, as illustrated in Figure 5-20.

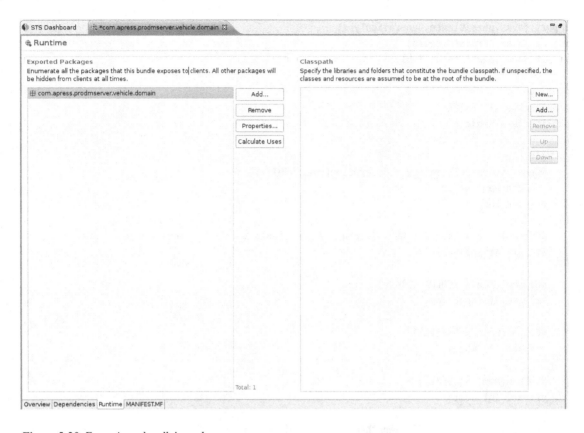

Figure 5-20. *Exporting a bundle's packages*

The completed `MANIFEST.MF` source code is as follows:

```
Manifest-Version: 1.0
Bundle-Name: Vehicle Domain Bundle
Bundle-Description: APRESS
Bundle-ManifestVersion: 2
Bundle-SymbolicName: com.apress.prodmserver.vehicle.domain
Bundle-Version: 1.0.0
Import-Bundle: com.springsource.javax.persistence;version="[1.0.0,1.0.0]"
Export-Package: com.apress.prodmserver.vehicle.domain
```

Since the model bundle will not require or offer any OSGi service, there is no need to add any Spring-DM configuration as was done for the infrastructure bundle.

Next, I will describe the vehicle system's repository interface bundle, which will contain the operations performed on the model bundle.

Creating the Repository Interface Bundle

Following the same process as the two previous bundles, create a dm Server bundle project with the name com.apress.prodmserver.vehicle.repository and add it to the PAR project created at the outset.

Since this bundle will define operations to be performed on the model bundle, it will require access to the application's domain classes and as such will need to import the com.apress.prodmserver.vehicle.domain package into the MANIFEST.MF file. Perform this import dependency process as you did for earlier bundles.

Now that all dependencies are defined, I will describe the code that will be included in this bundle. For demonstration purposes, the vehicle system will only define a single DAO method for accessing the vehicle data. The interface of this DAO is defined as follows:

```
package com.apress.prodmserver.vehicle.repository;
import java.util.List;
import com.apress.prodmserver.vehicle.model.Vehicle;

public interface VehicleDao {

    public void store(Vehicle vehicle);
    public Vehicle load(Long id);
    public List<Vehicle> findAll();
}
```

To complete this bundle, export com.apress.prodmserver.vehicle.repository from Eclipse's Runtime tab. This will allow the DAO interface to be accessed from other application bundles. The completed MANIFEST.MF source code should look like the following:

```
Manifest-Version: 1.0
Bundle-Name: Vehicle Repository Interface Bundle
Bundle-Description: APRESS
Bundle-ManifestVersion: 2
Bundle-SymbolicName: com.apress.prodmserver.vehicle.repository
Bundle-Version: 1.0.0
Import-Package: com.apress.prodmserver.vehicle.domain
Export-Package: com.apress.prodmserver.vehicle.repository
```

Like the model bundle, the repository interface bundle will not access or offer any OSGi service to other bundles, so there is no need to add any Spring-DM configuration files.

It should also be mentioned that the simplicity in the repository interface bundle is achieved thanks to the design choice described earlier, that of splitting the repository bundle in two. One bundle contains the interface logic and another the implementation details, making it easier to switch between repository technologies (JPA, JDBC, or JDO).

Creating the JPA-based Repository Implementation Bundle

Now let's create a dm Server bundle project to provide a JPA-based implementation for the repository, naming it `com.apress.prodmserver.vehicle.repository.jpa`. Right after creating it, add it to the application's PAR project like the previous bundles.

Before implementing the repository with JPA, you must first download the following library (containing the current versions at the time of writing) to the dm Server's repository so you can use EclipseLink as the JPA engine:

- The EclipseLink JPA library `org.eclipse.persistence` version 1.0.0, which will be used by the Spring Framework library (particularly its ORM module) to provide JPA support to your bundle.

■ **Warning** The EclipseLink JPA library defines a transitive dependency on the bundle `com.springsource.javax.persistence-1.99.0.jar`, which is the source of a bug (`https://issuetracker.springsource.com/browse/DMS-807`). You will need to remove this bundle, which is automatically downloaded to `/repository/bundles/usr/`—the repository—in order for EclipseLink to function properly on dm Server 2.0.

After you have downloaded the library using the dm Server's Bundle Repository Browser (See Figure 5-17), you will need to import these artifacts along with other bundles that come preinstalled with the dm Server, as well as other application packages you created earlier. From the bundle's Dependencies tab import the following:

- The Java Persistence API bundle `com.springsource.javax.persistence` version 1.0.0 for implementing the repository with JPA.
- The EclipseLink bundle `com.springsource.org.eclipselink.persistence` version 1.0.0 because the JPA engine will need to use some classes of EclipseLink at runtime. Note that this bundle is included in the EclipseLink JPA library of version 1.0.0 you downloaded.
- The AspectJ bundle `com.springsource.org.aspectj.weaver` version 1.6.5.RELEASE because the JPA engine will need to use weaving on the application's domain classes at runtime. Note that this bundle comes preinstalled with the dmServer.
- The Spring Framework library `org.springframework.spring` version 3.0.0 for utilizing Spring's JPA support and transaction management facilities. Note that this library comes preinstalled with the dm Server.
- The `javax.sql` package needed by the data source service.
- The domain package `com.apress.prodmserver.vehicle.domain` for accessing the domain classes.
- The repository package `com.apress.prodmserver.vehicle.repository` for accessing the DAO interfaces.

After importing all the preceding bundles, libraries, and packages, modify the MANIFEST.MF source code to extend the EclipseLink bundle's import scope to the entire application, making it visible to all bundles belonging to the PAR file. Here's the revised code:

```
Manifest-Version: 1.0
Bundle-Name: Vehicle Repository JPA-based Implementation Bundle
Bundle-Description: APRESS
Bundle-ManifestVersion: 2
Bundle-SymbolicName: com.apress.prodmserver.vehicle.repository.jpa
Bundle-Version: 1.0.0
Import-Library: org.springframework.spring;version="[3.0.0,3.0.0]"
Import-Bundle: com.springsource.javax.persistence;version="[1.0.0,1.0.0]",
 com.springsource.org.eclipse.persistence;version=8
"(1.0.0,1.0.0)";import-scope:=application,
com.springsource.org.aspectj.weaver;version="[1.6.5.RELEASE,1.6.5.RELEASE]"
Import-Package: com.apress.prodmserver.vehicle.domain,
 com.apress.prodmserver.vehicle.repository,
 javax.sql
```

The reason it's necessary to extend the import scope was briefly addressed in Chapter 3 in the "Application Boundary Support" section, but I will elaborate further here. When you employ EclipseLink for persistence, the persistent classes (in this case the domain classes) and thus the domain bundle will depend on EclipseLink, since it relies on persistence annotations. A possible solution is to import the EclipseLink bundle explicitly to the domain bundle; however, this breaks bundle modularity, as the domain bundle shouldn't be aware of the underlying persistence technology, requiring you to modify the domain bundle's MANIFEST.MF file when you switch to another persistence technology.

To solve this problem and enhance bundle modularity, the dm Server supports the notion of an *import scope*. By default, a bundle's import scope is the current bundle, but you can extend this scope to the entire application so that the dm Server will automatically import the bundle to every bundle of the same application. However, note that the application scope works only for bundles within a PAR file.

Now that you've defined dependencies, you can proceed with the bundle's code, which in this case will be one class that implements the VehicleDao interface with JPA and Spring's transaction. The class is illustrated next:

```
package com.apress.prodmserver.vehicle.repository.jpa;

import java.util.List;

import javax.persistence.EntityManager;
import javax.persistence.PersistenceContext;
import javax.persistence.Query;

import org.springframework.stereotype.Repository;
import org.springframework.transaction.annotation.Transactional;

import com.apress.prodmserver.vehicle.domain.Vehicle;
import com.apress.prodmserver.vehicle.repository.VehicleDao;
```

```
@Repository
@Transactional
public class JpaVehicleDao implements VehicleDao {

    @PersistenceContext
    private EntityManager entityManager;

    public void store(Vehicle vehicle) {
        entityManager.merge(vehicle);
    }

    @Transactional(readOnly = true)
    public Vehicle load(Long id) {
        return entityManager.find(Vehicle.class, id);
    }

    @SuppressWarnings("unchecked")
    @Transactional(readOnly = true)
    public List<Vehicle> findAll() {
        Query query = entityManager.createQuery("select v from Vehicle v");
        return query.getResultList();
    }
}
```

This DAO is implemented with both standard JPA and Spring's transaction support. First, EntityManager is the core JPA resource interface that provides methods for object persistence. Note that the field entityManager is annotated with the JPA annotation @PersistenceContext to apply JPA's context injection. Spring will inject a thread-safe entity manager to this field, and when you call methods on this, it will automatically obtain the entity manager for the current transaction and delegate your calls to it. As a result, you don't need to maintain an entity manager for each transaction by yourself.

Second, note that you have annotated Spring's @Repository annotation at the class level to have Spring translate native JPA exceptions thrown by this class (e.g. PersistenceException and other Java SE exceptions like IllegalArgumentException and IllegalStateException) into runtime exceptions in Spring's well-defined DataAccessException hierarchy. Moreover, you annotated Spring's @Transactional annotation at the class level to indicate that all methods in this class should have transactions enabled by default. Then you overrode the @Transactional annotation at certain method levels with the readOnly attribute set to true. This is to indicate that the operations within these methods will not update data, so that the database engine can apply strategies to optimize their performance.

As described in the JPA specification, by default the JPA engine will load persistence unit configurations from persistence.xml, which is located in the META-INF directory of the classpath root. A persistence unit defines its persistent classes and persistence details. The persistence.xml file for this application is as follows:

```
<persistence xmlns="http://java.sun.com/xml/ns/persistence"
    xmlns:xsi="http://www.w3.org/2001/XMLSchema-instance"
    xsi:schemaLocation="http://java.sun.com/xml/ns/persistence
        http://java.sun.com/xml/ns/persistence/persistence_1_0.xsd"
    version="1.0">

    <persistence-unit name="vehicle" transaction-type="RESOURCE_LOCAL">
        <class>com.apress.prodmserver.vehicle.domain.Vehicle</class>

        <exclude-unlisted-classes>true</exclude-unlisted-classes>
    </persistence-unit>
</persistence>
```

In this file, you define a persistence unit named vehicle, which includes the domain class
Vehicle as a persistent class. JPA supports scanning and detecting annotated persistent classes from the
classpath automatically. And though this process works for JPA applications running on a unified classpath
environment, for OSGi applications it does not work as expected. The reason is that OSGi uses separate
class loaders for each bundle, which is what permits it to offer finer-grained dependency resolution rules
and constraints. In this case, since the domain classes are present in another bundle, this JPA automatic
classpath scanning feature will not work. Therefore, you specify the persistent classes explicitly and disable
the scanning by setting exclude-unlisted-classes to true.

To configure the application context for this repository bundle, create module-context.xml in
the META-INF/spring directory with the following contents:

```
<beans xmlns="http://www.springframework.org/schema/beans"
    xmlns:xsi="http://www.w3.org/2001/XMLSchema-instance"
    xmlns:context="http://www.springframework.org/schema/context"
    xmlns:tx="http://www.springframework.org/schema/tx"
    xsi:schemaLocation="http://www.springframework.org/schema/beans
        http://www.springframework.org/schema/beans/spring-beans-2.5.xsd
        http://www.springframework.org/schema/context
        http://www.springframework.org/schema/context/spring-context-2.5.xsd
        http://www.springframework.org/schema/tx
        http://www.springframework.org/schema/tx/spring-tx-2.5.xsd">

    <context:annotation-config />

    <context:load-time-weaver aspectj-weaving="on"/>

    <bean id="entityManagerFactory"
        class="org.springframework.orm.jpa.LocalContainerEntityManagerFactoryBean">
        <property name="dataSource" ref="dataSource" />
        <property name="jpaVendorAdapter">
            <bean class="org.springframework.orm.jpa.vendor. ↵
```

```
        EclipseLinkJpaVendorAdapter">
        <property name="databasePlatform"↵
            value="org.eclipse.persistence.platform.database.DerbyPlatform" />
        <property name="showSql" value="true" />
        <property name="generateDdl" value="true" />
      </bean>
    </property>
  </bean>

  <bean class="org.springframework.dao.annotation.↵
      PersistenceExceptionTranslationPostProcessor" />

  <tx:annotation-driven mode="aspectj"/>

  <bean id="transactionManager"
      class="org.springframework.orm.jpa.JpaTransactionManager">
      <property name="entityManagerFactory" ref="entityManagerFactory" />
  </bean>

  <bean id="vehicleDao"
      class="com.apress.prodmserver.vehicle.repository.jpa.JpaVehicleDao" />
</beans>
```

In this bean configuration file you first define an entity manager factory using the factory bean LocalContainerEntityManagerFactoryBean, which allows you to utilize Spring's facilities to configure the target entity manager factory. The factory will be created using the data source that will be imported from the OSGi service registry in the next bean configuration file, along with the vendor adapter that uses EclipseLink as the JPA engine. In this adapter you can configure vendor details such as the database platform, whether to output the executed SQL statements, and whether to update the database schema automatically.

Also, you enable Spring's annotation processing feature via <context:annotation-config> so that Spring will inject an entity manager annotated with @PersistenceContext. When you call methods on this, it will automatically obtain the entity manager for the current transaction and delegate your calls to it.

Spring can translate native JPA exceptions thrown by classes annotated with @Repository into runtime exceptions in Spring's DataAccessException hierarchy. The purpose of this last hierarchy is to let code find and handle errors without specifying the details of a particular data access API (e.g. JDBC, JPA, or JDO). This is done by the PersistenceExceptionTranslationPostProcessor instance, so you next had to register that instance in the application context.

Finally, you defined a JPA transaction manager to manage transactions for entity managers. Then, when annotation-driven transaction management is enabled via <tx:annotation-driven>, Spring will automatically manage transactions for methods annotated with @Transactional or whose enclosing class is annotated with @Transactional, using the transaction manager named transactionManager.

For the next step, create osgi-context.xml in META-INF/spring to import and export OSGi services for this bundle. The contents are as follows:

```
<beans:beans xmlns="http://www.springframework.org/schema/osgi"
    xmlns:xsi="http://www.w3.org/2001/XMLSchema-instance"
    xmlns:beans="http://www.springframework.org/schema/beans"
    xsi:schemaLocation="http://www.springframework.org/schema/beans
        http://www.springframework.org/schema/beans/spring-beans-2.5.xsd
        http://www.springframework.org/schema/osgi
        http://www.springframework.org/schema/osgi/spring-osgi.xsd">

    <reference id="dataSource" interface="javax.sql.DataSource" />

    <service ref="transactionManager"
        interface="org.springframework.transaction.PlatformTransactionManager" />

    <service ref="vehicleDao"
        interface="com.apress.prodmserver.vehicle.repository.VehicleDao" />
</beans:beans>
```

In this Spring-DM configuration file you import the data source exported by the infrastructure bundle for creating the entity manager factory. Then you export the JPA transaction manager and the JPA-based vehicle DAO implementation as OSGi services. The reason for exporting the transaction manager is that you will need to apply transaction management in the service bundle, which also requires a transaction manager. The PlatformTransactionManager interface is the root interface for all types of Spring transaction managers.

Creating the Service Layer Bundle

For the service bundle, create a bundle project named com.apress.prodmserver.vehicle.service and add it to the vehicle PAR project. Dependencies for this bundle include the com.apress.prodmserver.vehicle.domain package and the com.apress.prodmserver.vehicle.repository package. In addition, this bundle will also utilize Spring's facilities for transaction management, so you will also need to import the Spring Framework library org.springframework.spring version 3.0.0. Import these artifacts as you've done for other bundles' MANIFEST.MF files.

With dependencies for the bundle defined, you can define the service bundle's business logic. For simplicity, the vehicle system will have a limited set of services, whose interface is defined as follows:

```
package com.apress.prodmserver.vehicle.service;

import java.util.List;

import com.apress.prodmserver.vehicle.domain.Vehicle;
import com.apress.prodmserver.vehicle.domain.Status;
```

```
public interface VehicleService {

    public void register(Vehicle vehicle);
    public void updateStatus(Long vehicleId, Status status);
    public List<Vehicle> list();
}
```

Then you can implement this interface with the help of a VehicleDao instance, which will be injected via setter injection. Remember that this class should be put in a different package (e.g. in the impl subpackage) to ensure that it can't be accessed by other bundles even if you export the interface package. The source code is as follows:

```
package com.apress.prodmserver.vehicle.service.impl;

import java.util.List;

import com.apress.prodmserver.vehicle.domain.Vehicle;
import com.apress.prodmserver.vehicle.domain.Status;

import com.apress.prodmserver.vehicle.repository.VehicleDao;

import com.apress.prodmserver.vehicle.service.VehicleService;

import org.springframework.beans.factory.annotation.Autowired;
import org.springframework.transaction.annotation.Transactional;

@Transactional
public class VehicleServiceImpl implements VehicleService {

    private VehicleDao vehicleDao;

    @Autowired
    public void setVehicleDao(VehicleDao vehicleDao) {
        this.vehicleDao = vehicleDao;
    }

    public void register(Vehicle vehicle) {
        vehicle.setStatus(Status.ACTIVE);
        vehicleDao.store(vehicle);
    }
```

```
public void updateStatus(Long vehicleId, Status status) {
    Vehicle vehicle = vehicleDao.load(vehicleId);
    vehicle.setStatus(status);
    vehicleDao.store(vehicle);
}

@Transactional(readOnly = true)
public List<Vehicle> list() {
    return vehicleDao.findAll();
}
}
```

The setVehicleDao() method is annotated with Spring's @Autowired annotation to indicate that Spring should automatically inject a bean of the VehicleDao type into this property. Also note that the @Transactional annotation presented at the class level indicates that all methods in this class should have transactions enabled. Then you can override @Transactional in the read-only methods with the readOnly attribute set to true. At runtime, transactions opened by these methods will propagate to the DAO methods.

To configure the application context for this service bundle, create module-context.xml in the META-INF/spring directory with the following contents:

```
<beans xmlns="http://www.springframework.org/schema/beans"
    xmlns:xsi="http://www.w3.org/2001/XMLSchema-instance"
    xmlns:context="http://www.springframework.org/schema/context"
    xmlns:tx="http://www.springframework.org/schema/tx"
    xsi:schemaLocation="http://www.springframework.org/schema/beans
        http://www.springframework.org/schema/beans/spring-beans-2.5.xsd
        http://www.springframework.org/schema/context
        http://www.springframework.org/schema/context/spring-context-2.5.xsd
        http://www.springframework.org/schema/tx
        http://www.springframework.org/schema/tx/spring-tx-2.5.xsd">

    <context:annotation-config />

    <tx:annotation-driven  mode="aspectj"/>

    <bean id="vehicleService"
        class="com.apress.prodmserver.vehicle.service.impl.VehicleServiceImpl" />
</beans>
```

With <context:annotation-config> enabled, Spring will automatically inject beans of appropriate types into properties annotated with @Autowired. On the other hand, enabling <tx:annotation-driven> causes Spring to manage transactions for transactional methods, using the specific transaction manager named transactionManager, which will be imported from the OSGi service registry in the next configuration file.

Then create osgi-context.xml in META-INF/spring to import and export OSGi services for this bundle, as shown following:

```
<beans:beans xmlns="http://www.springframework.org/schema/osgi"
    xmlns:xsi="http://www.w3.org/2001/XMLSchema-instance"
    xmlns:beans="http://www.springframework.org/schema/beans"
    xsi:schemaLocation="http://www.springframework.org/schema/beans
        http://www.springframework.org/schema/beans/spring-beans-2.5.xsd
        http://www.springframework.org/schema/osgi
        http://www.springframework.org/schema/osgi/spring-osgi.xsd">

    <reference id="transactionManager"
        interface="org.springframework.transaction.PlatformTransactionManager" />

    <reference id="vehicleDao"
        interface="com.apress.prodmserver.vehicle.repository.VehicleDao" />

    <service ref="vehicleService"
        interface="com.apress.prodmserver.vehicle.service.VehicleService" />
</beans:beans>
```

Because this bundle requires a transaction manager that is defined in and exported by the repository implementation bundle, you must import it using the name transactionManager so that Spring can locate it by default. You must also import the vehicle DAO from the OSGi service registry and export the vehicle service to that registry.

Finally, export the com.apress.prodmserver.vehicle.service package for other bundles to access the service interfaces. The completed MANIFEST.MF source code for this bundle should look like the following:

```
Manifest-Version: 1.0
Bundle-Name: Vehicle Service Bundle
Bundle-Description: APRESS
Bundle-ManifestVersion: 2
Bundle-SymbolicName: com.apress.prodmserver.vehicle.service
Bundle-Version: 1.0.0
Import-Library: org.springframework.spring;version="[3.0.0,3.0.0)"
Import-Package: com.apress.prodmserver.vehicle.domain,
 com.apress.prodmserver.vehicle.repository
Export-Package: com.apress.prodmserver.vehicle.service
```

Next, to finish up the vehicle system, you will create the last bundle in the form of a web bundle. First, I will provide a brief introduction to the topic of web bundles.

Developing Web Bundles for the dm Server

In addition to supporting packaging and deploying web applications in the WAR format, the dm Server supports the *web bundle* format, which has the following characteristics:

- A web bundle is a standard OSGi bundle designed to operate on an OSGi standard (RFC-66) web container and on which the dm Server is built.

- A web bundle can import dependencies from the dm Server's repository instead of from a directory like WEB-INF/lib, which is the norm for declaring dependencies in standard WARs. The dm Server also supports the inspection of dependencies in the WEB-INF/lib directory, a topic you will learn more about when we discuss migrating Web applications to the dm Server in the next chapter.

- Public web resources (e.g. static HTML pages, images, CSS files, and JavaScript files) should be packaged in the root directory of a web bundle. Private web resources (e.g. JSP templates and configuration files) should be packaged in the WEB-INF directory of a web bundle. And compiled classes belonging to a web bundle should be placed inside the WEB-INF/classes directory. In this case, the directory layout is identical to that of a standard WAR.

- A web deployment descriptor (web.xml) is required for a web bundle since it will contain the various web application parameters to operate on an OSGi web container. In this sense, a web bundle is also similar to a standard WAR.

- A web bundle will have its application context created by Spring-DM and can import services from the OSGi service registry. This allows a web bundle to access OSGi services provided by other application bundles. This is unlike a standard WAR, which can only access business logic contained in its own structure.

- A web bundle must have a .war extension to be properly detected as a web-bound bundle by the dm Server's underlying OSGi web container.

- A web bundle must have a MANIFEST.MF file like any standard OSGi bundle to specify package imports and exports. In addition to these values, a web bundle's MANIFEST.MF file can also include the optional Web-ContextPath header, used to configure the context path on which the OSGi web container will deploy the web bundle (e.g. http://localhost:8080/vehicle/).

Now that you're familiar with a web bundle's characteristics, you can set out to create one for the vehichle system.

Creating the Web Layer Bundle

First, create a Dynamic Web Project in Eclipse to generate the basic structure needed by a web bundle. Select the New menu ➤ Other. Next, from the pop-up window descend into the Web section and select the Dynamic Web Project wizard option as shown in Figure 5-21.

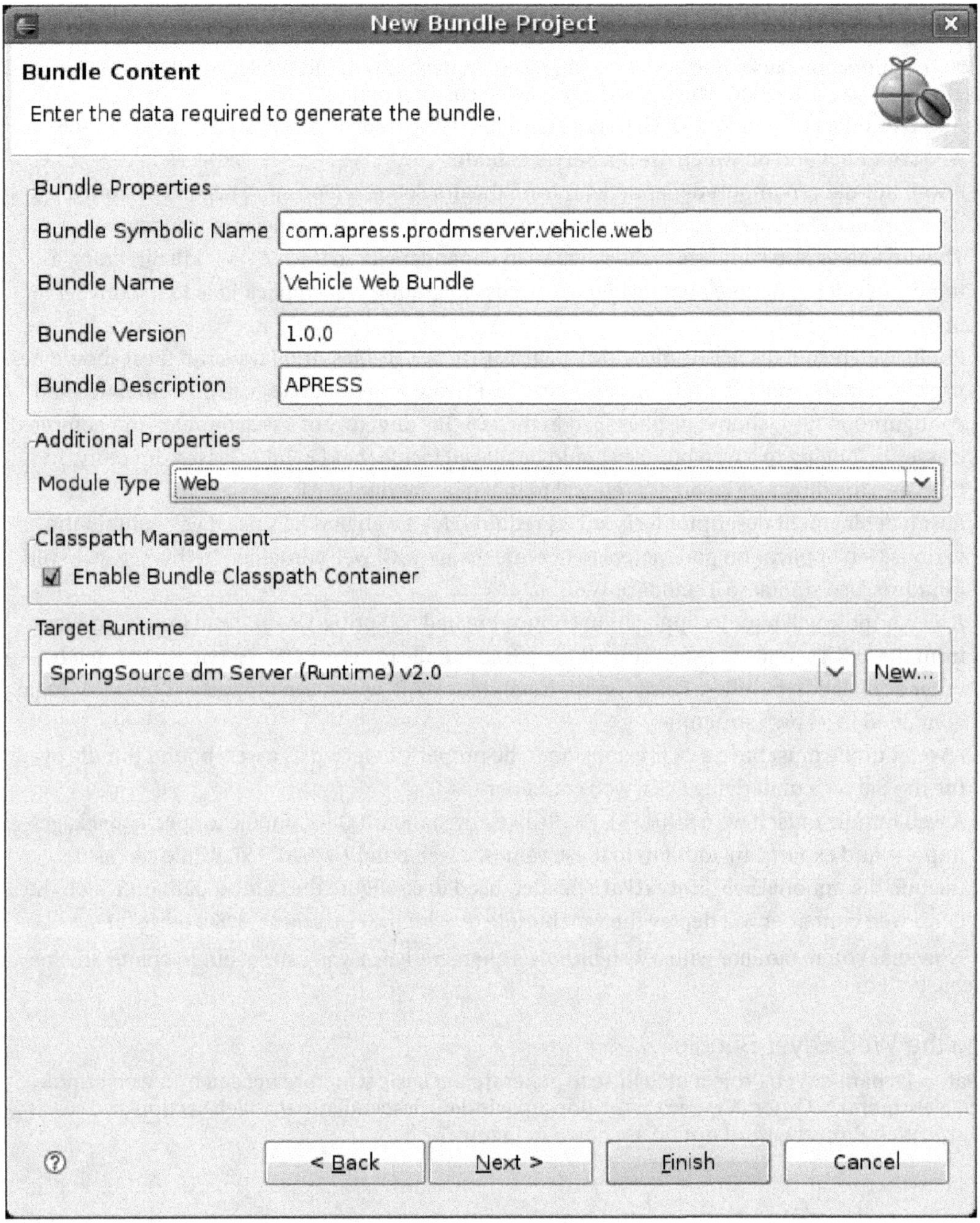

Figure 5-21. *Creating a Dynamic Web Project for a web bundle*

In the next window, assign a project name of com.apress.prodmserver.vehicle.web. This name is in line with the naming conventions used by the other project bundles. Next, click Finish. At this juncture, the Dynamic Web Project is a standard WAR. One additional step is necessary to convert this project into a web bundle.

With the Dynamic Web Project selected, right-click your mouse. From the pop-up menu select the option Spring Tools ➤ Add OSGi Bundle Project Nature, as illustrated in Figure 5-22.

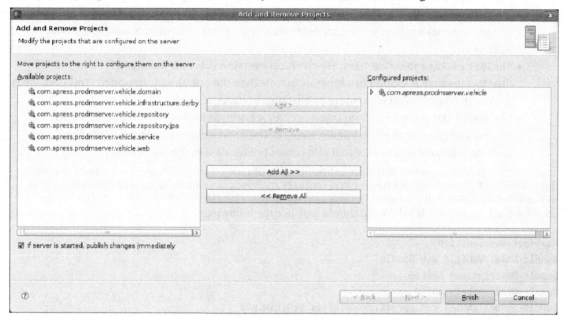

Figure 5-22. *Converting a Dynamic Web Project into a web bundle*

After performing this last step, right-click again. Next, descend into Spring Tools and a new set of options will appear. Select the Enable Bundle Classpath Container option. This will allow the web bundle access to the dm Server's repository to fulfill dependencies.

These two steps are all that's needed to convert a Dynamic Web Project into a web bundle, allowing it to be associated with a PAR file and providing access to the dm Server's repository to load bundle dependencies, as well as all the other OSGi bundle behaviors associated with Bundle Projects.

I opted to use this route of creating a Dynamic Web Project—or standard WAR—and then assigning it an OSGi Bundle Project Nature, because a web bundle's structure has more common elements with a Dynamic Web Project than a Bundle Project.

Instead of using a Bundle Project as you've done for the previous bundles, this route of creating a Dynamic Web Project for a web bundle and then performing these last two configuration tasks will save you additional setup steps.

Prior to developing the web bundle, you should add it to the vehicle PAR project as you've done for previous bundles. Then import the following bundles, libraries, and packages into the web bundle:

- The Apache Standard Taglibs bundle `com.springsource.org.apache.taglibs.standard` version `1.1.2` of the JSTL implementation for using JSTL tags in JSP files. This bundle comes preinstalled in the dm Server.
- The Spring Framework library `org.springframework.spring` version `3.0.0` for using the Spring MVC Framework to build the web module.
- The domain package `com.apress.prodmserver.vehicle.domain` for accessing the domain classes.
- The service package `com.apress.prodmserver.vehicle.service` for accessing the service interfaces.
- The JSTL package `javax.servlet.jsp.jstl.core` version `1.1.2` for accessing JSTL tags in JSP files; this package is located in a separate bundle than the one already imported. This package is present in a bundle that also comes preinstalled in the dm Server.
- The Spring-DM package `com.springsource.server.web.dm` for accessing a bundle's OSGi context and granting the web bundle access to OSGi services present in other bundles. This package is present in a bundle that also comes preinstalled in the dm Server.

After you've imported all the preceding bundles, libraries, and packages, you will need to modify the `MANIFEST.MF` file and add the header `Web-ContextPath:vehicle` so that the target web application is deployed to the OSGi web container in this path (e.g. `http://localhost:8080/vehicle/`). The source code for this bundle's `MANIFEST.MF` file should look like the following:

```
Manifest-Version: 1.0
Bundle-Name: Vehicle Web Bundle
Bundle-Description: APRESS
Bundle-ManifestVersion: 2
Bundle-SymbolicName: com.apress.prodmserver.vehicle.web
Bundle-Version: 1.0.0
Import-Library: org.springframework.spring;version="[3.0.0,3.0.0)"
Import-Bundle: com.springsource.org.apache.taglibs.standard;version="[1.1.2,1.1.2]"
Import-Package: com.apress.prodmserver.vehicle.domain,
 com.apress.prodmserver.vehicle.service,
 javax.servlet.jsp.jstl.core;version="[1.1.2,1.1.2]",
 com.springsource.server.web.dm;version="[2.0.0,3.0.0)"
Web-ContextPath: vehicle
```

Next, let's take a look at the classes that will be incorporated into this web bundle, which include some that are found in many other Java web applications: a web controller class, Java Server Page (JSP), and other configuration files. Suppose you would like to develop a user interface that lists all vehicles in the system. In Spring MVC, create a controller class as follows:

```
package com.apress.prodmserver.vehicle.web;

import com.apress.prodmserver.vehicle.service.VehicleService;

import org.springframework.beans.factory.annotation.Autowired;
import org.springframework.stereotype.Controller;
import org.springframework.ui.Model;
import org.springframework.web.bind.annotation.RequestMapping;

import com.apress.prodmserver.vehicle.service.VehicleService;
@Controller
public class VehicleListController {

    private VehicleService vehicleService;

    @Autowired
    public void setVehicleService(VehicleService vehicleService) {
        this.vehicleService = vehicleService;
    }

    @RequestMapping("/vehicleList.htm")
    public String list(Model model) {
        model.addAttribute("vehicles", vehicleService.list());
        return "vehicleList";
    }
}
```

Beginning in Spring 2.5, a controller class can be an ordinary Java class that does not implement a specific interface or extend a specific base class. The preceding controller class is defined in the com.apress.prodmserver.vehicle.web package (the base package for component scanning) and annotated with @Controller so that it will be auto-detected as a web controller. Also, the list() method is mapped by the @RequestMapping annotation to handle web requests for the URI /vehicleList.htm. When handling requests, this method will retrieve all vehicles from the vehicle service and store the result into the model under the key vehicles, and then return the view name vehicleList, which will be mapped to /WEB-INF/jsp/vehicleList.jsp by the view resolver.

Next, inside the project's WebContent directory, create a JSP named vehicleList.jsp located at /WEB-INF/jsp/vehicleList.jsp. This JSP file's major function is to iterate the vehicles model attribute and generate an HTML table for the entries:

```
<%@ page contentType="text/html; charset=utf-8" pageEncoding="utf-8" %>
<%@ taglib prefix="c" uri="http://java.sun.com/jsp/jstl/core" %>

<html>
<head>
<title>Vehicle List</title>
</head>

<body>
<table border="1">
  <tr>
    <th>Vehicle No</th>
    <th>Color</th>
    <th>Wheel</th>
    <th>Seat</th>
  </tr>
  <c:forEach items="${vehicles}" var="vehicle">
  <tr>
    <td>${vehicle.vehicleNo}</td>
    <td>${vehicle.color}</td>
    <td>${vehicle.wheel}</td>
    <td>${vehicle.seat}</td>
  </tr>
  </c:forEach>
</table>
<a href="vehicleRegister.htm">Register</a>
</body>
</html>
```

Suppose you have to develop another web interface for users to register a new vehicle by filling its information in a form. Create another controller class for this purpose as follows:

```
package com.apress.prodmserver.vehicle.web;

import com.apress.prodmserver.vehicle.service.VehicleService;
import com.apress.prodmserver.vehicle.domain.Vehicle;
import com.apress.prodmserver.vehicle.web.validation.VehicleValidator;
import org.springframework.beans.factory.annotation.Autowired;
import org.springframework.stereotype.Controller;
import org.springframework.ui.Model;
import org.springframework.validation.BindingResult;
import org.springframework.web.bind.annotation.ModelAttribute;
import org.springframework.web.bind.annotation.RequestMapping;
```

```
import org.springframework.web.bind.annotation.RequestMethod;
import org.springframework.web.bind.support.SessionStatus;

@Controller
@RequestMapping("/vehicleRegister.htm")
public class VehicleRegisterController {

    private VehicleService vehicleService;

    @Autowired
    public void setVehicleService(VehicleService vehicleService) {
        this.vehicleService = vehicleService;
    }

    @RequestMapping(method = RequestMethod.GET)
    public String setupForm(Model model) {
        Vehicle vehicle = new Vehicle();
        model.addAttribute("vehicle", vehicle);
        return "vehicleRegister";
    }

    @RequestMapping(method = RequestMethod.POST)
    public String processSubmit(@ModelAttribute("vehicle") Vehicle vehicle,
            BindingResult result, SessionStatus status) {
        new VehicleValidator().validate(vehicle, result);
        if (result.hasErrors()) {
            return "vehicleRegister";
        } else {
            vehicleService.register(vehicle);
            status.setComplete();
            return "redirect:vehicleList.htm";
        }
    }
}
```

In this controller, you first map the URI /vehicleRegister.htm at the class level, and then the HTTP GET method of this URI to the setupForm() method, and the HTTP POST method to the processSubmit() method. When a client requests this URI with the HTTP GET method, the setupForm() method initializes the form object and stores it as a model attribute with the name vehicle. Then it returns the view name vehicleRegister, which will be resolved by the view resolver, for rendering the form view.

When the client submits the form with the POST method, the form field values will first be bound to the form object's properties of the same name. Then the processSubmit() method will validate the form object with a validator. If there are errors found with the object, the method will render the form view again to display the error messages. Otherwise, the method will call the service to register this vehicle and redirect to the list page upon completion.

As you will note, this last controller also make use of a special validator class. The VehicleValidator class includes a validate() method for validating a vehicle object's fields as shown following:

```
package com.apress.prodmserver.vehicle.web.validation;

import com.apress.prodmserver.vehicle.domain.Vehicle;

import org.springframework.util.StringUtils;
import org.springframework.validation.Errors;


public class VehicleValidator {

    public void validate(Vehicle vehicle, Errors errors) {
        if (!StringUtils.hasLength(vehicle.getVehicleNo())) {
            errors.rejectValue("vehicleNo", "required", "required");
        }
        if (!StringUtils.hasLength(vehicle.getColor())) {
            errors.rejectValue("color", "required", "required");
        }
        if (vehicle.getWheel() <= 0) {
            errors.rejectValue("wheel", "invalid", "invalid");
        }
        if (vehicle.getSeat() <= 0) {
            errors.rejectValue("seat", "invalid", "invalid");
        }
    }
}
```

If the vehicle number or the color is empty, this validator will create an error for that field with the code required, which will be resolved by the message source into a message in a resource bundle. If the wheel or seat number is zero or negative, an error will be created for that field with the code invalid. In order for the message source to resolve the codes into text messages, you have to include the following file messages.properties in the top-level directory of the bundle (WebContent):

```
required=Required
invalid=Invalid
```

Next, create the form /WEB-INF/jsp/vehicleRegister.jsp with the following contents:

```jsp
<%@ page contentType="text/html; charset=utf-8" pageEncoding="utf-8" %>
<%@ taglib prefix="form" uri="http://www.springframework.org/tags/form" %>

<html>
<head>
<title>Vehicle Register</title>
<style>
.errors {
  color: #ff0000;
  font-weight: bold;
}
</style>
</head>

<body>
<form:form modelAttribute="vehicle">
<table>
  <tr>
    <td>Vehicle No</td>
    <td>
      <form:input path="vehicleNo" />
      <form:errors path="vehicleNo" cssClass="errors" />
    </td>
  </tr>
  <tr>
    <td>Color</td>
    <td>
      <form:input path="color" />
      <form:errors path="color" cssClass="errors" />
    </td>
  </tr>
  <tr>
    <td>Wheel</td>
    <td>
      <form:input path="wheel" />
      <form:errors path="wheel" cssClass="errors" />
    </td>
  </tr>
  <tr>
    <td>Seat</td>
```

```
        <td>
          <form:input path="seat" />
          <form:errors path="seat" cssClass="errors" />
        </td>
      </tr>
      <tr>
        <td colspan="2">
          <input type="submit" value="Register" />
        </td>
      </tr>
    </table>
  </form:form>
</body>
</html>
```

This JSP file utilizes Spring's form tag library to bind the fields of the form object, which is passed to this file as a model attribute with the name vehicle, with HTML input fields for users to input their values. If there are errors with the field values, the error messages will be displayed next to the fields.

Finally, create the welcome.html file in the WebContent directory of the web bundle, with the following contents:

```
<html>
<head>
<title>Welcome</title>
</head>

<body>
<h1>Welcome</h1>
<a href="vehicleList.htm">List all vehicles</a>
<br />
<a href="vehicleRegister.htm">Register a new vehicle</a>
</body>
</html>
```

Now that you have the various parts that will make up a web bundle's code, its necessary to create the corresponding configuration files for the web bundle. First up is the web.xml file, of which there is a pre-existing template inside the web bundle's /WEB-INF/ directory. Modify this file to reflect the following:

```
<web-app version="2.5" xmlns="http://java.sun.com/xml/ns/javaee"
    xmlns:xsi="http://www.w3.org/1999/XMLSchema-instance"
    xsi:schemaLocation="http://java.sun.com/xml/ns/javaee
        http://java.sun.com/xml/ns/javaee/web-app_2_5.xsd">
```

```xml
<display-name>com.apress.prodmserver.vehicle.web</display-name>
 <session-config>
      <session-timeout>60</session-timeout>
 </session-config>

 <context-param>
    <param-name>contextClass</param-name>
   <param-value>
      com.springsource.server.web.dm.ServerOsgiBundleXmlWebApplicationContext
   </param-value>
</context-param>

<listener>
    <listener-class>
      org.springframework.web.context.ContextLoaderListener
    </listener-class>
</listener>

 <servlet>
     <servlet-name>
        vehicle
     </servlet-name>
     <servlet-class>
        org.springframework.web.servlet.DispatcherServlet
     </servlet-class>

</servlet>

<servlet-mapping>
     <servlet-name>
        vehicle
     </servlet-name>
     <url-pattern>*.htm</url-pattern>
</servlet-mapping>

  <welcome-file-list>
    <welcome-file>index.html</welcome-file>
    <welcome-file>index.htm</welcome-file>
    <welcome-file>index.jsp</welcome-file>
    <welcome-file>default.html</welcome-file>
```

```
    <welcome-file>default.htm</welcome-file>
        <welcome-file>default.jsp</welcome-file>
        <welcome-file>welcome.html</welcome-file>
    </welcome-file-list>
</web-app>
```

The first two declarations of the web.xml file should be familiar if you've done standard Java web applications. One is used to declare a web bundle's name and the other its session timeout.

The next declaration deserves closer attention. The context parameter named contextClass, which is assigned a value of com.springsource.server.web.dm.ServerOsgiBundleXmlWebApplication-Context, is used by the web bundle to access its OSGi context, making it possible to access OSGi services offered by other application bundles.

Next, you will find a <listener> element, which is used to define a <listener-class> element. The class assigned to this last element is used to set up a context for the web bundle. If you've written standard Java web applications with Spring, this web.xml declaration should also be familiar.

The next statements are necessary to set up the web bundle's dispatcher Servlet. In this case, an org.springframework.web.servlet.DispatcherServlet named vehicle is mapped to all URL patterns ending in .htm. These dispatcher statements should also be familiar to Spring developers.

Finally, the <welcome-file-list> and <welcome-file> elements are used to define a series of default landing pages for the web bundle. These last elements are also in line with a standard WAR's web.xml file.

Once you've defined a web bundle's web.xml file, it's necessary to include the additional configuration files that will be expected upon processing this last web.xml file. In this case, a context is expected to be configured in a file named applicationContext.xml and a dispatcher Servlet in a file named vehicle-servlet.xml. These are conventions used by standard web applications using Spring that are also applicable to web bundles.

The web bundle's applicationContext.xml file should be placed inside the web bundle's / WEB-INF/ directory and look like the following listing:

```
<beans:beans xmlns="http://www.springframework.org/schema/osgi"
    xmlns:xsi="http://www.w3.org/2001/XMLSchema-instance"
    xmlns:beans="http://www.springframework.org/schema/beans"
    xsi:schemaLocation="http://www.springframework.org/schema/beans
        http://www.springframework.org/schema/beans/spring-beans-2.5.xsd
        http://www.springframework.org/schema/osgi
        http://www.springframework.org/schema/osgi/spring-osgi.xsd">

    <reference id="vehicleService"
        interface="com.apress.prodmserver.vehicle.service.VehicleService" />
</beans:beans>
```

Notice how this listing relies on the Spring-OSGi namespace and the <reference> element to locate an OSGi service registered with the interface com.apress.prodmserver.vehicle.service.VehicleService. This is sure to be in contrast with other web application contexts you've configured, since this is an OSGi web bundle context. Access to this context is made possible by the special <context-param> element and class com.springsource.server.web.dm. ServerOsgiBundleXmlWebApplicationContext declared in the web bundle's web.xml file.

Let's now examine the OSGi service. This service belongs to another application bundle, com.apress.prodmserver.vehicle.service, which registered it for further use by other bundles. Once the OSGi service is located by the web bundle, it will be referenced by an id value of vehicleService.

By using this reference value, the web bundle will inject the reference into the web bundle's controller Servlet—note the id=vehicleService– which is precisely the setter reference used in the web bundle's controller class. For Spring users, this mechanism is identical to the injection of bean values into controller Servlets, except that in this case it's being performed with OSGi services.

Once a web bundle's context is configured to access the OSGi services it requires, you can next configure the Servlets declared in a web bundle's web.xml file. In this case, given the only Servlet's name, it should be configured in a file named vehicle-servlet.xml with the following contents:

```xml
<beans xmlns="http://www.springframework.org/schema/beans"
    xmlns:xsi="http://www.w3.org/2001/XMLSchema-instance"
    xmlns:context="http://www.springframework.org/schema/context"
    xsi:schemaLocation="http://www.springframework.org/schema/beans
        http://www.springframework.org/schema/beans/spring-beans-2.5.xsd
        http://www.springframework.org/schema/context
        http://www.springframework.org/schema/context/spring-context-2.5.xsd">

    <context:component-scan base-package="com.apress.prodmserver.vehicle.web"/>

    <bean
        class="org.springframework.web.servlet.view.InternalResourceViewResolver">
        <property name="prefix" value="/WEB-INF/jsp/" />
        <property name="suffix" value=".jsp" />
    </bean>

    <bean id="messageSource"
        class="org.springframework.context.support.ResourceBundleMessageSource">
        <property name="basename" value="messages" />
    </bean>
</beans>
```

In this Servlet configuration file, you first enable Spring's component scanning feature via <context:component-scan> and specify the base package for scanning. This feature will scan and detect components annotated with Spring's stereotype annotations. The main purpose of enabling the feature here is to auto-detect Spring MVC web controllers that have the @Controller annotation, as well as other annotations that might be present in a Spring MVC web controller like @Autowired.

The InternalResourceViewResolver bean resolves logical view names into JSP files in the /WEB-INF/jsp/ directory of the web bundle. The ResourceBundleMessageSource bean resolves codes into text messages of different locales, using resource bundles located in the classpath root and with the base name messages. For example, messages_en.properties stores messages for the English locale, and messages.properties stores default messages.

CHANGING A WEB BUNDLE'S CONFIGURATION FILE NAMES AND LOCATIONS

Just like a standard WAR, a web bundle's web.xml file elements can be configured to locate configuration files in different location and by different names. For example, the default location for dispatcher Servlets can be overridden by adding the following statement to the <servlet> element:

```
<init-param>
 <param-name>contextConfigLocation</param-name>
 <param-value>
   /WEB-INF/spring/*.xml
 </param-value>
</init-param>
```

If you add this last statement to a web bundle's web.xml file, the bundle would look for a servlet configuration file named vehicle-servlet.xml under the bundle's /WEB-INF/spring/ directory, instead of the default directory /WEB-INF/.

Similarly, a web bundle's context can be configured to use a configuration other than the default applicationContext.xml file, by adding the following elements to the bundle's web.xml file:

```
<context-param>

    <param-name>contextConfigLocation</param-name>

    <param-value>/WEB-INF/spring/webbundleconfig.xml</param-value>

</context-param>
```

Adding this last statement would make a web bundle search for its context configuration in a file named webbundleconfig.xml inside the bundle's /WEB-INF/spring/ directory.

With this we conclude designing the sixth and final bundle that will compose the vehicle application. Next, I will describe the deployment process to the dm Server directly within Eclipse.

Deploying Applications in the dm Server Tools

With all bundles of the vehicle system ready, you can deploy the PAR file that includes these bundles to the dm Server.

To deploy the application using dm Server Tools, right-click the dm Server instance in the Servers view and choose Add and Remove Projects. Then, in the pop-up dialog, add the PAR project com.apress.prodmserver.vehicle from Available projects to Configured projects, as shown in Figure 5-23.

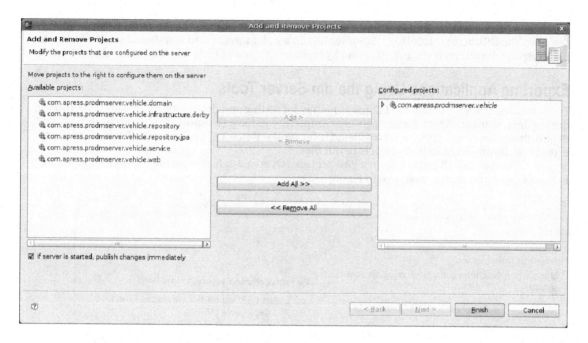

Figure 5-23. Adding the vehicle PAR project to the dm Server

If everything goes well, when you start the dm Server you should see that all bundles and the PAR project are in the Synchronized status, as shown in Figure 5-24.

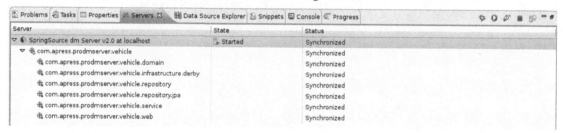

Figure 5-24. Starting the dm Server with the PAR project deployed

---

■ **Note** You can also use drag-and-drop to deploy an application, by dragging the application name represented in the main window onto the server instance icon illustrated in Figure 5-24.

Because you specified vehicle as the context path in the Web-ContextPath manifest header, you can open the URL http://localhost:8080/vehicle in a web browser; and you should see the welcome page displayed. You can test the application by registering a new vehicle and listing all vehicles.

Exporting Applications Using the dm Server Tools

The dm Server instance defined in Eclipse is mainly for testing and debugging bundle and PAR projects during development. When the projects are complete, you have to export them to archive files and deploy these files to another dm Server instance for production use. The dm Server Tools allow you to export bundle projects and PAR projects to JAR files.

To export a PAR project, from a PAR project's Overview tab, choose the Export PAR link from Eclipse's PAR Actions area, as shown in Figure 5-25.

Figure 5-25. Exporting a PAR project or a PAR file

Then, from the pop-up window, select the PAR project in the Eclipse workspace to export, as shown in Figure 5-26.

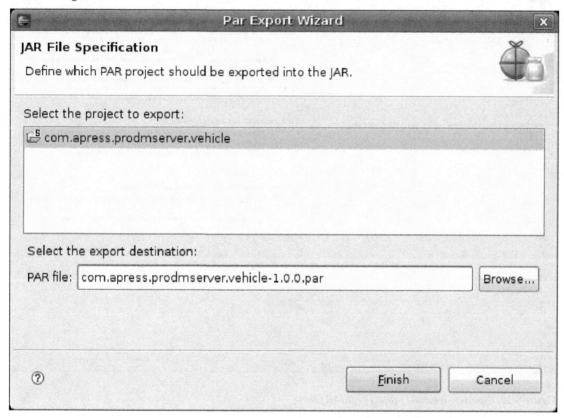

Figure 5-26. *Selecting a PAR project to export*

Similarly, if all you wanted to export was an individual bundle project to a JAR file, from the bundle project's Overview tab, select the Export Bundle link from the Bundle Actions area, as shown in Figure 5-27.

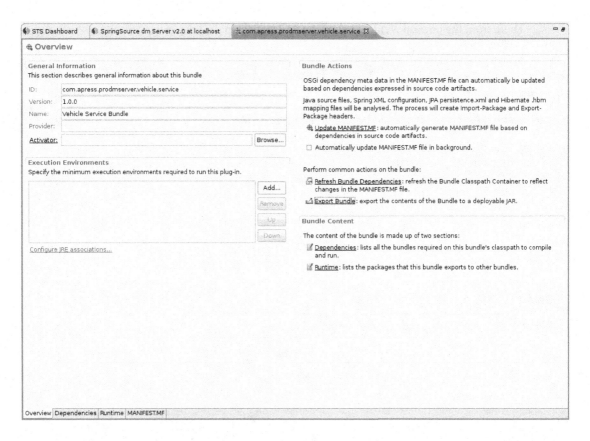

Figure 5-27. *Exporting a bundle project or a JAR file*

Then from the pop-up window, select the bundle project in the Eclipse workspace to export, as shown in Figure 5-28.

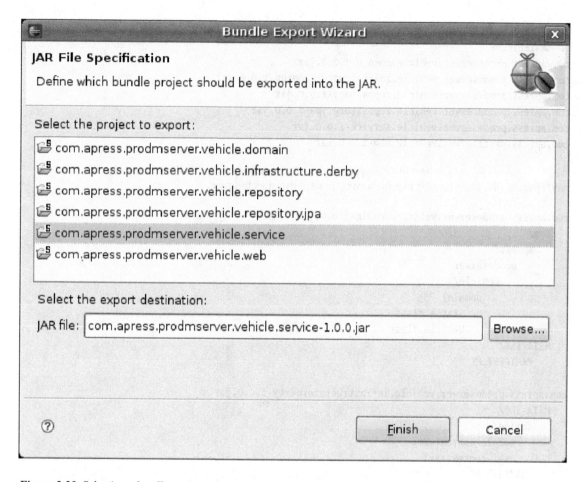

Figure 5-28. Selecting a bundle project to export

By default, the export destination is relative to the root of the Eclipse workspace directory. For your vehicle system, all composing bundles are included in a PAR project, so you only need to export the PAR project, not individual bundle projects. For a PAR project, the default filename has the form [Application-SymbolicName]-[Application-Version].par (in this case, com.apress.prodmserver. vehicle-1.0.0.par). If you use an archive utility to browse the file contents, you should see the following:

```
META-INF/
    MANIFEST.MF
com.apress.prodmserver.vehicle.domain-1.0.0.jar
com.apress.prodmserver.vehicle.infrastructure.derby-1.0.0.jar
com.apress.prodmserver.vehicle.repository-1.0.0.jar
com.apress.prodmserver.vehicle.repository.jpa-1.0.0.jar
com.apress.prodmserver.vehicle.service-1.0.0.jar
com.apress.prodmserver.vehicle.web-1.0.0.war
```

As you can see, a PAR file simply archives all composing bundle JAR files together with a MANIFEST.MF file. Each bundle JAR file's contents are listed as follows:

```
com.apress.prodmserver.vehicle.domain-1.0.0.jar
    com/
        apress/
            prodmserver/
                vehicle/
                    domain/
                        Status.class
                        Vehicle.class
    META-INF/
        MANIFEST.MF

com.apress.prodmserver.vehicle.infrastructure.derby-1.0.0.jar
    META-INF/
        spring/
            module-context.xml
            osgi-context.xml
        MANIFEST.MF

com.apress.prodmserver.vehicle.repository-1.0.0.jar
    com/
        apress/
            prodmserver/
                vehicle/
                    repository/
                        VehicleDao.class
    META-INF/
        MANIFEST.MF
```

```
com.apress.prodmserver.vehicle.repository.jpa-1.0.0.jar
    com/
        apress/
            prodmserver/
                vehicle/
                    repository/
                        jpa/
                            JpaVehicleDao.class
    META-INF/
        spring/
            module-context.xml
            osgi-context.xml
        MANIFEST.MF
        persistence.xml

com.apress.prodmserver.vehicle.service-1.0.0.jar
    com/
        apress/
            prodmserver/
                vehicle/
                    service/
                        impl/
                            VehicleServiceImpl.class
                        VehicleService.class
    META-INF/
        spring/
            module-context.xml
            osgi-context.xml
        MANIFEST.MF

com.apress.prodmserver.vehicle.web-1.0.0.war
WEB-INF/
    classes/
        com/
        apress/
            prodmserver/
                vehicle/
                    web/
                        validation/
                            VehicleValidator.class
                        VehicleListController.class
                        VehicleRegisterController.class
```

```
META-INF/

    MANIFEST.MF

    WEB-INF/
        jsp/
            vehicleList.jsp
            vehicleRegister.jsp
        web.xml
        vehicle-servlet.xml
        applicationContext.xml
    welcome.html
messages.properties
```

Finally, you can deploy this PAR file to a production dm Server instance either by uploading it in the admin console or by copying it to the `pickup` directory of the dm Server home.

Summary

In this chapter, you first installed the dm Server Tools plug-in in Eclipse or the SpringSource Tools Suite (STS), itself also an Eclipse environment, both of which serve to develop applications for the dm Server and deploy applications in a development environment. With either of these tools, you can define a dm Server instance, start and stop the server, and add and remove projects for the server.

Before starting to develop applications to run on the dm Server, you had an overview of the general bundle architecture and dependencies of an enterprise application, which are divided by application layers. You also saw the specific bundle architecture and dependencies of the sample application, which uses JPA (with EclipseLink as the engine) to persist objects into the Derby database and uses Spring MVC as the web application framework.

Prior to developing bundles for the sample applications, you first created a PAR project in Eclipse to group all bundles of the application in a single deployment unit so that they can be deployed, refreshed, and undeployed as a whole. Later you added each bundle project to this PAR project after creation.

By creating the dm Server bundle projects in Eclipse, you in turn created bundles for the sample application's infrastructure, domain model, repository layer, service layer and web layer, which helped you become familiar with their functions, responsibilities, and how they communicate with each other.

You finally learned how the dm Server Tools plug-in allows you to add bundle projects and PAR projects to the dm Server instance defined in Eclipse for testing and debugging purposes. The tools also allow you to export these projects to JAR files and PAR files so that you can deploy them to another dm Server instance for production use.

In the next chapter, you will learn how to migrate traditional Java EE web applications to the dm Server to take advantage of OSGi and the dm Server features.

■■■

CHAPTER 6

Migrating Web Applications to the dm Server

In the previous chapter, you learned how to develop modular and OSGi-based enterprise Java applications for the dm Server. In this chapter, you will see how to migrate existing Java EE web applications to the dm Server gradually.

Because of the popularity and relatively long history of Java EE, enterprises may already have a number of standard web applications developed, packaged, and deployed in the WAR format. It would be hard for them to give up these applications and convert them into OSGi bundles all at once to take advantage of OSGi. For this reason, the dm Server supports a clear migration path for developers to migrate existing Java EE web applications in the standard WAR format to an OSGi web bundle. This chapter covers the following topics:

- Introducing the migration path for standard Java EE WARs into web bundles
- Developing and packaging a Java EE web application in a standard WAR file
- Migrating a standard WAR file to a shared libraries WAR web bundle
- Migrating a shared libraries WAR web bundle to a shared services WAR web bundle
- Incorporating a shared services WAR web bundle into a PAR file

Before reading this chapter, you should have a basic knowledge of Java web application development. I also assume that you have read Chapter 5, which introduced how to develop applications to run on the dm Server. Therefore, I won't repeat those topics here.

Introduction to the Migration Path

The dm Server operates atop an OSGi standard (RFC 66) web container. Unlike conventional web containers—used in Java EE applications—which rely on the WAR format as a deployment unit, an OSGi web container defines its own deployment unit, known as a web bundle.

A web bundle differs from a WAR in that it incorporates OSGi features into web applications. Such OSGi features can range from the basic, like the incorporation of a MANIFEST.MF file to take advantage of OSGi versioning, to more advanced cases, like using OSGi services provided by other bundles in a web application.

Because there are different OSGi features a web bundle can take advantage of, *web bundle* is an "umbrella term," since the bundle doesn't need to abide to a strict set of OSGi features, but rather a gradual incorporation of them.

OSGi features aside, a web bundle's directory and content structure is similar to that of a WAR. This makes a WAR—which by definition has no OSGi dynamics—capable of being deployed as a web bundle, a structure that can be gradually modified to incorporate OSGi features. It is this evolving nature of a web bundle that creates a migration path and allows us to group different sets of features under the umbrella of "web bundle."

This process also helps developers gradually migrate existing Java EE web applications in the standard WAR format to take full advantage of the OSGi feature set provided by the dm Server. The migration path for a web bundle from having no OSGi features to taking full advantage of them is the following:

Standard WAR: A standard Java EE WAR file contains all library JAR files and services required by the application.

Shared libraries WAR: A shared libraries WAR web bundle doesn't contain library JAR files. It imports the libraries from the dm Server's bundle repository at runtime.

Shared services WAR: A shared services WAR web bundle doesn't contain library JAR files or services. It imports the libraries from the bundle repository and the services from the OSGi service registry at runtime.

As an overview, Figure 6-1 illustrates the migration path for web bundles from a standard WAR file to a shared services WAR web bundle.

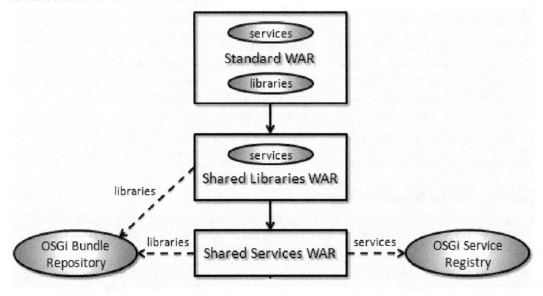

Figure 6-1. *The migration path for web bundles from a standard WAR file to a shared services WAR*

A standard WAR file packages all dependent libraries and application services in a single archive, which makes them hard to manage and reuse. The first step in the migration path of a web bundle is to remove the libraries from the WAR file and install them as OSGi bundles. Then the WAR file can import the libraries from the bundle repository at runtime, which produces a shared libraries WAR web bundle in the end. The second step in the migration path of a web bundle is to extract the application services from the WAR file to form a service bundle and register the services as OSGi services. Then the WAR file can import the services from the OSGi service registry at runtime, which produces a shared services WAR web bundle in the end. As an additional step, once a web bundle reaches it final migration phase—that of a shared services WAR web bundle—a web bundle can be packaged alongside other bundles in a PAR file, to take further advantage of dm Server OSGi features. In the case of a PAR, these features include providing a single deployment unit and OSGi service scoping.

Note that this migration path is applicable to any Java EE web applications that can be developed with any web application framework; it is not specific to Spring MVC.

The following sections use a simple web application as an example to demonstrate the migration process in detail.

Standard WAR Files

In this section, I will first demonstrate the process of developing a Java EE web application and packaging and deploying it in the standard WAR format. Then, in the upcoming sections, you will gradually migrate this web application to take advantage of OSGi. You are free to develop the web application with any web application framework, such as Struts, JSF, or any of the others available. Here I will use Spring MVC 2.5 so that developers who are familiar with the Spring Framework can get started quickly.

Note that the standard WAR file developed and packaged in this section can be deployed to any Java EE-compliant web application server, such as Tomcat, Jetty, or others. To save you the trouble of installing an extra application server, I will demonstrate how to deploy it to the dm Server. The advantages of deploying a standard WAR file to the dm Server compared to other Java EE application servers include per-application tracing and first failure data capture (FFDC). Many developers choose to deploy their existing web applications to the dm Server as a starting point of migrating to OSGi.

Suppose you are going to develop a web application for finding the distance between two cities. To develop, package, and deploy this application in the standard WAR format, you can create a Dynamic Web Project in Eclipse to take advantage of its Java EE and web support features, as shown in Figure 6-2.

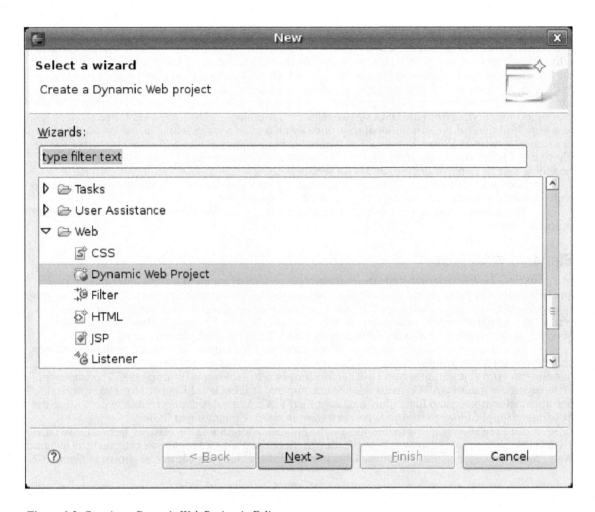

Figure 6-2. *Creating a Dynamic Web Project in Eclipse*

In the next screen, enter `com.apress.prodmserver.city` as the project name for this project. If you have the dm Server Tools plug-in installed and a dm Server instance configured properly, you will be able to select SpringSource dm Server (Runtime) v2.0 as the target runtime for this project, as shown in Figure 6-3.

Figure 6-3. *Selecting the target runtime for the project*

Next, you can modify the context root to `city-war`, used to indicate the context to which the project will be deployed, and the directories for storing web contents and Java sources, as shown in Figure 6-4.

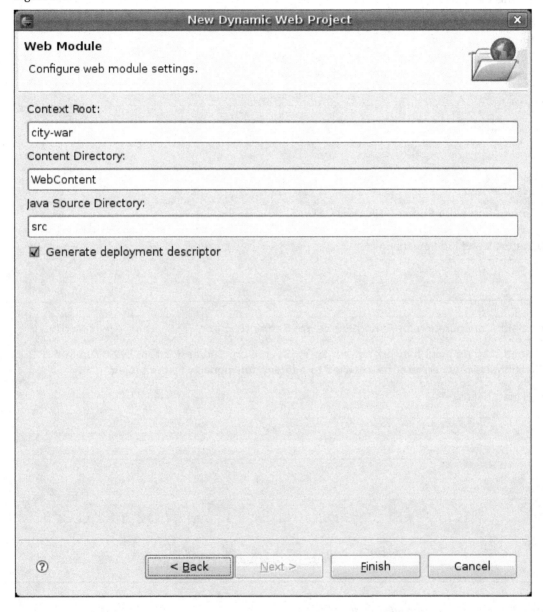

Figure 6-4. *Configuring the context root and directories for the project*

Before developing and packaging this application in the standard WAR format, you must prepare the library JAR files required by the application. Since you are going to use Spring MVC as the web application framework, you have to retrieve its corresponding JAR files. I recommend that you download the Spring Framework release with dependencies (e.g. version 2.5.5 or 3.0.0) from the SpringSource web site (http://www.springsource.org/download) and extract the file to a directory of your choice (e.g. c:\spring-framework-2.5.5 or c:\spring-framework-3.0.0). Then copy the JAR files listed in Table 6-1 to the WEB-INF/lib directory of your web application. You perform this last step by placing your mouse over the WEB-INF/lib directory, right-clicking, and selecting New ➤ File from the pop-up menu. In the resulting pop-up window, click the Advanced>> icon, check the box Link to File in the File System, and browse for the required JARs. In an Eclipse dynamic web project, JAR files in the WEB-INF/lib directory will automatically be added to the project's classpath. If a dynamic web project is exported as a WAR, the JAR files in the WEB-INF/lib directory files will be copied automatically to the WAR.

Table 6-1. *Required JAR Files for the Web Application*

JAR File	Description
dist/spring.jar	Collection of the Spring Framework's standard modules
dist/modules/spring-webmvc.jar	The Spring Web MVC module
lib/jakarta-commons/commons-logging.jar	Apache Commons Logging
lib/j2ee/jstl.jar	The JavaServer Pages Standard Tag Library (JSTL) API
lib/jakarta-taglibs/standard.jar	Jakarta's standard tag library implementation for JSTL

Once you've added the JAR files described in Table 6-1 to the dynamic project, you can define the following service interface for finding the distance between a source city and a destination city:

```
package com.apress.prodmserver.city.service;

public interface CityService {

    public Double findDistance(String srcCity, String destCity);
}
```

If this application were intended for production use, you might implement this interface by storing the static distances of cities in a database, or storing the geographical coordinates of cities in a database and calculating the distances on demand. However, for simplicity's sake, let's use a Java map to store the distances.

```
package com.apress.prodmserver.city.service.impl;

import java.util.Map;

import com.apress.prodmserver.city.service.CityService;

public class CityServiceImpl implements CityService {

    private Map<String, Map<String, Double>> distanceMap;

    public void setDistanceMap(Map<String, Map<String, Double>> distanceMap) {
        this.distanceMap = distanceMap;
    }

    public Double findDistance(String srcCity, String destCity) {
        Map<String, Double> destinationMap = distanceMap.get(srcCity);
        if (destinationMap == null) {
            return null;
        }
        return destinationMap.get(destCity);
    }
}
```

This map's keys are source cities, while its values are nested maps that contain destination cities and their distance from the source city. The map can be injected via setter injection so that it can be configured in the Spring IoC container. Finally, if no source city or no destination city matches the arguments, the findDistance() method will return null.

The application contexts of a Spring MVC–based web application should be organized in a hierarchical manner to separate web components from service components. For this purpose, you can define service components in the root application context and web components in the web application context, which refers to the root application context as its parent and thus can access its components. Now in the web deployment descriptor (WEB-INF/web.xml), define a ContextLoaderListener to load the root application context and a DispatcherServlet to load the web application context and handle requests mapped to this Servlet:

```
<web-app version="2.5" xmlns="http://java.sun.com/xml/ns/javaee"
    xmlns:xsi="http://www.w3.org/2001/XMLSchema-instance"
    xsi:schemaLocation="http://java.sun.com/xml/ns/javaee
        http://java.sun.com/xml/ns/javaee/web-app_2_5.xsd">

    <listener>
        <listener-class>
            org.springframework.web.context.ContextLoaderListener
        </listener-class>
    </listener>
```

```
<servlet>
    <servlet-name>city</servlet-name>
    <servlet-class>
        org.springframework.web.servlet.DispatcherServlet
    </servlet-class>
</servlet>

<servlet-mapping>
    <servlet-name>city</servlet-name>
    <url-pattern>*.htm</url-pattern>
</servlet-mapping>
</web-app>
```

By default, the ContextLoaderListener will load the applicationContext.xml file from the root of WEB-INF as the bean configuration file for the root application context. In this file, you can define a bean instance of type CityServiceImpl and configure its distance map with some hard-coded distances for several major cities in the world:

```
<beans xmlns="http://www.springframework.org/schema/beans"
    xmlns:xsi="http://www.w3.org/2001/XMLSchema-instance"
    xsi:schemaLocation="http://www.springframework.org/schema/beans
        http://www.springframework.org/schema/beans/spring-beans-2.5.xsd">

    <bean id="cityService"
        class="com.apress.prodmserver.city.service.impl.CityServiceImpl">
        <property name="distanceMap">
            <map>
                <entry key="New York">
                    <map>
                        <entry key="London" value="5574" />
                        <entry key="Beijing" value="10976" />
                    </map>
                </entry>
            </map>
        </property>
    </bean>
</beans>
```

Similarly, the DispatcherServlet will by default load a bean configuration file for its web application context from the root of WEB-INF by joining the Servlet name with -servlet.xml as the file name (city-servlet.xml in this case). You can create the city-servlet.xml file with the following contents:

```xml
<beans xmlns="http://www.springframework.org/schema/beans"
    xmlns:xsi="http://www.w3.org/2001/XMLSchema-instance"
    xmlns:context="http://www.springframework.org/schema/context"
    xsi:schemaLocation="http://www.springframework.org/schema/beans
        http://www.springframework.org/schema/beans/spring-beans-2.5.xsd
        http://www.springframework.org/schema/context
        http://www.springframework.org/schema/context/spring-context-2.5.xsd">

    <context:component-scan base-package="com.apress.prodmserver.city.web"/>

    <bean
        class="org.springframework.web.servlet.view.InternalResourceViewResolver">
        <property name="prefix" value="/WEB-INF/jsp/" />
        <property name="suffix" value=".jsp" />
    </bean>
</beans>
```

In this bean configuration file, you first enable Spring's component scanning feature and specify the base package com.apress.prodmserver.city.web for scanning. As a result, Spring MVC web controllers that are defined in this package (and also in its subpackages) and annotated with @Controller will be auto-detected. On the other hand, the view resolver bean resolves logical view names into JSP files of the same name in the WEB-INF/jsp directory.

To allow users to input the source and destination cities and find the distance, create a Spring MVC controller to handle the form as follows:

```java
package com.apress.prodmserver.city.web;

import org.springframework.beans.factory.annotation.Autowired;
import org.springframework.stereotype.Controller;
import org.springframework.ui.Model;
import org.springframework.web.bind.annotation.RequestMapping;
import org.springframework.web.bind.annotation.RequestMethod;
import org.springframework.web.bind.annotation.RequestParam;

import com.apress.prodmserver.city.service.CityService;

@Controller
@RequestMapping("/distance.htm")
public class DistanceController {

    private CityService cityService;
```

```
@Autowired
public void setCityService(CityService cityService) {
    this.cityService = cityService;
}

@RequestMapping(method = RequestMethod.GET)
public String setupForm() {
    return "distance";
}

@RequestMapping(method = RequestMethod.POST)
public String processSubmit(
        @RequestParam(value = "srcCity", required = false) String srcCity,
        @RequestParam(value = "destCity", required = false) String destCity,
        Model model) {
    Double distance = cityService.findDistance(srcCity, destCity);
    model.addAttribute("distance", distance);
    return "distance";
}
}
```

Note that you have mapped the controller class to the /distance.htm URI, the setupForm() method to the HTTP GET method, and the processSubmit() method to the HTTP POST method. When the URI is requested by the GET method, the controller method will render the distance view, which will be resolved into WEB-INF/jsp/distance.jsp. When the URI is requested by the POST method, the controller method will pass the srcCity and destCity request parameters to the city service for finding the distance, which will be added to the model and passed to the distance view for rendering.

Finally, you have to create the distance.jsp file in the WEB-INF/jsp directory for rendering the form as follows:

```
<%@ taglib prefix="c" uri="http://java.sun.com/jsp/jstl/core" %>
<%@ taglib prefix="fmt" uri="http://java.sun.com/jsp/jstl/fmt" %>

<html>
<head>
<title>City Distance</title>
</head>

<body>
<form method="POST">
```

```
<table>
  <tr>
    <td>Source City</td>
    <td><input type="text" name="srcCity" value="${param.srcCity}" /></td>
  </tr>
  <tr>
    <td>Destination City</td>
    <td><input type="text" name="destCity" value="${param.destCity}" /></td>
  </tr>
  <tr>
    <td>Distance</td>
    <td>
      <c:if test="${distance == null}">Not found</c:if>
      <c:if test="${distance != null}">
        <fmt:formatNumber groupingUsed="true" value="${distance}" /> km
      </c:if>
    </td>
  </tr>
  <tr>
    <td colspan="2"><input type="submit" value="Find" /></td>
  </tr>
</table>
</form>
</body>
</html>
```

Note that this JSP file has used JSTL tags such as <c:if> and <fmt:formatNumber> to help render the HTML contents.

Now the web application in the standard WAR format is complete. You can deploy it to the dm Server embedded in Eclipse for testing purposes. Right-click the dm Server instance in the Servers view and choose Add and Remove Projects. Then add the web project city-war from Available Projects to Configured Projects, as shown in Figure 6-5.

When you start the dm Server in Eclipse, the application will be deployed to the city-war context path, which you specified in the New Project wizard. If nothing is missing, you should see the following output in the dm Server console:

```
...
<SPSC1000I> Creating web application '/city-war'.
<SPSC1001I> Starting web application '/city-war'.
<SPDE0010I> Deployment of 'city-war.war' version '0' completed.
```

It's important to note that at deployment time, the dm Server treats a standard WAR as a web bundle. This is because the dm Server runs atop an OSGi web container.

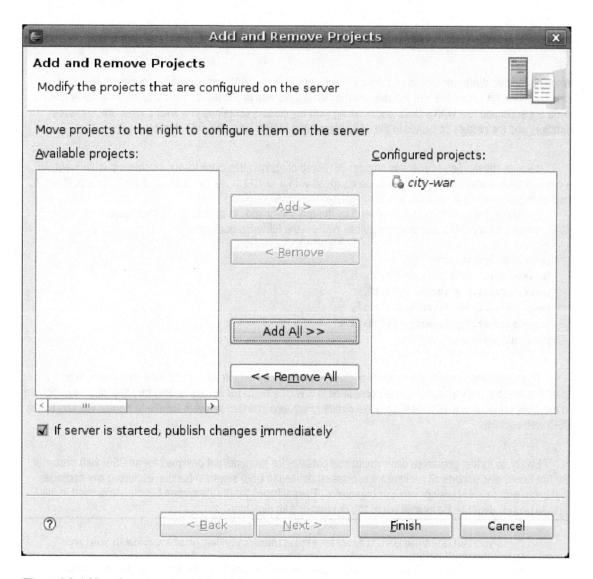

Figure 6-5. *Adding the web project to the dm Server*

HOW ARE STANDARD WARS TREATED AS WEB BUNDLES?

When a standard WAR is deployed on a Java EE web container, the WAR has access to a series of JARs (e.g. `servlet.jar`, `jstl.jar`) that are typically used by most Java web applications. The classes contained in these JARs are appended to a WAR's class loader, along with the classes contained in a WAR's `/WEB-INF/classes` directory and the classes contained in the JARs placed in a WAR's `/WEB-INF/lib` directory.

Because the dm Server operates atop an OSGi web container, this class loader mechanism is different. As a consequence, a standard WAR needs to be equipped with a `MANIFEST.MF` file in which it explicitly indicates the packages (i.e. classes) it needs access to.

By default, the OSGi web container used by the dm Server adds to all web deployment units—standard WARs, shared library WARs and shared services WARs—the following packages:

```
javax.servlet;version="2.5",
javax.servlet.http;version="2.5",
javax.servlet.jsp";version="2.1",
javax.servlet.jsp.el;version="2.1",
javax.servlet.jsp.tagext;version="2.1"
javax.el";version="1.0".
```

These packages include the majority of classes available by default on Java EE web containers. In addition to all the previous packages, the classes contained in a WAR's `/WEB-INF/classes` directory and classes contained in the JARs placed in a WAR's `/WEB-INF/lib` directory are also included in a web bundle to ensure visibility by the OSGi web container.

Finally, to further guarantee deployment compatibility for elements not designed for an OSGi web container, the dm Server also imports all packages (i.e. classes) defined in OSGi's system bundle, excluding any packages that begin with `org.eclipse` or `com.springsource`. The packages for OSGi's system bundle are defined in the `java6-server-profile` file located under the dm Server's lib directory.

Next, you can open the URL `http://localhost:8080/city-war/distance.htm` in your web browser to test the application.

If you would like to deploy this application to an application server outside Eclipse, you first have to export the web project as a WAR file. Right-click the project and choose Export ➤ WAR File, and then specify the WAR file as shown in Figure 6-6.

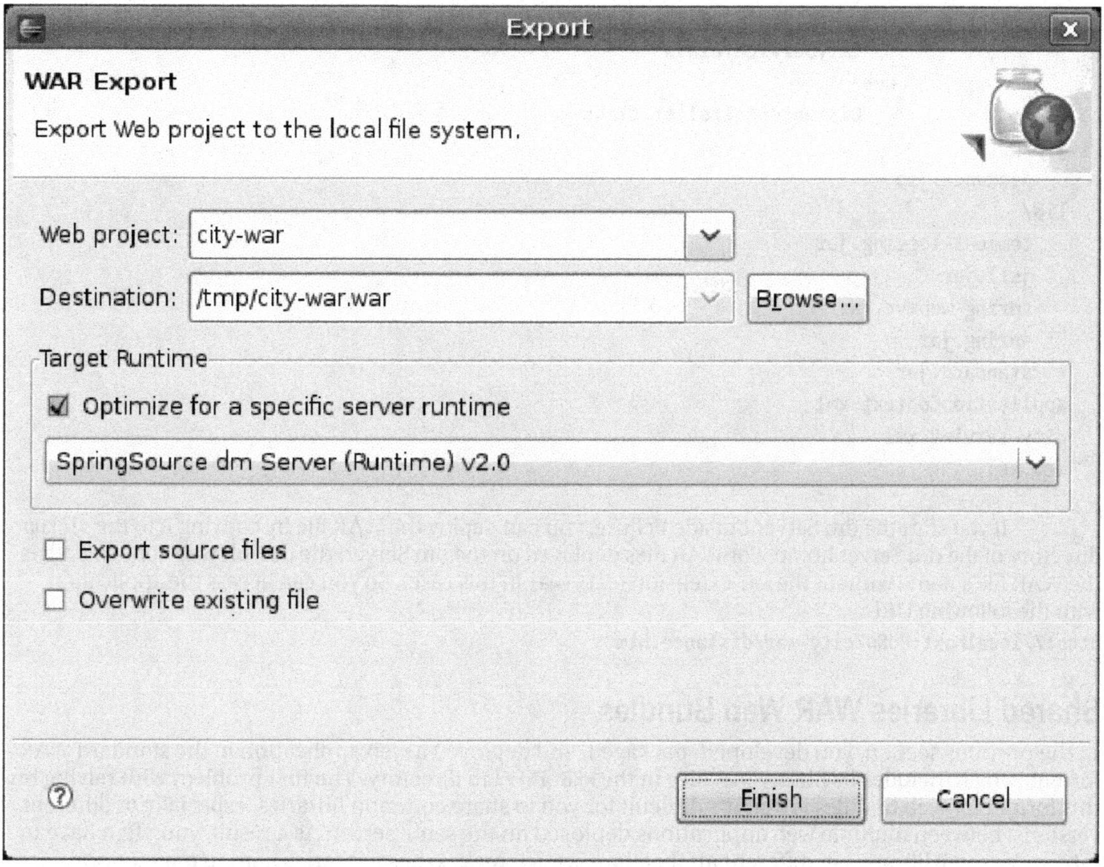

Figure 6-6. Exporting the web project as a WAR file

Assume that you have exported this project to the city-war.war file. If you use an archive utility to browse its contents, you should see the following:

```
META-INF/
    MANIFEST.MF
WEB-INF/
    classes/
        com/
            apress/
                prodmserver/
                    city/
                        service/
                            impl/
```

```
                    CityServiceImpl.class
                  CityService.class
                web/
                    DistanceController.class
        jsp/
            distance.jsp
        lib/
            commons-logging.jar
            jstl.jar
            spring-webmvc.jar
            spring.jar
            standard.jar
        applicationContext.xml
        city-servlet.xml
        web.xml
```

If you start the dm Server outside Eclipse, you can deploy the WAR file by copying it to the pickup directory of the dm Server home. For WAR files deployed on the dm Server, the default web context path is the WAR file's name without the war extension (city-war in this case). So you can access the application with the following URL:

`http://localhost:8080/city-war/distance.htm`

Shared Libraries WAR Web Bundles

In the previous section, you developed, packaged, and deployed a web application in the standard WAR format, which includes its library JAR files in the WEB-INF/lib directory. The first problem with relying on this format for web bundles is that it's difficult for you to share common libraries, especially of different versions, between multiple web applications deployed on the same server. As a result, you often have to repeat the same libraries in different applications, which makes these libraries hard to manage and reuse.

The first step of migrating to OSGi is to remove the libraries from the WAR file and import them from the dm Server's bundle repository at runtime. The dm Server supports a web bundle in the shared libraries WAR format for this purpose. By using a shared library WAR web bundle you obtain the following benefits:

Centralized management of JARs: Once installed on the dm Server, the same JARs (i.e. bundles) can be used by multiple applications.

Smaller footprint WARs: Since JARs (bundles) are centralized and managed by the dm Server, this results in smaller WARs that have no JARs in their structure.

Multiple versions of JARs: Because the dm Server is built on OSGi, it can host multiple versions of the same JAR without conflict (unlike the standard Java classpath). WARs can pick and choose different JAR versions with ease.

Provisioning of transient run-time dependencies: WARs that use certain JARs often need to incorporate transient run-time dependencies. (For example, a WAR using a JPA implementation like Hibernate or EclipseLink will need to incorporate not only the JARs that compose such a library, but also several transient run-time dependencies needed by the library's core JARs.)

Detecting these dependencies can be an error-prone process in a WAR. By relying on the dm Server, you only need to worry about a single dependency in a shared library WAR; the dm Server will manage transient run-time dependencies for every JAR at installation or warn you if they are missing.

To begin the migration, you first have to install the JARs required by your WAR file to the dm Server in the form of bundles. Then use the manifest headers Import-Package, Import-Bundle, and Import-Library to import the JARs directly used by your WAR file.

Now let's migrate the city-war web project from the standard WAR format to the shared libraries WAR web bundle format. First, you must ensure that all the JARs of the same versions have been installed in the dm Server properly. Fortunately, the dm Server comes preinstalled with common Java JARs in its bundle repository, and all dependent JARs of your web application (i.e., Spring, Spring MVC, Commons Logging, JSTL, and Jakarta's standard taglibs) fall into this category. So there's no need to download and install these JARs manually. Next, remove all JAR files from the WEB-INF/lib directory and delete the directory.

Note that once you delete the JAR files from the WEB-INF/lib directory, your web project immediately has errors because some package imports and JSP tag libraries can't be resolved from the project classpath. Before importing the JARs from the dm Server's bundle repository, you should enable the OSGi nature as well as the Bundle Classpath Container for the project so that the dm Server tools will set up the project classpath using the manifest headers in the MANIFEST.MF file. To enable the OSGi nature for a project, right-click the project and choose Spring Tools ➤ Add OSGi Bundle Project Nature. To enable the Project Classpath Container for a project, right-click the project and choose Spring Tools ➤ Enable Bundle Classpath Container.

Then modify the META-INF/MANIFEST.MF file located in the WebContent root to include the OSGi bundle headers as follows:

```
Manifest-Version: 1.0
Bundle-Name: City WAR
Bundle-Description: APRESS
Bundle-ManifestVersion: 2
Bundle-SymbolicName: com.apress.prodmserver.city.web
Bundle-Version: 1.0.0
Web-ContextPath: city-sharedlib-war
Import-Package: javax.servlet.jsp.jstl.core;version="[1.1.2,1.1.2]"
Import-Library: org.springframework.spring;version="[3.0.0,3.0.0]"
Import-Bundle: com.springsource.org.apache.taglibs.standard;version="[1.1.2,1.1.2]"
```

■ **Note** If you still receive the errors after saving the MANIFEST.MF file, verify that you have enabled the Bundle Classpath Container option, too, as this will allow the project's MANIFEST.MF file declarations to be picked up. If you still receive errors after this, you will have to clean and rebuild your project using the Clean menu item under the Project menu.

The Web-ContextPath: city-sharedlib-war defines the deployment context for the shared library WAR web bundle. The deployment context is an optional parameter, but by defining it explicitly, you guarantee that the web bundle is deployed under the `city-sharedlib-war` context (e.g. `http://localhost:8080/city-sharedlib-war/`). If this parameter is omitted, the web bundle is deployed by its file name. (For example, a web bundle named `country-war.war` would be deployed by default at `http://localhost:8080/country-war/`.)

The imported `javax.servlet.jsp.jstl.core` package is necessary because the web bundle relies on the JSTL to display its contents. Though JSTL is fairly common in Java web applications and its bundles are included in the dm Server distribution, this particular JSTL package does not form part of the default group of packages added by the dm Server's OSGi web container; therefore it needs to be added explicitly.

The imported `org.springframework.spring` library definition contains all the standard Spring Framework modules, including the Spring Web MVC module. Notice the use of version `3.0.0` of the Spring Framework. This version is used because dm Server 2.0 comes equipped by default with this library, and the application is compatible with versions `2.5.x` and `3.0.0` of the library. You could have equally opted to use version `2.5.x` of the Spring Framework, but this would have required the extra step of downloading and installing the library in the dm Server.

The Spring Framework internally uses Apache Commons Logging for logging purposes, but since this library is not used directly by your web application, you needn't import it in the `MANIFEST.MF` file. The `com.springsource.org.apache.taglibs.standard` bundle is the OSGi version of Jakarta's standard tag library implementation, which requires the JSTL API internally. Since you are using JSTL tags in your JSP files, you have to import this bundle to provide a tag library implementation.

If you start the dm Server in Eclipse, the web application will be deployed to the `city-sharedlib-war` context path, and the dm Server console will output the following messages:

```
...
<SPSC1000I> Creating web application '/city-sharedlib-war'.
<SPSC1001I> Starting web application '/city-sharedlib-war'.
<SPDE0010I> Deployment of 'com.apress.prodmserver.city_sharedlib_war' version '1' completed.
```

Now you can open the URL `http://localhost:8080/city-sharedlib-war/distance.htm` in your web browser to test the application.

If you would like to deploy this application to the dm Server outside Eclipse, you must export this web project as a WAR file. For example, suppose you have exported this web project to the `city-shared-libraries-war.war` file, which has the following contents:

```
META-INF/
    MANIFEST.MF
WEB-INF/
    classes/
        com/
            apress/
                prodmserver/
                    city/
                        service/
                            impl/
                                CityServiceImpl.class
                        CityService.class
```

```
        web/
            DistanceController.class
jsp/
    distance.jsp
applicationContext.xml
city-servlet.xml
web.xml
```

If you start the dm Server outside Eclipse, you can deploy the web bundle by copying it to the pickup directory of the dm Server home. Since the web context path of the web bundle is configured through the Web-ContextPath: city-sharedlib-war header, you can access the application with the following URL:

http://localhost:8080/city-sharedlib-war/distance.htm

Shared Services WAR Web Bundles

In the previous section, you migrated your web application from the standard WAR format to the shared libraries WAR web bundle format by extracting the JARs in a WAR's /WEB-INF/lib directory and instead relying on the dm Server's bundle repository. As a result, JARs across different web applications can be better reused and managed. You have taken a step toward migrating your web application to OSGi.

However, there is still a problem with a shared libraries WAR web bundle. A typical enterprise web application offers a series of functionalities to solve business problems, but in the standard WAR format all these functionalities are packaged in a single WAR file—locked away, if you will. So if you need to update any of these functionalities in your application, you have to repackage, redeploy, and restart the entire application. Moreover, this format makes it difficult to reuse common functionality across multiple applications.

By exposing functionality as OSGi services, applications gain a greater degree of flexibility. OSGi's service model allows applications to share functionality (services). This creates a loosely coupled architecture whereby bundles are not directly dependent on other bundles, but rather depend on services that can be provided by any bundle at a given time. Such run-time dynamics also make it easier to repackage, redeploy, and restart individual parts or bundles of an application without disturbing the whole.

So the second step of migrating to OSGi is to extract the application services from the web bundle shared libraries WAR file to form a service bundle, which registers the services to the OSGi service registry to allow the web bundle to import the services at runtime. The dm Server supports the shared services WAR web bundle format in the migration path for this purpose. In this section I will show you how to migrate the city-war web project from the shared libraries WAR web bundle format to the shared services WAR web bundle format.

Extracting the Services to Form a Bundle

Now let's extract the services from the city-war web project to form a bundle. First, just as in the bundle creation process in Chapter 5, create a dm Server bundle project with the name com.apress. rodmserver.city.service for the purpose of hosting the migrated services.

Then, move the CityService interface and the CityServiceImpl class as well as their packages from the city-war web project to this com.apress.prodmserver.city.service for dm Server bundle project, by selecting them and dragging and dropping into the new project. Finally, edit the MANIFEST.MF file to export the com.apress.prodmserver.city.service package that defines the service interface (not the com.apress.prodmserver.city.service.impl package that provides the implementation), as follows:

```
Manifest-Version: 1.0
Bundle-Name: Service Bundle
Bundle-Description: APRESS
Bundle-ManifestVersion: 2
Bundle-SymbolicName: com.apress.prodmserver.city.service
Bundle-Version: 1.0.0
Export-Package: com.apress.prodmserver.city.service
```

To configure the application context for this service bundle, create `module-context.xml` in the `META-INF/spring` directory. You have to migrate the beans that provide services to the web application from the `city-war` web project to this bundle project. You can copy the following bean definitions from the web project's `applicationContext.xml` file to this file:

```xml
<beans xmlns="http://www.springframework.org/schema/beans"
    xmlns:xsi="http://www.w3.org/2001/XMLSchema-instance"
    xsi:schemaLocation="http://www.springframework.org/schema/beans
        http://www.springframework.org/schema/beans/spring-beans-2.5.xsd">

    <bean id="cityService"
        class="com.apress.prodmserver.city.service.impl.CityServiceImpl">
        <property name="distanceMap">
            <map>
                <entry key="New York">
                    <map>
                        <entry key="London" value="5574" />
                        <entry key="Beijing" value="10976" />
                    </map>
                </entry>
            </map>
        </property>
    </bean>
</beans>
```

Then create `osgi-context.xml` in the `META-INF/spring` directory to export the service beans as OSGi services, as follows:

```
<beans:beans xmlns="http://www.springframework.org/schema/osgi"
    xmlns:xsi="http://www.w3.org/2001/XMLSchema-instance"
    xmlns:beans="http://www.springframework.org/schema/beans"
    xsi:schemaLocation="http://www.springframework.org/schema/beans
        http://www.springframework.org/schema/beans/spring-beans-2.5.xsd
        http://www.springframework.org/schema/osgi
        http://www.springframework.org/schema/osgi/spring-osgi.xsd">

    <service ref="cityService"
        interface="com.apress.prodmserver.city.service.CityService" />
</beans:beans>
```

With this step the service bundle is complete and you can deploy it to the dm Server in Eclipse. Right-click the dm Server instance and choose Add and Remove Projects, and then move this bundle from Available Projects to Configured Projects.

You can also export this bundle project as a JAR file to deploy it to the dm Server outside Eclipse. Please refer to Chapter 5 for the steps of exporting a bundle as a JAR file. The bundle JAR file com.apress.prodmserver.city.service-1.0.0.jar should contain the following:

```
com/
    apress/
        prodmserver/
            city/
                service/
                    impl/
                        CityServiceImpl.class
                    CityService.class
META-INF/
    spring/
        module-context.xml
        osgi-context.xml
    MANIFEST.MF
```

If you start the dm Server outside Eclipse, you can deploy the bundle JAR file by copying it to the pickup directory of the dm Server home.

Modifying the Web Bundle to Import the Services

After extracting the services from the city-war web project to form a bundle, you can migrate the web project from the shared libraries WAR web bundle format to a shared services WAR web bundle format to import the services. However, as you have removed the com.apress.prodmserver.city.service package from the web project, the project will have errors because the CityService interface can no longer be resolved. To fix these errors, you must import this package in the MANIFEST.MF file as follows:

```
Manifest-Version: 1.0
Bundle-Name: City WAR
Bundle-Description: APRESS
Bundle-ManifestVersion: 2
Bundle-SymbolicName: com.apress.prodmserver.city_war
Bundle-Version: 1.0.0
Web-ContextPath: city-sharedservices-war
Import-Library: org.springframework.spring;version="[3.0.0,3.0.0]"
Import-Bundle: com.springsource.org.apache.taglibs.standard;version="[1.1.2.1.1.2]"
Import-Package: com.apress.prodmserver.city.service,
  javax.servlet.jsp.jstl.core;version="[1.1.2.1.1.2]",
  com.springsource.server.web.dm;version="[2.0.0,3.0.0)",
```

In addition to importing the com.apress.prodmserver.city.service package, you also need to import the javax.servlet.jsp.jstl.core package to support JSTL, as well as the com.springsource.server.web.dm package to access OSGi services via the web bundle's application context.

Although you have imported the com.apress.prodmserver.city.service package exported by the service bundle in the MANIFEST.MF file, the city-war web project still cannot access this package unless you explicitly configure a project reference to the service bundle project.

■ **Note** In Chapter 5 you did not face this visibility issue, because a PAR project automatically references all bundles thanks to its scoped behavior.

You can configure a web project's references in its Properties dialog, shown in Figure 6-7, which can be brought up by choosing Properties from the project's pop-up menu.

After configuring a reference to the service bundle project, you must refresh the bundle dependencies of the city-war project by right-clicking the project and choosing Spring Tools ➤ Refresh Bundle Classpath Container. Once you complete this step, the web project can access the package, and therefore all project errors will be solved.

Then, in the applicationContext.xml file, replace the service bean definition with an OSGi service reference as follows:

```
<beans:beans xmlns="http://www.springframework.org/schema/osgi"
    xmlns:xsi="http://www.w3.org/2001/XMLSchema-instance"
    xmlns:beans="http://www.springframework.org/schema/beans"
    xsi:schemaLocation="http://www.springframework.org/schema/beans
        http://www.springframework.org/schema/beans/spring-beans-2.5.xsd
        http://www.springframework.org/schema/osgi
        http://www.springframework.org/schema/osgi/spring-osgi.xsd">

    <reference id="cityService"
        interface="com.apress.prodmserver.city.service.CityService" />
</beans:beans>
```

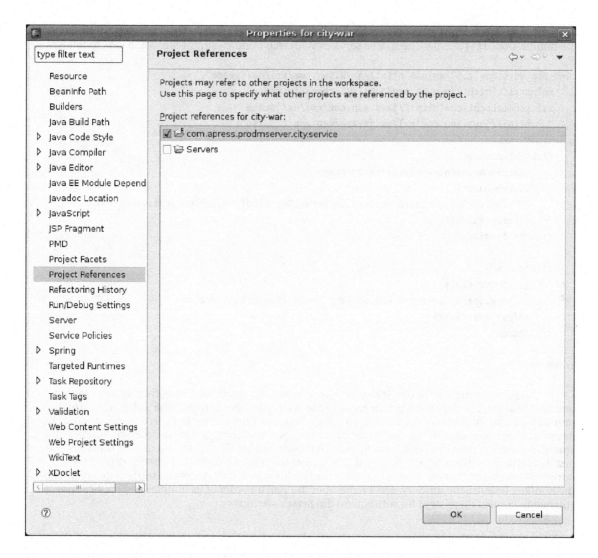

Figure 6-7. *Configuring project references explicitly*

The final step to complete the shared services WAR web bundle is to configure an OSGi-enabled application context for it. A web application that requires a Spring application context has to define a ContextLoaderListener in web.xml to load the root application context. By default, the ContextLoaderListener instantiates an application context class that is not OSGi-enabled and therefore cannot import OSGi services from the service registry. If you need to import OSGi services using the <reference> element in the root application context, you must specify an application context class that is OSGi-enabled. For web bundles deployed on the dm Server, you can specify ServerOsgiBundleXmlWebApplicationContext as the context class for the ContextLoaderListener in web.xml. Note that this last class belongs to the com.springsource.server.web.dm package specified in the bundle's MANIFEST.MF file. The shared services WAR web bundle web.xml file would look as follows:

```
<web-app version="2.5" xmlns="http://java.sun.com/xml/ns/javaee"
    xmlns:xsi="http://www.w3.org/2001/XMLSchema-instance"
    xsi:schemaLocation="http://java.sun.com/xml/ns/javaee
        http://java.sun.com/xml/ns/javaee/web-app_2_5.xsd">

    <context-param>
        <param-name>contextClass</param-name>
        <param-value>
            com.springsource.server.web.dm.ServerOsgiBundleXmlWebApplicationContext
        </param-value>
    </context-param>

    <listener>
        <listener-class>
            org.springframework.web.context.ContextLoaderListener
        </listener-class>
    </listener>
    ...
</web-app>
```

Now you can start the dm Server in Eclipse to test this web bundle together with the service bundle. However, this may not work, because of the uncertain startup order. The web bundle has to import packages from the service bundle, so it must start after the service bundle; otherwise, its package imports cannot be resolved. The dm Server did not support specifying a startup order for bundles and applications at the time this book went to press. A recommended workaround is to start the dm Server first with only the service bundle deployed. Then, after the service bundle has started, deploy the web bundle file to ensure that the service bundle is ready. This step is only necessary the first time you deploy the bundles, because the dm Server will remember the startup order of its bundles and applications, so you needn't repeat these steps for subsequent dm Server startups.

■ **Note** Future versions of dm Server will support specifying startup order for applications. However, at the time this book went to press the approach had yet to be implemented.

To deploy this application to the dm Server outside Eclipse, you must export this web project as a WAR file. For example, suppose that you have exported this web project to the city-shared-services-war.war file, which has the following contents:

```
META-INF/
    MANIFEST.MF
WEB-INF/
    classes/
        com/
            apress/
                prodmserver/
                    city/
                        web/
                            DistanceController.class
    jsp/
        distance.jsp
    applicationContext.xml
    city-servlet.xml
    web.xml
```

If you start the dm Server outside Eclipse, you can deploy the web bundle by copying it to the pickup directory of the dm Server home. Since the context path of the web bundle is already configured in the MANIFEST.MF file through the Web-ContextPath: city-sharedservices-war header, you can access the application with the following URL:

`http://localhost:8080/city-war/distance.htm`

Remember that you must ensure that the service bundle starts before the web bundle. To do this, you can first start the dm Server with only the service bundle deployed. Then deploy the WAR file after the service bundle has started. This startup order issue can be avoided altogether if you package bundles inside a PAR file, as discussed in the next section.

Web Bundles Within PAR Files

In the previous section, you migrated your web application from a shared libraries WAR web bundle format to a shared services WAR web bundle format by extracting the application services from the WAR file to form a service bundle and importing the services to the WAR file at runtime. As a result, when you update a single module of your application, you needn't repackage, redeploy, and restart the entire application. Also, you can easily reuse common modules and services across multiple applications.

However, there is still an additional step you can take to simplify and safeguard the deployment of bundles belonging to an application. You can use a PAR file to join the entire set of bundles belonging to an application. A PAR simplifies deployment because an application's bundles are repackaged, redeployed, and restarted as unit. This eases the management of bundles and guarantees that OSGi services are properly detected irrespective of installation order. In addition, a PAR file also defines an application boundary for its bundles, guaranteeing that its OSGi services are isolated from those of other PAR files, thus avoiding conflicts with similarly named OSGi services belonging to other applications.

Create a PAR project with the name com.apress.prodmserver.city for your web application, which will include the service bundle and the web bundle. In the project wizard, select the service bundle com.apress.prodmserver.city.service and the web bundle com.apress.prodmserver.city.web to be included in this PAR project. Next, ensure that the MANIFEST.MF file of this PAR project is as follows:

```
Manifest-Version: 1.0
Application-SymbolicName: com.apress.prodmserver.city
Application-Version: 1.0.0
Application-Description: APRESS
Application-Name: City PAR
```

Next, modify the web bundle's MANIFEST.MF file, adding city-web as the web context path to distinguish it from the other web context paths used in the earlier bundles. The bundle's MANIFEST.MF file should look as follows:

```
Manifest-Version: 1.0
Bundle-Name: Web Bundle
Bundle-Description: APRESS
Bundle-ManifestVersion: 2
Bundle-SymbolicName: com.apress.prodmserver.city.web
Bundle-Version: 1.0.0
Import-Package: com.apress.prodmserver.city.service,
  javax.servlet.jsp.jstl.core;version="[1.1.2,1.1.2]",
 com.springsource.server.web.dm;version="[2.0.0,3.0.0)"
Import-Library: org.springframework.spring;version="[3.0.0,3.0.0]"
Import-Bundle: com.springsource.org.apache.taglibs.standard;version="1.1.2"
Import-Package: com.apress.prodmserver.city.service

Web-ContextPath: city-web
```

Once you've modified the web bundle, you can deploy it as part of a PAR file to the dm Server in Eclipse. Right-click the dm Server instance and choose Add and Remove Projects. Add the PAR project, not individual bundles and web bundles, to the dm Server. When you start the dm Server, the PAR will be deployed to the city-web context path, which is specified in the web bundle's Web-ContextPath manifest header, and the dm Server console will output the following messages.

```
...
<SPSC1000I> Creating web application '/city-web'.
<SPSC1001I> Starting web application '/city-web'.
<SPDE0010I> Deployment of 'com.apress.prodmserver.city' version '1' completed.
```

You can then open the URL http://localhost:8080/city-web/distance.htm to test the application.

WHAT HAPPENED TO DM SERVER WEB MODULES?

If you used dm Server in its 1.0 release, you were exposed to a type of element named *web modules*, which have been deprecated in the dm Server 2.0 release in favor of web bundles. The semantics of web bundles are more general than those of web modules. If you were an early adopter of web modules, there are a few distinctions you need to be aware of in case you need to migrate them:

- Web bundles do not support the special `MANIFEST.MF` headers that were used by web modules (e.g. `Web-DispatcherServletUrlPatterns`, `Web-FilterMappings`, and so on). Instead, Web bundles rely on Java's standard `web.xml` file to specify such behaviors. The only special header that continues to be supported in web bundles is `Web-ContextPath`.
- Web bundles need a `.war` extension in order to be detected by the dm Server as web artifacts (for example, to be deployed to a web context path). Web modules relied on the use of a `Module-Type` header and scanning process for this.
- Web bundle configuration parameters (e.g. context and Servlets) are configured in standard Java web application files (e.g. `applicationContext.xml` and `city-servlet.xml`). Web modules required configuration parameters to be placed inside the directory `/META-INF/spring/` in order to be processed.
- Web bundles need to have their classes placed in a bundle's `/WEB-INF/classes/` directory in order to be detected. Web modules placed a bundle's packages in the root path of a bundle.

The emergence of web bundles came from the incorporation of the OSGi standard (RFC-66) web container into the dm Server 2.0 release. The dm Server 1.0 release was based on a standard Java Tomcat web container, and thus web modules were an ad-hoc format used to run bundles in a non-OSGi web container. With the advent of an OSGi standard web container, the dm Server now supports the standard format used for the deployment of OSGi web applications, which is the web bundle.

If you would like to deploy this application to the dm Server outside Eclipse, you have to export the PAR project as a PAR file. Please refer to Chapter 5 for instructions on exporting a PAR file from Eclipse. The exported PAR file `com.apress.prodmserver.city-1.0.0.par` should include the following contents:

```
META-INF/
   MANIFEST.MF
com.apress.prodmserver.city.service-1.0.0.jar
com.apress.prodmserver.city.web-1.0.0.war
```

The web bundle, `com.apress.prodmserver.city.web-1.0.0.war`, packaged in the PAR file, has the following contents:

```
META-INF/

    MANIFEST.MF

    WEB-INF/
    classes/
        com/
            apress/
                prodmserver/
                    city/
                        web/
                            DistanceController.class
        jsp/
            distance.jsp
    applicationContext.xml
    city-servlet.xml
    web.xml
```

If you start the dm Server outside Eclipse, you can deploy the PAR file by copying it to the `pickup` directory of the dm Server home. The context path of the web bundle in the PAR file is `city-web`, as specified in the `Web-ContextPath` manifest header. So you can open the following URL to use the application:

`http://localhost:8080/city-web/distance.htm`

Summary

In this chapter, you were first introduced to the migration path from a standard WAR file to an OSGi web bundle and then walked through the process of migrating a Java EE web application developed with Spring MVC.

The first step in the migration path is to remove the libraries from a WAR file and import them from the dm Server's bundle repository at runtime. The dm Server supports the shared libraries WAR web bundle format for this purpose. First you install the libraries required by a web bundle to the dm Server in the form of bundles. Then you can import the libraries directly used by your web bundle.

The second step in the migration path is to extract the application services from a web bundle to form a service bundle, which registers the services to the OSGi service registry to allow the web bundle to import the services at runtime. The dm Server supports the shared services WAR web bundle format for this purpose.

Finally, you learned how to package a web bundle and other bundles in a PAR file as a single deployment unit.

In the next chapter, you will have an introduction to the dm Server's serviceability—its capacity for diagnosing errors—and learn how to trace applications deployed on the dm Server.

■■■

CHAPTER 7

Tracing Applications on the dm Server

In the previous two chapters, you learned about application development and migration for the dm Server. In this chapter, you will see how to trace applications running on the dm Server so that you can better understand the runtime behavior of your applications and diagnose errors when they occur. The dm Server includes a dedicated serviceability (logging and tracing) subsystem for this purpose. This chapter covers the following topics:

- Introducing the dm Server's serviceability
- Configuring serviceability for the dm Server
- Tracing application output and logs

Even though you may have dealt with error diagnosis on multiple servers throughout your career and think to yourself, "I've seen one, I've seen them all," the logging and tracing system of the dm Server is substantially different. Therefore, I recommend that administrators and developers alike give this chapter a detailed read.

Introduction to the dm Server's Serviceability

In general, a system's *serviceability* refers to the ability to diagnose errors when they occur. The dm Server has a dedicated serviceability subsystem that can output log files, trace files, and service dumps. The information in these files can help the dm Server's users and service team to trace and diagnose errors.

Log Files

At runtime, the dm Server writes log messages of significant server events to the `logging.log` file, which is located in the dm Server home's `serviceability/logs` directory by default. This file contains only log messages written by the dm Server itself, not by any applications. Each log message is of the following form:

```
[timestamp]   thread-name   <log-code>   text
```

For ease of reading and to retain a consistent layout, the thread name in each log message has a fixed length of 24 characters. If the thread name has more than 24 characters, only the last 24 characters will be logged. For example, the thread name `scheduled-executor-thread-1` will be logged as `eduled-executor-thread-1`.

As you can see, each log message has a log code to help describe the event context. Each log code has nine characters of the form *SPSS0000L*, where *SP* stands for the Spring platform, *SS* denotes the subsystem code, *0000* denotes the event number, and *L* denotes the event severity level. Tables 7-1 and

7-2 list the subsystem codes and the event severity levels. For each log code's detailed description, please refer to the "Log Error Codes" section of the dm Server's user guide.

Table 7-1. *The dm Server's Subsystem Codes*

Code	Subsystem
CC	Concurrent
CN	Control
CO	Config
DE	Deployer
FF	FFDC
KB	Bootstrap
KE	Kernel
OP	OSGi
PM	Profile
SC	Servlet
WE	Web

Table 7-2. *The dm Server's Event Severity Levels*

Code	Severity Level
E	Error
W	Warn
I	Info

As an example, when the dm Server starts with no user application deployed, it will write the following log messages:

```
-----------------------------------------------------------------------------
|
| SpringSource dm Server
|
-----------------------------------------------------------------------------
[2009-06-07 10:18:25.109] main                    <SPKB0001I> Server starting.
[2009-06-07 10:18:26.140] main                    <SPOF0001I> OSGi telnet console↵
available on port 2401.
[2009-06-07 10:18:28.984] main                    <SPKE0000I> Boot subsystems↵
installed.
[2009-06-07 10:18:30.218] main                    <SPKE0001I> Base subsystems↵
installed.
[2009-06-07 10:18:31.875] server-dm-2             <SPPM0000I> Installing profile↵
'web'.
[2009-06-07 10:18:33.140] server-dm-2             <SPPM0001I> Installed profile↵
'web'.
[2009-06-07 10:18:33.359] server-dm-4             <SPSC0001I> Creating HTTP/1.1↵
connector with scheme http on port 8080.
[2009-06-07 10:18:33.437] server-dm-4             <SPSC0001I> Creating HTTP/1.1↵
connector with scheme https on port 8443.
[2009-06-07 10:18:33.453] server-dm-4             <SPSC0001I> Creating AJP/1.3↵
connector with scheme http on port 8009.
[2009-06-07 10:18:33.484] server-dm-4             <SPSC0000I> Starting↵
ServletContainer.
[2009-06-07 10:18:34.421] server-dm-9             <SPPM0002I> Server open for↵
business with profile 'web'.
[2009-06-07 10:18:35.296] Deployer Recovery       <SPSC1000I> Creating web↵
application '/'.
[2009-06-07 10:18:35.437] async-delivery-thread-1 <SPSC1001I> Starting web↵
application '/'.
[2009-06-07 10:18:35.937] Deployer Recovery       <SPDE0010I> Deployment of↵
'com.springsource.server.servlet.splash' version '0' completed.
[2009-06-07 10:18:36.781] Deployer Recovery       <SPSC1000I> Creating web↵
application '/admin'.
[2009-06-07 10:18:37.046] async-delivery-thread-1 <SPSC1001I> Starting web↵
application '/admin'.
[2009-06-07 10:18:37.421] Deployer Recovery       <SPDE0010I> Deployment of↵
'com.springsource.server.servlet.admin' version '2.0.0.RELEASE' completed.
[2009-06-07 10:18:37.437] fs-watcher              <SPDE0048I> Processing 'INITIAL'↵
event for file 'server.admin.splash-2.0.0.RELEASE.war'.
[2009-06-07 10:18:37.437] fs-watcher              <SPDE0031I> File↵
'server.admin.splash-2.0.0.RELEASE.war' already deployed.
[2009-06-07 10:18:37.437] fs-watcher              <SPDE0048I> Processing 'INITIAL'↵
event for file 'server.admin.web-2.0.0.RELEASE.jar'.
[2009-06-07 10:18:37.453] fs-watcher              <SPDE0031I> File↵
'server.admin.web-2.0.0.RELEASE.jar' already deployed.
```

In addition to logging significant server events, the dm Server configures its embedded Tomcat to write access log files to the `access` subdirectory of the `serviceability/logs` directory. Tomcat writes access logs of each web context to both a global access log file and a per-context access log file:

Global access log file (`SpringSource-AP.yyyy-MM-dd.log`): This file contains daily access logs of all web contexts.

Per-context access log file (`SpringSource-AP.[context-path].yyyy-MM-dd.log`): This file contains daily access logs of a particular web context.

As an example, the following access logs are taken from the access log file of the Admin application (`access/SpringSource-AP.admin.2009-06-07.log`), which is deployed to the admin context path by default:

```
127.0.0.1 - admin [07/Jun/2009:10:26:41 +0800]↩
    "GET /admin/web/applications/list.htm HTTP/1.1" 200 9661↩
    "http://localhost:8080/"↩
    "Mozilla/4.0 (compatible; MSIE 6.0; Windows NT 5.1; SV1)"
127.0.0.1 - admin [07/Jun/2009:10:26:41 +0800]↩
    "GET /admin/styles/main.css HTTP/1.1" 200 4565↩
    "http://localhost:8080/admin/web/applications/list.htm"↩
    "Mozilla/4.0 (compatible; MSIE 6.0; Windows NT 5.1; SV1)"
127.0.0.1 - admin [07/Jun/2009:10:26:41 +0800]↩
    "GET /admin/styles/print.css HTTP/1.1" 200 772↩
    "http://localhost:8080/admin/web/applications/list.htm"↩
    "Mozilla/4.0 (compatible; MSIE 6.0; Windows NT 5.1; SV1)"
```

As you can see, each access log message has nine parts in total, separated by spaces. Each part is described as follows:

1. Remote host name (or remote IP address if it can't be resolved)
2. Remote logical username from the Ident protocol (always "–")
3. Authenticated remote user ("–" if the user has not been authenticated)
4. Access time (in the format *dd/ MMM/ yyyy: HH: mm: ss ZZZZ*)
5. The request's first line (the request method, request URI, and HTTP version)
6. The response's HTTP status code (e.g. 200 OK or 404 Not Found)
7. Total bytes sent in the response's body ("–" for zero bytes)
8. The URL by which the request is referred to (the `Referer` header)
9. The user agent that makes the request (the `User-Agent` header)

Trace Files

In addition to logging significant server events, the dm Server supports tracing internal server events and application events, output, and logs in great detail for diagnosing problems. Each trace entry has the following form:

```
[timestamp]  thread-name  source  level  text
```

For ease of reading, the thread name also has a fixed length of 24 characters and aligns to the left (the same as in a log message), while the source has a fixed length of 64 characters but aligns to the right. The trace level is represented by a single character (for example, I denotes info and E denotes error).

Trace files are created in the dm Server home's serviceability/trace directory by default. The dm Server creates two types of trace files, global and per-application:

Global trace file: The dm Server traces all internal server events and application events, output, and logs in the global trace.log file located in the trace directory's root. This trace file is intended for the dm Server's service team, not application developers and server administrators, to diagnose problems.

Per-application trace file: The dm Server traces events, output, and logs of each deployed application in the trace.log file located in the [*application-name*]-[*version*] subdirectory (e.g. com.apress.prodmserver.app-1) of the trace directory. In contrast to the global trace file, this file is intended for application developers and server administrators to diagnose problems for each application independently. Note that, in addition to being placed in its own separate trace file, application trace information is also output to the global trace file.

As an example, the following traces are taken from the Admin application's trace file (i.e. com.springsource.server.servlet.admin-2.0.0.RELEASE/trace.log):

```
--------------------------------------------------------------------------------
|
| SpringSource dm Server
|
--------------------------------------------------------------------------------
[2009-06-07 10:41:00.062] Deployer Recovery⏎
    com.springsource.server.servlet.admin-2.0.0.RELEASE I⏎
    Trace configuration: {com.springsource.server.*=WARN, *=INFO}
[2009-06-07 10:41:00.187] server-dm-1⏎
    pringframework.beans.factory.xml.XmlBeanDefinitionReader.unknown I⏎
    Loading XML bean definitions from URL⏎
    [bundleentry://72/META-INF/spring/module-context.xml]
[2009-06-07 10:41:00.203] server-dm-1⏎
    pringframework.beans.factory.xml.XmlBeanDefinitionReader.unknown I⏎
    Loading XML bean definitions from URL⏎
    [bundleentry://72/META-INF/spring/osgi-context.xml]
...
```

Trace files are also where all application debugging and logging information is output. This is to say, output from application calls made to System.out() and System.err(), as well as output from calls performed using logging libraries (e.g. Log4J/Logback, Jakarta Commons) is placed in trace files. You'll find details about using such calls in dm Server applications in the later section "Tracing Application Output and Logs."

■ **Note** Logback is a successor to Log4J. However, Log4J is still in wide use in many applications. Thus it's common to refer to both versions together as "Log4J/Logback."

Once the size of a trace file (global or per-application) reaches 100 MB, the dm Server will automatically roll it over to a new file of the form trace-*yyyy-MM-dd_hh-mm-ss*.log, which reflects the rollover time in the file name. Only the last four rolled-over trace files in addition to the current trace file (trace.log) will be kept by the dm Server for historical reference.

Service Dumps

If it detects a server failure or thread deadlock at runtime, the dm Server will create a service dump to capture a snapshot of all necessary server information. It implements the first failure data capture (FFDC) feature to capture important server states for diagnostic purposes when a server failure (in particular an unchecked exception thrown in the dm Server code) occurs for the first time. Therefore, application developers and system administrators needn't reproduce the failure but simply send the service dump files for the server service team to diagnose the problem.

Service dumps contain large volumes of information intended to help the dm Server's service team diagnose problems. Application developers and server administrators can also use service dumps to gain insight into problems that may be related to poor application design. A service dump will be saved to a file of the form *yyyy-MM-dd_hh-mm-ss*.dump, which reflects the creation time in the file name. By default, service dumps are stored in the dm Server home's serviceability/dump directory.

Configuring Serviceability for the dm Server

The dm Server has its serviceability configured in the serviceability.config file located in the config directory of the dm Server home. In this file, you can find the following default configuration:

```
{
    "trace": {
        "global" : {
                "directory": "serviceability/trace",
                "levels": {
                        "*" : "warn"
                }
        },
         "trickle": {
                "windowSize": 10000,
                "levels": {
                    "*" : "debug",
                    "org.apache.commons.digester.*" : "warn"
                 }
        }
    },
    "logs": {
        "directory": "serviceability/logs"
    },
    "dump": {
        "directory": "serviceability/dump"
    },
```

```
    "heapDump": {
        "enabled":  false
    }
}
```

In this file you can see that by default the dm Server outputs its trace files, log files, and service dumps to the trace, logs, and dump subdirectories, respectively, of the serviceability directory. If you have to output the files to other directories for particular reasons, you can simply specify the directory paths in this file and then restart the dm Server to have them take effect. Note that the directory paths are relative to the dm Server's home directory.

As well as setting the output directory, trace configurations allow you to set the trace levels at which logs should be traced. Trace levels set in this file become defaults for the dm Server and all applications deployed on it. In the next section, you will see that you can also set application-specific trace levels, which always override the global dm Server trace levels. But let's take a closer look at the global default for the dm Server:

```
"global": {
        "directory": "serviceability/trace",
        "levels": {
           "*" : "warn"
}
```

The dm Server supports five trace levels. Listed in descending order of severity, they are error, warn, info, debug, and verbose. You can see that in the default dm Server configuration, only logs at the warn and higher levels are traced for all classes and packages.

You can modify this default level as well as configure specific levels for individual classes and packages, where class-level and subpackage-level configurations always override package-level configurations. Classes that can't be matched with any of the configured trace levels will have trace disabled. The following example configures trace levels at the package, class, and subpackage levels, respectively:

```
"global": {
    "directory": "serviceability/trace",
    "levels": {
        "*" : "warn",
        "mypackage.*" : "debug",
        "mypackage.MyClass" : "verbose",
        "mypackage.mysubpackage.*" : "verbose"
    }
}
```

As you can see, this last configuration listing assigns specific trace levels to a package, class, and subpackage, with all other elements assigned a default trace level (global, thanks to the *) of warn.

Following the global section, the dm Server serviceability.config file also includes a trickle section for configuring trace output. The trickle section is intended to generate trace output, but not for application developers or server administrators, but rather for the dm Server's service team to help diagnose problems.

In this section the windowSize is used to specifiy the size of an in-memory circular buffer—measured in the number of entries that the buffer can hold—into which trace output is placed. By in-memory and circular, it's implied that the trickle buffer always maintains the latest trace output and is never archived—unlike the global section, which is configured to archive data to a directory.

In the event of a dm Server crash, a trickle file is written with the contents of this buffer to the dm Server's dump folder. The trickle section's levels subsection has the same syntax as the global section; it can be configured globally or per package, class, or subpackage. (It's not recommended to modify the trickle section unless recommended by the dm Server's service team.)

Next in the serviceability.config configuration file, you will observe the logs and dump sections, both of which have a single configuration parameter, an output directory relative to the dm Server's home. And finally, the heapDump section allows you to configure the dmServer to generate (or not) Java heap dumps for the purpose of post-crash diagnostics.

Tracing Application Output and Logs

In the previous section, you had an introduction to the dm Server's serviceability features. In this section, I will use a simple calculator application to show how dm Server supports application tracing. The dm Server traces events, output, and logs of each application in the application's own trace.log file so that they are isolated from those of other applications. To develop this application, first create a PAR project named com.apress.prodmserver.calculator, whose MANIFEST.MF file looks like the following:

```
Manifest-Version: 1.0
Application-SymbolicName: com.apress.prodmserver.calculator
Application-Version: 1.0.0
Application-Description: APRESS
Application-Name: Calculator PAR
```

Next, create a bundle project with the name com.apress.prodmserver.calculator.service to provide calculation services, and add this project to the PAR project. Then create the following interface to define the operations supported by this calculator:

```
package com.apress.prodmserver.calculator.service;

public interface CalculatorService {

    public double add(double a, double b);
    public double sub(double a, double b);
    public double mul(double a, double b);
    public double div(double a, double b);
}
```

For demonstration purposes, the calculator supports only very simple operations. You can implement this interface as follows:

```
package com.apress.prodmserver.calculator.service.impl;

import com.apress.prodmserver.calculator.service.CalculatorService;

public class CalculatorServiceImpl implements CalculatorService {

    public double add(double a, double b) {
        return a + b;
    }

    public double sub(double a, double b) {
        return a - b;
    }

    public double mul(double a, double b) {
        return a * b;
    }

    public double div(double a, double b) {
        return a / b;
    }
}
```

In the MANIFEST.MF file, export the com.apress.prodmserver.calculator.service package so that other bundles can access the interface:

```
Manifest-Version: 1.0
Bundle-Name: Service Bundle
Bundle-Description: APRESS
Bundle-ManifestVersion: 2
Bundle-SymbolicName: com.apress.prodmserver.calculator.service
Bundle-Version: 1.0.0
Export-Package: com.apress.prodmserver.calculator.service
```

To configure the application context for this service bundle, create module-context.xml in the META-INF/spring directory with the following contents:

```
<beans xmlns="http://www.springframework.org/schema/beans"
    xmlns:xsi="http://www.w3.org/2001/XMLSchema-instance"
    xsi:schemaLocation="http://www.springframework.org/schema/beans
        http://www.springframework.org/schema/beans/spring-beans-2.5.xsd">
```

```
<bean id="calculatorService" class="com.apress.prodmserver.calculator.↵
    service.impl.CalculatorServiceImpl" />
</beans>
```

Then create osgi-context.xml in the META-INF/spring directory to export this service bean as an OSGi service as follows:

```
<beans:beans xmlns="http://www.springframework.org/schema/osgi"
    xmlns:xsi="http://www.w3.org/2001/XMLSchema-instance"
    xmlns:beans="http://www.springframework.org/schema/beans"
    xsi:schemaLocation="http://www.springframework.org/schema/beans
        http://www.springframework.org/schema/beans/spring-beans-2.5.xsd
        http://www.springframework.org/schema/osgi
        http://www.springframework.org/schema/osgi/spring-osgi.xsd">

    <service ref="calculatorService"
        interface="com.apress.prodmserver.calculator.service.CalculatorService" />
</beans:beans>
```

Now the service bundle is complete and you can create a client bundle to test its services. Create a new bundle project with the name com.apress.prodmserver.calculator.client and add this to the PAR project. Then import the com.apress.prodmserver.calculator.service package in the MANIFEST.MF file:

```
Manifest-Version: 1.0
Bundle-Name: Client Bundle
Bundle-Description: APRESS
Bundle-ManifestVersion: 2
Bundle-SymbolicName: com.apress.prodmserver.calculator.client
Bundle-Version: 1.0.0
    Import-Package: com.apress.prodmserver.calculator.service
```

You can create the following Client class to access each operation exposed by the calculator service in the calculate() method:

```
package com.apress.prodmserver.calculator.client;

import com.apress.prodmserver.calculator.service.CalculatorService;

public class Client {

    private CalculatorService calculatorService;
```

```java
public void setCalculatorService(CalculatorService calculatorService) {
    this.calculatorService = calculatorService;
}

public void calculate() {
    calculatorService.add(3, 2);
    calculatorService.sub(3, 2);
    calculatorService.mul(3, 2);
    calculatorService.div(3, 2);
}
}
```

Next, you need to define a client bean in the application context. You can ask Spring to call the calculate() method at initialization time (every time the bundle starts, which creates the application context), so that you can see output and logs written by the operations with statements added later. Create module-context.xml in the META-INF/spring directory with the following contents:

```xml
<beans xmlns="http://www.springframework.org/schema/beans"
    xmlns:xsi="http://www.w3.org/2001/XMLSchema-instance"
    xsi:schemaLocation="http://www.springframework.org/schema/beans
        http://www.springframework.org/schema/beans/spring-beans-2.5.xsd">

    <bean id="client"
        class="com.apress.prodmserver.calculator.client.Client"
        init-method="calculate">
        <property name="calculatorService" ref="calculatorService" />
    </bean>
</beans>
```

Finally, create osgi-context.xml in the META-INF/spring directory to import the calculator service as a bean as follows:

```xml
<beans:beans xmlns="http://www.springframework.org/schema/osgi"
    xmlns:xsi="http://www.w3.org/2001/XMLSchema-instance"
    xmlns:beans="http://www.springframework.org/schema/beans"
    xsi:schemaLocation="http://www.springframework.org/schema/beans
        http://www.springframework.org/schema/beans/spring-beans-2.5.xsd
        http://www.springframework.org/schema/osgi
        http://www.springframework.org/schema/osgi/spring-osgi.xsd">

    <reference id="calculatorService"
        interface="com.apress.prodmserver.calculator.service.CalculatorService" />
</beans:beans>
```

Now the calculator application is complete and you can deploy the PAR project to the dm Server. After the application starts, its traces will be available in the `trace.log` file located in the `com.apress.prodmserver.calculator-1` subdirectory of the `serviceability/trace` directory. If you look at this trace file, you will find the application startup events are traced at the `warn` level.

Tracing System.out and System.err

A Java application can use the built-in `System.out` and `System.err` streams to output messages to the console. However, on a Java application server with many applications deployed, each application's messages will be output to the same console or directed to the same log file. As a result, all these messages will be mixed together with the application server's messages, so it's hard for developers and administrators to know which application has output a particular message. Therefore, using the `System.out` and `System.err` streams to output messages is not recommended in an application server environment.

The dm Server can solve this problem by partitioning system output on a per-application basis by directing it to the application's own `trace.log` file. To demonstrate how this feature works, you can insert a `System.out.println()` statement into each calculator operation to output the arguments and result as follows:

```
package com.apress.prodmserver.calculator.service.impl;

import com.apress.prodmserver.calculator.service.CalculatorService;

public class CalculatorServiceImpl implements CalculatorService {

    public double add(double a, double b) {
        double result = a + b;
        System.out.println(a + " + " + b + " = " + result);
        return result;
    }

    public double sub(double a, double b) {
        double result = a - b;
        System.out.println(a + " - " + b + " = " + result);
        return result;
    }

    public double mul(double a, double b) {
        double result = a * b;
        System.out.println(a + " * " + b + " = " + result);
        return result;
    }
```

```
public double div(double a, double b) {
    double result = a / b;
    System.out.println(a + " / " + b + " = " + result);
    return result;
}
}
```

After you update and restart the application, if you look at the application's own trace.log file you will find nothing. This is because the global trace threshold for the dm Server is set to the warn level, and messages written to the System.out stream are traced at the info level. (The System.err stream is traced at the error level and could appear because it is a lower threshold than the default warn level, but no System.err calls are made in the application.)

Therefore, you will need to modify the dm Server's serviceability.config file to the following:

```
"global": {
    "directory": "serviceability/trace",
    "levels": {
        "*" : "info"
    }
}
```

Notice that the trace levels section is now set globally (*) to the info level. If you restart the dm Server and look once again at the application's own trace.log file, you will see all System.out output written by the application into its own trace.log file, as shown in the following fragment:

```
[2009-06-07 14:41:02.812] server-dm-2 System.out I 3.0 + 2.0 = 5.0
[2009-06-07 14:41:02.812] server-dm-2 System.out I 3.0 - 2.0 = 1.0
[2009-06-07 14:41:02.812] server-dm-2 System.out I 3.0 * 2.0 = 6.0
[2009-06-07 14:41:02.812] server-dm-2 System.out I 3.0 / 2.0 = 1.5
```

Other configuration options for outputting System.out—and System.err—trace messages can include configuring an individual class or package's trace levels (e.g. com.apress.prodmserver.calculator.*: ìdebugî) or setting a lower global threshold (e.g. for System.out, using info or the lower trace levels debug or verbose).

Tracing Log Messages

Compared to using System.out and System.err, a better way of tracing applications is using a logging API (e.g. Commons Logging and Log4J/Logback) to log your messages. In a typical Java EE application, you have to configure the logging details, which include the output file, logging level, message pattern, and so on.

The dm Server relies on SLF4J for its logging operations. SLF4J is capable of funneling logging calls used by frameworks like Commons Logging, Log4J/Logback, and other logging APIs to direct log messages output to the dm Server's global trace.log file as well as the application's own trace.log file.

To demonstrate how this feature works, you first have to import the Commons Logging or Log4J/Logback package in the MANIFEST.MF file, depending on which API you will use for logging purposes. Because this application will use the Commons Logging API, let's import the org.apache.commons.logging package as follows:

```
Manifest-Version: 1.0
Bundle-Name: Service Bundle
Bundle-Description: APRESS
Bundle-ManifestVersion: 2
Bundle-SymbolicName: com.apress.prodmserver.calculator.service
Bundle-Version: 1.0.0
Import-Package: org.apache.commons.logging;version="[1.1.1,1.1.1]"
Export-Package: com.apress.prodmserver.calculator.service
```

Now you can replace the System.out.println() calls and use Commons Logging calls as you would do with any other Java application using this logging API. For this class, I will use logging calls at the beginning and ending of each method, as well as their method arguments and return values for debugging purposes:

```java
package com.apress.prodmserver.calculator.service.impl;

import org.apache.commons.logging.Log;
import org.apache.commons.logging.LogFactory;

import com.apress.prodmserver.calculator.service.CalculatorService;

public class CalculatorServiceImpl implements CalculatorService {

    private Log log = LogFactory.getLog(this.getClass());

    public double add(double a, double b) {
        log.debug("The method add() begins with " + a + ", " + b);
        double result = a + b;
        log.info(a + " + " + b + " = " + result);
        log.debug("The method add() ends with " + result);
        return result;
    }

    public double sub(double a, double b) {
        log.debug("The method sub() begins with " + a + ", " + b);
        double result = a - b;
        log.info(a + " - " + b + " = " + result);
```

```
        log.debug("The method sub() ends with " + result);
        return result;
    }

    public double mul(double a, double b) {
        log.debug("The method mul() begins with " + a + ", " + b);
        double result = a * b;
        log.info(a + " * " + b + " = " + result);
        log.debug("The method mul() ends with " + result);
        return result;
    }

    public double div(double a, double b) {
        log.debug("The method div() begins with " + a + ", " + b);
        double result = a / b;
        log.info(a + " / " + b + " = " + result);
        log.debug("The method div() ends with " + result);
        return result;
    }
}
```

Commons Logging supports six logging levels. Listed in descending order of severity, they are fatal, error, warn, info, debug, and trace. The fatal level is not supported by the dm Server, while the trace level maps to the dm Server's verbose level. As you can see from the preceding class, the method beginnings and endings are logged at the debug level, while the calculation results are logged at the info level.

If you update and restart the application on the dm Server, you will find that only the logs at the info level are traced, as shown in the following fragment:

```
[2009-06-07 15:06:26.281] server-dm-4↵
    rodmserver.calculator.service.impl.CalculatorServiceImpl.unknown I↵
    3.0 + 2.0 = 5.0
[2009-06-07 15:06:26.281] server-dm-4↵
    rodmserver.calculator.service.impl.CalculatorServiceImpl.unknown I↵
    3.0 - 2.0 = 1.0
[2009-06-07 15:06:26.281] server-dm-4↵
    rodmserver.calculator.service.impl.CalculatorServiceImpl.unknown I↵
    3.0 * 2.0 = 6.0
[2009-06-07 15:06:26.281] server-dm-4↵
    rodmserver.calculator.service.impl.CalculatorServiceImpl.unknown I↵
    3.0 / 2.0 = 1.5
```

Because of the earlier modification of the dm Server's serviceability.config file, only info and higher levels are traced, so logs at the debug level are not traced.

As already noted, you can modify the trace levels for the dm Server in the serviceability.config file, allowing you to set trace levels globally or for specific classes and packages.

However, constantly modifying the dm Server's serviceability.config file can become tedious. As an alternative, the dm Server also supports configuring trace levels in an application's MANIFEST.MF file via the Application-TraceLevels manifest header, a mechanism that overrides any values set in the dm Server's serviceability.config file.

If your application is packaged and deployed in a PAR file, you can use this header in the PAR file's MANIFEST.MF file. This header is not taken into account if placed in the MANIFEST.MF files of individual bundles *belonging* to a PAR file. However, if your application is packaged and deployed in a single bundle, not in a PAR file, you can use this header in the bundle's MANIFEST.MF file.

Because your calculator application is packaged in a PAR file with two bundles, you should add this header to the PAR file's MANIFEST.MF file as follows:

```
Manifest-Version: 1.0
Application-SymbolicName: com.apress.prodmserver.calculator
Application-Version: 1.0.0
Application-Description: APRESS
Application-Name: Calculator PAR
Application-TraceLevels: *=info,com.apress.prodmserver.calculator.*=debug
```

The Application-TraceLevels manifest header's value can contain a list of package-level entries separated by commas, a convention similar to the one used in the dm Server's serviceability.config file. The preceding value indicates that the dm Server traces logs output by classes in the com.apress.prodmserver.calculator package and its subpackages at the debug level, and logs output by other packages at the info level. If you update and restart the application again, you should see the following logs, including those at the debug level, in the trace file:

```
[2009-06-07 15:13:12.500] server-dm-3↵
    rodmserver.calculator.service.impl.CalculatorServiceImpl.unknown D↵
    The method add() begins with 3.0, 2.0
[2009-06-07 15:13:12.500] server-dm-3↵
    rodmserver.calculator.service.impl.CalculatorServiceImpl.unknown I↵
    3.0 + 2.0 = 5.0
[2009-06-07 15:13:12.500] server-dm-3↵
    rodmserver.calculator.service.impl.CalculatorServiceImpl.unknown D↵
    The method add() ends with 5.0
[2009-06-07 15:13:12.500] server-dm-3↵
    rodmserver.calculator.service.impl.CalculatorServiceImpl.unknown D↵
    The method sub() begins with 3.0, 2.0
[2009-06-07 15:13:12.500] server-dm-3↵
    rodmserver.calculator.service.impl.CalculatorServiceImpl.unknown I↵
    3.0 - 2.0 = 1.0
[2009-06-07 15:13:12.500] server-dm-3↵
    rodmserver.calculator.service.impl.CalculatorServiceImpl.unknown D↵
    The method sub() ends with 1.0
[2009-06-07 15:13:12.500] server-dm-3↵
    rodmserver.calculator.service.impl.CalculatorServiceImpl.unknown D↵
    The method mul() begins with 3.0, 2.0
```

```
[2009-06-07 15:13:12.500] server-dm-3↵
    rodmserver.calculator.service.impl.CalculatorServiceImpl.unknown I↵
    3.0 * 2.0 = 6.0
[2009-06-07 15:13:12.500] server-dm-3↵
    rodmserver.calculator.service.impl.CalculatorServiceImpl.unknown D↵
    The method mul() ends with 6.0
[2009-06-07 15:13:12.500] server-dm-3↵
    rodmserver.calculator.service.impl.CalculatorServiceImpl.unknown D↵
    The method div() begins with 3.0, 2.0
[2009-06-07 15:13:12.500] server-dm-3↵
    rodmserver.calculator.service.impl.CalculatorServiceImpl.unknown I↵
    3.0 / 2.0 = 1.5
[2009-06-07 15:13:12.500] server-dm-3↵
    rodmserver.calculator.service.impl.CalculatorServiceImpl.unknown D↵
    The method div() ends with 1.5
```

Summary

In this chapter, you were introduced to the dm Server's serviceability subsystem, which is able to output log files, trace files, and service dumps for tracing and diagnosing errors. The dm Server writes log messages of significant server events to a global log file, and it configures the embedded Tomcat to write access logs. The dm Server also traces internal server events in a global trace file, and application events, output, and logs in both the global trace file and each application's own trace file. If a server failure is detected at runtime, the dm Server's FFDC feature will capture all necessary server information in a service dump so that the dm Server's users needn't reproduce the failure for the service team to diagnose the problem.

The dm Server's serviceability can be configured in the dm Server's serviceability.config configuration file. Supported configurations include the output directory of log files, trace files, and service dumps, global and trickle dm Server trace levels, as well as the ability to generate Java heap dumps on server crashes.

The dm Server traces events, output, and logs of each application in the application's own trace file. First, it partitions the System.out and System.err output on a per-application basis by directing it to the application's own trace file. It also directs log messages output with Commons Logging and Log4J/Logback to the application's trace file. You can set an application's trace levels with the Application-TraceLevels manifest header, and these levels will override the global dm Server trace levels.

■ ■ ■

CHAPTER 8

Managing Application Growth on the dm Server

In the previous chapters you learned how to develop and migrate applications for the dm Server, familiarizing yourself with topics like OSGi services, application modularity, OSGi versioning, and more specific dm Server topics like platform archives (PARs) and libraries.

While these foundations can now help you develop or migrate practically any application to operate on the dm Server, as an application starts to grow, you may find it more difficult to adapt the application to certain requirements. This chapter will introduce you to more advanced topics related to constructs, tools, and configuration setups for the dm Server. These topics include

- dm Server plan files, configuration provisioning, and cloning
- Bundlor and bundle dependency management
- SpringSource slices for the dm Server

When reading this chapter, keep in mind that the growth scenarios and examples will be based on the vehicle application described in Chapter 5, so familiarity with the structure of this application is recommended. In addition, the topics covered in the chapter pertain only to the dm Server's 2.0 release.

Application Constructs for Managing Growth

So far you've learned about OSGi's standard bundle format, as well as the dm Server's PAR and library formats. These constructs, which provide OSGi's building blocks in the case of a bundle, or make it easier to develop and deploy modular applications for the dm Server in the case of PARs and libraries, have particular sets of rules and behaviors.

Each of these rules and behaviors serves a purpose, such as scoping an application's OSGi services in the case of PARs or providing a shortcut for using multiple bundles in the case of libraries. But the creators of the dm Server have also devised other constructs that can make it even easier or possible to solve certain scenarios as an application enters a greater growth phase.

Plan Files

A *plan file* is a construct to generalize PAR behavior. As you've already seen in the previous chapters, a PAR file allows you to group an application's bundles (modules) into a single file. Because the purpose of a plan file is to generalize a PAR's behavior, it's useful to recap the characteristics of a PAR.

One of the primary characteristics of using a PAR file is that it introduces the concept of an application in OSGi. An application is made up of a collection of bundles assembled in an atomic unit, which is to say that either all of the application's bundles are installed, started, stopped, and uninstalled successfully or none of them are. For large modular applications this can be especially important, since it guarantees that the multiple parts operate in sync at deployment time.

Another characteristic of a PAR file is its scoping behavior. Since an OSGi environment hosts services on a global namespace, a PAR file limits the visibility of services to an application, thus avoiding potential name clashes. In addition, a PAR file also makes it possible to scope packages on an application basis—via the import-scope:=application directive—allowing the import of packages to be performed on a single application bundle and making them visible to all bundles belonging to a PAR.

Finally, another characteristic of a PAR file is that it requires grouping an application's bundles into the same file. For large applications, the outcome can be unmanageably large (e.g. gigabyte) PAR files.

Now that I've recapped a PAR file's characteristics, here is how a plan file generalizes a PAR's behavior:

- A plan file can control whether the parts of an application are installed atomically. In other words, you can group an application's parts just as in a PAR, but you can also decide whether to tie their lifecycles together or not.

- A plan file can contain *artifacts* other than bundles. As illustrated earlier, a PAR file simply contains bundles; a plan file is more flexible and can contain general artifacts, as you will see shortly.

- A plan file can control scoping. Whereas a PAR file automatically scopes all its parts, a plan file can have its scoping behavior enabled or disabled. If scoping is disabled, a plan file's parts are visible globally.

- A plan file uses an XML structure to define its parts. Unlike a PAR file, which requires that its parts be zipped together in the same file, a plan file is a set of declarations that together point toward artifacts already installed in the repository, thus minimizing the size of deployment units and enhancing application bundle reusability.

Now that you're aware of the general behavior a plan file has with respect to a PAR file, we can explore a potential growth scenario for the vehicle application you created in Chapter 5; it involves plan files instead of PAR files.

Realizing that the vehicle application facilitates versioning and reusability of modules, the project stakeholders have decided to move forward with new initiatives similar to the vehicle application in areas like motorcycles and boats.

Initially, using PAR files for each application has no apparent drawbacks, but as an application grows or attempts to reuse modules between applications, you will gain a greater degree of flexibility by using multiple plan files instead of multiple PAR files.

For example, the infrastructure bundle defines a data source for the Derby database and exports it as an OSGi service. It's common to use the same database to host multiple applications, so reusing this bundle for the vehicle and newer motorcycle and boat applications would be a common scenario. But what happens if you discover a security bug in this bundle's code? Or if you simply upgrade the database version, which in turn requires updating the driver classes used in this bundle?

If you are using PAR files, this would require repackaging every application PAR to include the newly upgraded infrastructure bundle, since PAR files require a separate copy for each application. If you relied on plan files, however, you would only need to keep track of a single copy of the infrastructure bundle and modify a plan file's statements, which are XML-based.

This reusability scenario made possible by plan files can be equally applied to other bundles, such as web interfaces or persistence providers, where you can centralize a copy of an application bundle and reuse it in multiple applications without losing a PAR's behaviors (e.g. scoping).

Now that you have a better understanding of plan files, take a look at the following listing, which illustrates the vehicle application in the form of a plan file:

```
<?xml version="1.0" encoding="UTF-8"?>
<plan name="multi-artifact.plan" version="1.0.0" scoped="true" atomic="true"
xmlns="http://www.springsource.org/schema/dm-server/plan"
xmlns:xsi="http://www.w3.org/2001/XMLSchema-instance"
xsi:schemaLocation="http://www.springsource.org/schema/dm-server/plan
http://www.springsource.org/schema/dm-server/plan/springsource-dm-server-plan.xsd">
<artifact type="bundle"
name="com.apress.prodmserver.vehicle.domain"
version="[1.0.0, 1.0.0]"/>
<artifact type="bundle" name="com.apress.prodmserver.vehicle.infrastructure.derby"
version="[1.0.0, 1.0.0]"/>
<artifact type="bundle"
name="com.apress.prodmserver.vehicle.repository"
version="[1.0.0, 1.0.0]"/>
<artifact type="bundle"
name="com.apress.prodmserver.vehicle.repository.jpa"
version="[1.0.0, 1.0.0]"/>
<artifact type="bundle"
name="com.apress.prodmserver.vehicle.service"
version="[1.0.0, 1.0.0]"/>
<artifact type="bundle"
name="com.apress.prodmserver.vehicle.web"
version="[1.0.0, 1.0.0]"/>
</plan>
```

As you can see, a plan file is an XML file with its own schema that defines artifact elements. In this case, the only artifacts are of the type bundle, which correspond to the same application bundles that made up the PAR file in Chapter 5. Further note that each artifact element also declares a version attribute.

So for example, the element

```
<artifcat type="bundle" name="com.apress.prodmserver.vehicle.web" version="[1.0.0,1.0.0]">
```

refers to a bundle having a Bundle-SymbolicName of com.apress.prodmserver.vehicle.web and a Bundle-Version version value of 1.0.0.

The deployment of plan files is a two step process. First you need install a plan file's artifacts in the dm Server's repository—located under the dm Server's repository/bundles/usr/ directory. Once a plan file's artifacts are installed, the second step consists of placing the plan file (with a .plan extension) in the dm Server's deployment directory, which is located under the Server's pickup directory.

■ **Note** Unlike PAR projects, which are supported in dm Server tools for Eclipse/STS, plan files at the time of this writing are still not supported in dm Server Tools; therefore they need to be created as regular XML files and deployed manually to the dm Server.

Finally, it's worth mentioning the different values that can be assigned to a plan file. Table 8-1 illustrates a plan file's elements and element attributes.

Table 8-1. *Plan File Element and Attribute Values*

Element	Description	Restriction
<plan>	Top-level element for a plan file; has the attributes described next.	Needs to be the root element in XML file.
Attribute	Description	Value
name	Name assigned to a plan file, used to distinguish deployed units along with version attribute.	Required string value.
version	Version assigned to a plan file, used to distinguish deployed units along with name attribute.	Required version value, in accordance with OSGi version notation.
scoped	Defines whether a plan file is scoped.	Required Boolean (true/false) value.
atomic	Defines whether a plan file is atomic.	Required Boolean (true/false) value.
abstract	Defines whether a plan file is abstract. An abstract plan file is not deployed on its own, but rather referenced in an artifact element.	Optional Boolean (true/false) value. Defaults to false, which means the plan file is being deployed on its own.
<artifact>	Artifact element for plan file; has the attributes described next.	Needs to be nested within the <plan> element and occur at least once in a plan file.
Attribute	Description	Value
type	Defines the type of artifact.	Required string value. Currently supported types include bundle, properties and plan.

Table 8-1. Continued

name	Name assigned to the artifact.	Required string value. For a bundle type a bundle's Bundle-SymbolicName, for a properties type a property's file name, and for a plan type a plan's name.
version	Version assigned to the artifact.	Optional version value, in accordance with OSGi version notation. Defaults to 0, which in OSGi implies version 0 to infinity.

As you've now learned, plan files give you the same benefits as PAR files but with a greater degree of flexibility. You can control scope and atomicity and you can centralize a single copy of an application bundle to be reused by multiple applications.

WHAT IS THE DIFFERENCE BETWEEN A PLAN FILE AND A LIBRARY?

Though apparently similar, a dm Server library differs from a dm Server plan file in two ways:

- A library is a way to join a collection of bundles into a single deployment unit and reference it in other bundles. Once deployed, a library will be exploded into individual bundles with no scoping, atomicity, or any other behavior supported by plan files.
- A plan file is a way to join a collection of bundles into a single deployment unit strictly for administrative purposes—not for referencing inside other bundles. In addition, plan files support behaviors like scoping and atomicity, which allow greater control over their deployment process.

If you observed a plan file's structure closely, you will have noted that it uses the term artifact as a qualifier for assigning bundles. That's because a plan file can contain more than just bundles—unlike a PAR file. One of these other artifact types is the *properties* file, described next.

Properties Files—Configuration Provisioning

Properties files are fairly common in Java applications. These small text files, placed alongside Java classes, are used to place things like localized messages or parameters that can change at runtime, a more convenient approach than hard-coding such values into Java classes.

For example, depending on certain cues that are best determined at runtime (e.g. a user's language, a production vs. development environment), an application can be designed to use a particular value set in a properties file to "fill in" the application's information.

Configuration provisioning in the dm Server follows the same principle as properties files but applied to plan files. The purpose of properties files in the dm Server is to rely on simple text files containing properties, which can then be used to fill in certain parameters present in an application's bundles in the definition of a plan file.

Just as plan files go to the heart of avoiding bundle duplication and enhancing the management of dm Server applications, properties files allow application bundles to be customized at runtime depending on their use. I will continue to build on Chapter 5's application—now based on a plan file—to illustrate the purpose of properties files.

The applications you developed for the dm Server, including the initial vehicle and now the motorcycle and boat applications, have been extremely successful. In fact, the applications have had so many visitors that the database administrators have suggested splitting the workload into multiple databases to offload the work of a single server and make administrative tasks simpler.

Plan files allowed you to reuse the infrastructure bundle to define a data source for the Derby database and leverage it in multiple applications, without keeping track of multiple copies. But this scenario of multiple databases will apparently require you to use a different infrastructure bundle for each of the vehicle, motorcycle, and boat applications. Not so if you use properties files.

If you analyze the contents of the infrastructure bundle, you will realize that only a few parameters (e.g. username, password, and connection URL) differ if you create bundles for separate databases. In light of this, it becomes feasible to rely on a properties file to define such parameters for the bundle and determine which set to use in the definition of a plan file.

For example, the following listing illustrates what a properties file—contained in a file named prodmserver.vehicle.db—would look like for the vehicle application:

```
jdbc.url=jdbc:derby://localhost:1527/vehicle;create=true
jdbc.user=app
jdbc.password=app
jdbc.driver=org.apache.derby.jdbc.ClientDriver
```

Notice that this listing's syntax is like any other Java .properties file. Next, it's necessary to modify the hard-coded values in the infrastructure bundle to reference the values of these properties. For this task, the dm Server relies on Configuration Admin, part of the OSGi service compendium specification, which defines how to incorporate declarative data into OSGi bundles. The following listing illustrates how the infrastructure bundle's Spring configuration file module-context.xml would look using Configuration Admin:

```
<beans xmlns="http://www.springframework.org/schema/beans"
    xmlns:xsi="http://www.w3.org/2001/XMLSchema-instance"
    xmlns:osgix="http://www.springframework.org/schema/osgi-compendium"
    xmlns:ctx="http://www.springframework.org/schema/context"
    xsi:schemaLocation="http://www.springframework.org/schema/beans
        http://www.springframework.org/schema/beans/spring-beans-2.5.xsd
        http://www.springframework.org/schema/context
        http://www.springframework.org/schema/context/spring-context.xsd
      http://www.springframework.org/schema/osgi-compendium
      http://www.springframework.org/schema/osgi-compendium/↵
spring-osgi-compendium.xsd">
    <!-- Configuration Admin entry -->
    <osgix:cm-properties id="dbProps" persistent-id="prodmserver.db.vehicle">
        <prop key="jdbc.driver">org.apache.derby.jdbc.ClientDriver</prop>
    </osgix:cm-properties>
    <!-- Placeholder configurer -->
    <ctx:property-placeholder properties-ref="dbProps"/>
```

```
<bean id="dataSource" class="org.apache.commons.dbcp.BasicDataSource"
    init-method="createDataSource" destroy-method="close">
    <property name="driverClassName"
        value="${jdbc.driver}"/>
    <property name="url"
  value="${jdbc.url}"/>
    <property name="username" value="${jdbc.user}"/>
    <property name="password" value="${jdbc.password}"/>
</bean>
</beans>
```

The first modification to this file consists of two additional namespaces, the spring-osgi-compendium namespace used by Configuration Admin and the spring-context namespace used as a properties placeholder. Next, you will find the Configuration Admin entry defined in the <cm-properties> element. This element relies on two properties, the id property (with a dbProps value) used to define a reference name for the properties file and the persistence-id property (with a prodmserver.db.vehicle value) used to define the name of the properties file.

Nested inside the <cm-properties> element you will find the <prop> element, which is an optional statement that allows you to define local properties. The <prop> element relies on a key attribute to define a property's name, in this case jdbc.driver), and defines the value for the property as the element's character data, in this case org.apache.derby.jdbc.ClientDriver.

By default, Configuration Admin properties take precedence over local properties defined in <prop> elements. This means that if a properties file defines a property named jdbc.driver, its value will override the locally defined jdbc.driver property. Nevertheless, this behavior can be modified by including the attribute local-override="true", which would then have local properties take precedence over Configuration Admin properties.

Once the <cm-properties> element is defined, it is necessary to define a placeholder that will serve to reference properties inside the context, specifically Spring beans. For this purpose the <property-placeholder> element is used, and its properties-ref attribute is used to reference the <cm-properties> id attribute—which in this case has a value of dbProps.

Finally, you will see that the bean values that were once had hard-coded—jdbc:derby://localhost:1527/vehicle;create=true, app, app, and org.apache.derby.jdbc.ClientDriver—now have a syntax of the form ${*property.name*}. At runtime, the dm Server will take care of replacing this special syntax with the actual values defined in a properties file.

Once a properties file is defined and an application bundle configured to use it, you can assign the properties file in the definition of a plan file, as illustrated next:

```
<?xml version="1.0" encoding="UTF-8"?>
<plan name="multi-artifact.plan" version="1.0.0" scoped="true" atomic="true"
xmlns="http://www.springsource.org/schema/dm-server/plan"
xmlns:xsi="http://www.w3.org/2001/XMLSchema-instance"
xsi:schemaLocation="http://www.springsource.org/schema/dm-server/plan
http://www.springsource.org/schema/dm-server/plan/springsource-dm-server-plan.xsd">
```

```
<artifact type="properties" name="prodmserver.vehicle.db"
version="[1.0.0,1.0.0]"/>
<artifact type="bundle" name="com.apress.prodmserver.vehicle.infrastructure.derby"
version="[1.0.0,1.0.0]"/>
<artifact type="bundle"
name="com.apress.prodmserver.vehicle.domain"
version="[1.0.0,1.0.0]"/>
<artifact type="bundle"
name="com.apress.prodmserver.vehicle.repository"
version="[1.0.0,1.0.0]"/>
<artifact type="bundle"
name="com.apress.prodmserver.vehicle.repository.jpa"
version="[1.0.0,1.0.0]"/>
<artifact type="bundle"
name="com.apress.prodmserver.vehicle.service"
version="[1.0.0,1.0.0]"/>
<artifact type="bundle"
name="com.apress.prodmserver.vehicle.web"
version="[1.0.0,1.0.0]"/>
</plan>
```

Notice how this plan file defines an artifact of the type properties. In this case, the name of the artifact—prodmserver.vehicle.db—corresponds to the name of the properties file. Like all other artifacts referenced in a plan file, the properties file needs to be installed in the dm Server's repository, located under the dm Server's repository/bundles/usr/ directory.

At runtime, the dm Server will read the properties file defined in the plan file and use it to "fill-in" whatever declarations are made in a plan file's artifacts—which in this case correspond to the DB connection properties. An identical approach would be used for the plan files corresponding to the remaining applications, using properties files (e.g. prodmserver.motorcycle.db or prodmserver.boat.db) with different DB connection parameters. The result will be that you can continue to rely on a single copy of the infrastructure bundle.

Much as in the reusability scenarios for plan files, properties files can also be used for various tasks where an application bundle requires minimal changes to be reused. For example, production vs. development databases and multiple-language messages are among the areas where you would typically see standard Java properties files used.

Before leaving the topic of properties files and plan files, it's a good opportunity to introduce you to another related topic: *abstract plan files*. The following listing illustrates the use of an abstract plan file:

```
<?xml version="1.0" encoding="UTF-8"?>
<plan name="prodmserver.coreapp" version="1.0.0" abstract="true"
xmlns="http://www.springsource.org/schema/dm-server/plan"
xmlns:xsi="http://www.w3.org/2001/XMLSchema-instance"
xsi:schemaLocation="http://www.springsource.org/schema/dm-server/plan
http://www.springsource.org/schema/dm-server/plan/springsource-dm-server-plan.xsd">
<artifact type="bundle" name="com.apress.prodmserver.vehicle.infrastructure.derby"
```

```
version="[1.0.0,1.0.0]"/>
<artifact type="bundle"
name="com.apress.prodmserver.vehicle.domain"
version="[1.0.0,1.0.0]"/>
<artifact type="bundle"
name="com.apress.prodmserver.vehicle.repository"
version="[1.0.0,1.0.0]"/>
<artifact type="bundle"
name="com.apress.prodmserver.vehicle.repository.jpa"
version="[1.0.0,1.0.0]"/>
<artifact type="bundle"
name="com.apress.prodmserver.vehicle.service"
version="[1.0.0,1.0.0]"/>
<artifact type="bundle"
name="com.apress.prodmserver.vehicle.web"
version="[1.0.0,1.0.0]"/>
</plan>
<plan name="vehicle.plan" version="1.0.0" scoped="true" atomic="true">
 <artifact type="properties" name="prodmserver.vehicle.db" version="[1.0.0,1.0.0]"/>
 <artifact type="plan" name="prodmserver.coreapp" version="[1.0.0,1.0.0]"/>
</plan>
<plan name="motorcycle.plan" version="1.0.0" scoped="true" atomic="true">
 <artifact type="properties" name="prodmserver.motorcycle.db" version="[1.0.0,1.0.0]"/>
 <artifact type="plan" name="prodmserver.coreapp" version="[1.0.0,1.0.0]"/>
</plan>
<plan name="boat.plan" version="1.0.0" scoped="true" atomic="true">
 <artifact type="properties" name="prodmserver.boat.db" version="[1.0.0,1.0.0]"/>
 <artifact type="plan" name="prodmserver.coreapp" version="[1.0.0,1.0.0]"/>
</plan>
```

Notice how the top-level statement is declared with the attribute abstract=true. This tells the dm Server not to deploy the plan file directly. The purpose of the abstract attribute is to use a plan file as an artifact in another plan file.

Next, notice how the same plan file, prodmserver.coreapp, is referenced three times in other <plan> declarations—using a plan-type artifact—in addition to being combined with a properties-type artifact. This illustrates how an abstract plan file can simplify the use of plan files even further, since a single plan file declaration can be reused for multiple applications.

Bear in mind, this last example doesn't mean that an abstract plan file can only be used with properties files; you are free to use them in whatever way you see fit. I only opted to do so because properties files lend themselves to the use of abstract plan files.

Cloning

While plan files and properties files address issues related to packaging applications in the dm Server, *cloning* addresses an issue that affects the growth of OSGi applications in general. The technical concepts of cloning and the problem it attempts to solve—*pinning* or uses conflict—were thoroughly addressed in

Chapter 3's "Enhanced Dependency Management" section, so here I will concentrate on the dm Server's cloning behaviors.

There are two ways that cloning is triggered in the dm Server:

Automatically: When an application fails to resolve because of a uses constraint violation.

Manually: By specifying the sharing:=clone directive on an Import-Library or Import-Bundle header.

The dm Server is configured to trigger automatic cloning by default. This means that if the dm Server detects a particular usage pattern in an application that might lead to a pinning or uses conflict error, it will trigger the cloning of the conflicting bundles.

Because some uses constraint violations cannot be avoided, and the cloning process is driven by OSGi resolver failures, this can lead to a certain amount of overhead produced by various iterations of running the resolver and cloning process on one or more bundles.

This overhead can range from additional seconds to minutes in start-up time and can be avoided by disabling the dm Server's automatic cloning mode. However, if uses constraint violations are present, they will inevitably lead an application to be undeployable and in turn require you to address such issues by cloning an application's bundles manually. So unless the penalty for running an application with the dm Server's automatic cloning mode is severe, I strongly advise you not to deactivate it.

■ **Note** You can determine whether cloning is taking place in an application by analyzing the dm Server's console and log files, which contain detailed cloning messages.

If performance is of the utmost importance, you can rely on the dm Server's manual cloning option. The advantage to using manual cloning is that you don't incur additional start-up overhead, since you indicate exactly what bundles require cloning. The disadvantage, of course, is that you must determine exactly which bundles represent a potential pinning or uses conflict error. One approach I recommend when using manual cloning is to take advantage of the automatic cloning mode first, as follows:

1. Run the dm Server in automatic cloning mode and deploy the application.

2. Take note in the dm Server console or logs which bundles or libraries are being cloned upon deploying the application.

3. Disable the dm Server's automatic cloning mode.

4. Inspect an application's bundles and take note of those bundles whose Import-Library or Import-Bundle header values have bundles or libraries that are being cloned in automatic mode.

5. Modify these application bundles' header values to include the sharing:=clone directive, on a one by one basis, until the application is successfully deployed.

This trial-and-error process will make it easier to minimize the number of bundles being cloned, while also minimizing the effort to determine which bundles are the ones that represent a potential pinning or uses conflict error.

Now that we've reviewed the available constructs, next we'll move on to discuss the tools available in the dm Server for managing application growth.

Tools for Managing Growth

In Chapter 5 and Chapter 6 you relied on the dm Server Tools plug-in—part of the greater STS—to ease the development and migration of applications created using Eclipse. Although these chapters exposed you to most of the tools you will use on a regular basis for creating dm Server applications, there is also (as with the dm Server's constructs), a special set of tool features that can aid you once an application starts to grow.

Introducing Bundlor

So far you've relied on the availability of bundles in SpringSource's Enterprise Bundle Repository (http://www.springsource.com/repository/). Though this site is constantly updated to contain the newest JARs equipped with MANIFEST.MF files containing OSGi headers, what happens if you can't find a bundle in this public repository?

A little thought reveals that this may become a common occurrence as an application grows or a large application is migrated to take advantage of OSGi features. It may turn out that an application relies on an old Java JAR file that is absent from the SpringSource Enterprise Bundle Repository. Or you may rely on a new JAR file developed in-house or by a third-party that contains no OSGi header information.

Under such circumstances, you will need to add OSGi headers to a JAR's structure in order for it to be deployed on the dm Server's repository. Adding such OSGi headers is not a difficult process, but determining them can be. Since OSGi headers typically include the outside packages needed by a JAR (the Import-Package header) as well as the packages offered by a JAR to other JARs (the Export-Package header) this can become a lengthy inspection process.

In fact, it's a process that can be tedious even if you have access to a JAR's source code and even more difficult if all you have is binary JAR with compiled classes, requiring a decompilation process to determine such dependencies. In light of this, Bundlor offers an easy route to equip a JAR's MANIFEST.MF file with OSGi headers.

Simply put, Bundlor is an inspection tool for JARs. When executed on a JAR, Bundlor will use a series of criteria to inspect the JAR and determine the best possible OSGi headers in order to transform it into an OSGi-compliant bundle. These criteria include inspecting all the types used in a JAR's code (fields, classes, exceptions, instanceofs, and so on), as well as types that may be included in a JAR's configuration files (.properties files, persistence.xml, spring.xml, module-context.xml, and so on).

Since Bundlor determines all types used in a bundle, it is often unnecessary to assign every type included in a bundle to OSGi headers. As noted in earlier examples, it's not always convenient to expose or import every single type used in a bundle or application, since you lose out on OSGi's more stringent class loading approach, which enforces versioning and modularity. For this reason, Bundlor also relies on a manifest template to add more control over which OSGi headers are included in a JAR's MANIFEST.MF file.

You can think of a Bundlor manifest template as an additional filter at your disposal. Since you know beforehand the structure of a JAR file and the purpose behind many of its types, you can ensure that certain OSGi headers are included or avoided in the JAR's final MANIFEST.MF file.

Now that you know Bundlor's purpose, download it from http://www.springsource.org/bundlor/ and unpack it in a local directory on your workstation. To get started, create a file named template.mf on your workstation and place the following contents in it:

```
Bundle-SymbolicName: osgified.acmedb.driver
Bundle-Name: AcmeDB Driver
Bundle-Vendor: AcmeDB
Bundle-ManifestVersion: 2
```

This last file will serve as the initial Bundlor manifest template. Notice that it contains various OSGi-related MANIFEST.MF file headers, referring to a DB with a brand named Acme. Take note of this file's location, as you will use it next.

Next, descend into Bundlor's bin directory. There you will see two executables, one named bundlor.sh for Unix/Linux operating systems and one named bundlor.bat for Windows. Depending on your environment, execute the following instructions from the command line:

```
bundlor.sh manifest -b /<route_to_acme_jar>/acme-db-driver.jar -m↩
  /<route_to_bundlor_template>/template.mf
```

The first of part of this last instruction, bundlor.sh manifest, invokes Bundlor in its manifest mode. In this mode, Bundlor simply outputs what it deems to be an OSGi-compliant MANIFEST.MF for the JAR file specified using the -b flag, based on the Bundlor template specified using the -m flag. You can input any JAR available on your workstation to run this command; the DB Acme JAR name is just one example. Once you run this command you will see output like the following:

```
Manifest-Version: 1.0
Export-Package: com.acme.jdbc;version="0";uses:="com.acme.jdbc.log,c
 om.acme.jdbc.util,javax.naming",com.acme.jdbc.configs;version="0",c
 om.acme.jdbc.exceptions;version="0",com.acme.jdbc.integration.c3p0;
 version="0";uses:="com.mchange.v2.c3p0",com.acme.jdbc.jdbc2.optiona
 l;version="0";uses:="com.acme.jdbc,javax.naming,javax.naming.spi,
 javax.sql,javax.transaction.xa",com.acme.jdbc.log;↩
version="0",com.acme.jdbc.profiler;
 version="0";uses:="com.acme.jdbc",com.acme.jdbc.util;version="0";us
 es:="com.acme.jdbc,com.acme.jdbc.log",org.gjt.mm.acme;version="0";
 uses:="com.acme.jdbc"
Bundle-Vendor: AcmeDB
Ant-Version: Apache Ant 1.6.5
Bundle-Classpath: .
Built-By: acmedev
Bundle-Name: AcmeDB Driver
Bundle-ManifestVersion: 2
Created-By: 1.4.2-b28 (Sun Microsystems Inc.)
Bundle-SymbolicName: osgified.acmedb.driver
Import-Package: com.mchange.v2.c3p0,javax.naming,javax.naming.spi,java
 x.net,javax.net.ssl,javax.sql,javax.transaction.xa,org.apache.commons
 .logging,org.apache.log4j

SB0001W: The import of package com.mchange.v2.c3p0 does not specify a version.
SB0001W: The import of package javax.naming does not specify a version.
SB0001W: The import of package javax.naming.spi does not specify a version.
SB0001W: The import of package javax.net does not specify a version.
SB0001W: The import of package javax.net.ssl does not specify a version.
SB0001W: The import of package javax.sql does not specify a version.
SB0001W: The import of package javax.transaction.xa does not specify a version.
SB0001W: The import of package org.apache.commons.logging ↩
does not specify a version.
SB0001W: The import of package org.apache.log4j does not specify a version.
```

As you can see, Bundlor determines a series of packages present in a JAR file and generates a series of values corresponding to the OSGi `Import-Package` and `Export-Package` headers. In addition, Bundlor also appends the headers declared in the Bundlor template file, and it provides some warning messages indicating that versions for certain packages were not provided.

This output is Bundlor's "best guess" at generating an OSGi-compliant `MANIFEST.MF` file. However, after closer inspection you may decide it's convenient to omit or declare other packages in the `Import-Package` or `Export-Package` headers, in addition to adding other OSGi headers. Here again, since you will know the structure and contents of a JAR file beforehand, you are better prepared to determine what will make up the final OSGi-compliant `MANIFEST.MF` for the JAR.

To achieve better control of what Bundlor determines to be a JAR's `MANIFEST.MF`, you can fall back on Bundlor's template file. The Bundlor template file supports a series of headers that are defined in Table 8-2.

Table 8-2. *Bundlor Manifest Template Headers*

Header	Purpose
`Excluded-Exports`	A comma-separated list of packages that must not be added to the manifest's `Export-Package` header.
`Excluded-Imports`	By default, Bundlor will add imports for every package that it determines is referenced by the code or special files in the JAR. This header allows a comma-separated list of packages to be omitted from such imports.
`Export-Template`	By default, Bundlor versions are all exported packages by the `Bundle-Version` value. The `Export-Template` header allows individual exported packages to be exported at different versions. For example, `Export-Template com.foo.*;version="1.5"` will cause any `Export-Package` entries for `com.foo` or its subpackages to be versioned at `1.5`.
`Ignored-Existing-Headers`	For cases where a JAR already contains an OSGi-compliant manifest, this header can be used to list headers in the original manifest that Bundlor should ignore.
`Import-Template`	This header is used to augment package imports that Bundlor generates via bytecode and special file analysis. Typically this will be to version the imports and, in some cases, to mark them as optional. The header's value is in the form of a comma-separated list of package names and attributes.

From their names and descriptions, you can see that by using these headers in a Bundlor manifest template you gain greater control over what will be placed in a JAR's `MANIFEST.MF` file. In addition to these Bundlor headers, which are not placed verbatim in the final `MANIFEST.MF` file but interpreted as instructions, you can also place standard OSGi headers as you did in the first iteration of the Bundlor manifest template.

The following listing contains a second iteration of the Bundlor manifest template applied to the DB Acme JAR, illustrating the use of Bundlor headers listed in Table 6-1.

```
Bundle-SymbolicName: osgified.acmedb.driver
Bundle-Name: AcmeDB Driver
Bundle-Vendor: AcmeDB
Bundle-ManifestVersion: 2
Excluded-Exports: com.acme.jdbc.configs
Excluded-Imports: org.apache.log4j
Export-Template: com.acme.jdbc;version="2.5"
Import-Template: org.apache.commons.logging;version="[1.1.1, 2.0.0)"
Import-Package: org.acme.oldutilities;version="[2.0.0, 3.0.0)";resolution:=optional
```

The first additional header is Excluded-Exports, which tells Bundlor not to incorporate the package com.acme.jdbc.configs in the Export-Package value list of the generated MANIFEST.MF. The next header, Excluded-Imports, is similar, except that it tells Bundlor not to incorporate the package org.apache.log4j in the Import-Package value list of the generated MANIFEST.MF.

The Export-Template is used to set up Bundlor for adding information to packages that it will already add to the Export-Package value list of a MANIFEST.MF. In this case, the com.acme.jdbc; version:=2.5 value is telling Bundlor to append a version:=2.5 directive to the com.acme.jdbc package.

The Import-Template serves a similar purpose to Export-Template, except that it adds information to packages that Bundlor will already add to the Import-Package value list of a MANIFEST.MF. In this case, the value

```
org.apache.commons.logging;version="[1.1.1, 2.0.0)"
```

tells Bundlor to append a version="[1.1.1, 2.0.0)" directive to the org.apache.commons.logging package.

Finally, Import-Package, a standard OSGi header, when declared in a Bundlor template serves to append additional packages to those detected by Bundlor, for cases in which package auto-detection might fail. Like any other tool, Bundlor is not 100% infallible.

If you invoke the earlier Bundlor command using this last manifest template file instead of the first one, you will see a MANIFEST.MF file output like the following:

```
Manifest-Version: 1.0
Export-Package: com.acme.jdbc;version="2.5";uses:="com.acme.jdbc.log
 ,com.acme.jdbc.util,javax.naming",com.acme.jdbc.exceptions;version=
 "0",com.acme.jdbc.integration.c3p0;version="0";uses:="com.mchange.v2
 .c3p0",com.acme.jdbc.jdbc2.optional;version="0";uses:="com.acme.jdbc,javax.naming
 ,javax.naming.spi,javax.sql,javax.transaction.xa",com.acme.jdbc.log;
 version="0",com.acme.jdbc.profiler;version="0";uses:="com.acme.jdbc
 ",com.acme.jdbc.util;version="0";uses:="com.acme.jdbc,com.acme.jdb
 c.log",org.gjt.mm.acme;version="0";uses:="com.acme.jdbc"
Bundle-Vendor: AcmeDB
Ant-Version: Apache Ant 1.6.5
Bundle-Classpath: .
Built-By: acmedev
Bundle-Name: AcmeDB Driver
Bundle-ManifestVersion: 2
```

```
Created-By: 1.4.2-b28 (Sun Microsystems Inc.)
Bundle-SymbolicName: osgified.acmedb.driver
Import-Package: com.mchange.v2.c3p0,javax.naming,javax.naming.spi,java
 x.net,javax.net.ssl,javax.sql,javax.transaction.xa,org.acme.oldutilit
 ies;version="[2.0.0, 3.0.0)";resolution:=optional,org.apache.commons.
 logging;version="[1.1.1, 2.0.0)"


SB0001W: The import of package com.mchange.v2.c3p0 does not specify a version.
SB0001W: The import of package javax.naming does not specify a version.
SB0001W: The import of package javax.naming.spi does not specify a version.
SB0001W: The import of package javax.net does not specify a version.
SB0001W: The import of package javax.net.ssl does not specify a version.
SB0001W: The import of package javax.sql does not specify a version.
SB0001W: The import of package javax.transaction.xa does not specify a version.
```

Notice how the packages om.acme.jdbc.configs and org.apache.log4j are omitted in this last listing. In addition, observe how the corresponding version directives were added to the org.apache.commons.logging;version="[1.1.1, 2.0.0)" package and the com.acme.jdbc;version:=2.5 package, as well as the additional package import of org.acme.oldutilities;version="[2.0.0, 3.0.0)";resolution:=optional.

Bear in mind that if you are unsure about excluding or adding OSGi statements to a JAR via Bundlor's manifest template, it's best to let Bundlor determine the defaults. Generating a JAR's OSGi-compliant MANIFEST.MF file with Bundlor is that simple.

What you've done so far is generate the contents of a MANIFEST.MF file to the screen. However, Bundlor can also be run in transform mode, making the incorporation of a MANIFEST.MF file into a JAR automatic, as illustrated next:

```
bundlor.sh transform -b /<route_to_acme_jar>/acme-db-driver.jar -m↵
  /<route_to_bundlor_template>/template.mf -o/<route_to_new_acme_jar>/↵
osgified-acme-db-driver.jar
```

Notice that the initial command is changed from bundlor.sh manifest to bundlor.sh transform. Because we're using transform mode, Bundlor automatically incorporates the contents of the MANIFEST.MF file to a newly created OSGi-compliant JAR. In this case, the additional -o flag explicitly indicates the name of the new OSGi-compliant JAR. If this flag were omitted, Bundlor would overwrite the previously existing JAR with a new OSGi-compliant JAR containing OSGi-related headers.

Besides this additional execution mode, there is one more topic worth discussing related to Bundlor templates: *property substitution*.

The previous Bundlor templates all had hard-coded values, but it is also possible to use placeholders inside a Bundlor template and have them replaced by values specified at runtime. This makes a Bundlor template more reusable. For example, take a look at the following DB Acme JAR Bundlor template, which uses properties for both text and version values:

```
Bundle-SymbolicName: osgified.acmedb.driver
Bundle-Name: ${db.friendly.name} Driver
Bundle-Vendor: ${db.friendly.name}
Bundle-ManifestVersion: 2
Excluded-Exports: com.acme.jdbc.configs
Excluded-Imports: org.apache.log4j
Export-Template: com.acme.jdbc;version="${com.acme.jdbc:[=.=,=.=]"
Import-Template: org.apache.commons.logging;version=↵
"${org.apache.commons.logging:[=.=.=.=, +1.0.0.0)}"
Import-Package: org.acme.oldutilities;version=↵
"${org.db.utilities:[=.=.=.=, +1.=.=.=)}";resolution:=optional
```

The first placeholder, ${db.friendly.name}, illustrates text substitution. Whatever value is provided for the property db.friendly.name upon executing Bundlor (at runtime) will be substituted and form part of the final MANIFEST.MF.

The remaining placeholders illustrate version substitution. The notation for version substitution is a little more elaborate, since it relies on special syntax for specifying ranges. The first placeholder, ${com.acme.jdbc:[=.=,=.=], is the simplest. It indicates that whatever version value is provided for the property com.acme.jdbc, it should be placed in the same lower and upper (inclusive) range. In this case, if a value of 2.5 is provided for com.acme.jdbc Bundlor will replace the placeholder with [2.5,2.5]. The = sign is interpreted as the passed-in value in its position.

The second placeholder, {org.apache.commons.logging:[=.=.=.=, +1.0.0.0)}, shows a variation of this syntax, by incrementing the upper range and modifying it to be noninclusive. In this case, if a value of 1.1.1.0 is provided for the property org.apache.commons.logging, Bundlor will replace the placeholder with [1.1.1.0,2.0.0.0). The +1 sign is interpreted as incrementing by 1 the passed-in value in that position, where as the 0 sign is interpreted as zero (verbatim).

Finally, the third placeholder, ${org.db.utilities:[=.=.=.=, +1.=.=.=)}, shows another variation. In this case, if a value of 2.0.0.0 is provided for the property org.db.utilities, Bundlor will replace the placeholder with [2.0.0.0,3.0.0.0).

By relying on the use of property substitution in Bundlor, you can apply changes to a bundle's MANIFEST.MF more easily, since you don't have to modify a template but rather pass the values at runtime, as illustrated next:

```
bundlor.sh transform -b /<route_to_acme_jar>/acme-db-driver.jar -m
/<route_to_bundlor_template>/template.mf ↵
-o/<route_to_new_acme_jar>/osgified-acme-db-driver.jar -Ddb.friendly.name="AcmeDB" ↵
-Dcom.acme.jdbc="2.5" -Dorg.apache.commons.logging="1.1.1.0" -Dorg.db.utilities="2.0.0.0"
```

Note the use of the -D flag—the notation for a Java system property—to indicate the various Bundlor template properties for which specific values will be substituted in the template.

Besides running Bundlor from an OS command line as shown here, you can also integrate Bundlor to work with Apache Ant and Apache Maven. Consult Bundlor's documentation for instructions on these integration steps.

In addition, there is also another variant to Bundlor named BundlorEclipse, which as its name implies, aids in the creation of MANIFEST.MF files while developing applications on the Eclipse IDE or STS. The capabilities of BundlorEclipse are described next.

■ **Note** Besides Bundlor, there is another tool for converting JARs into OSGi-compliant bundles, named BND. It operates under the same principle—processing a JAR, applying a template, and outputting an OSGi-compliant bundle. You can read more about BND at `http://aqute.biz/Code/Bnd` or in the book *Pro Spring Dynamic Modules for OSGi Service Platforms.*[1]

Introducing BundlorEclipse

As you worked with Bundlor in the last section, you experienced how this tool facilitates the creation of a bundle's `MANIFEST.MF` by inspecting the contents of an existing JAR file. While this no doubt enhances the development of large OSGi applications that depend on legacy or extremely new JARs, it is also worthwhile to streamline creating a bundle's `MANIFEST.MF` in development, which is the purpose of BundlorEclipse.

In Chapter 5 and Chapter 6 you relied on Eclipse—or STS—to develop dm Server applications. You created `MANIFEST.MF` files for these applications' bundles using one of three tabs in a bundle's editor: the Dependencies tab to assign imported packages (illustrated in Figure 5-18), the Runtime tab to assign exported packages (Figure 5-20), or the MANIFEST.MF tab to edit the file manually.With BundlorEclipse, however, a bundle's `MANIFEST.MF` file can be created and updated automatically by scanning the bundle's source code.

If you are using STS or installed Eclipse as described in Chapter 5 to use dm Server Tools—which includes not only the dm Server Tools plug-in, but the entire series of Spring-related Eclipse plug-ins—then you already have BundlorEclipse installed. In fact, if you were curious in exploring the Spring Tools section in Eclipse/STS, you may have already stumbled upon BundlorEclipse's functionality. But in case you haven't, I will describe it next.

BundlorEclipse provides two functions that aid in generating a bundle's `MANIFEST.MF` file. One is an incremental generator, which incorporates changes as you are modifying a bundle's source code; the other is a manual generator, which updates a bundle's `MANIFEST.MF` file on demand.

You can activate any of these BundlorEclipse operations from the Spring Tools option, available in the pop-up menu that appears when you right-click a bundle project. Figure 8-1 illustrates this menu.

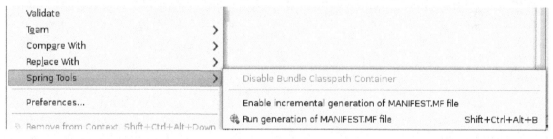

Figure 8-1. BundlorEclipse options

You can first try out the Run Generation of MANIFEST.MF File option, which can also be triggered by the keyboard combination Shift+Ctrl+Alt+B. When you do, BundlorEclipse will scan all the types (fields, classes, exceptions, `instanceofs`, and so on) used in the bundle project, as well as the types included in

---

[1] *Pro Spring Dynamic Modules for OSGi Service Platforms,* by Daniel Rubio. Apress, 2009.

configuration files (.properties files, persistence.xml, spring.xml, module-context.xml, and so on) belonging to the bundle project.

If you inspect the bundle's MANIFEST.MF tab in the bundle editor area, you will see MANIFEST. MF headers generated by BundlorEclipse. Bear in mind that just like Bundlor's basic version explored in the previous section, BundlorEclipse is a "best guess" attempt at generating a bundle's MANIFEST.MF. The result may or may not be what you're expecting.

For example, if you run BundlorEclipse on Chapter 5's Repository JPA implementation bundle, it will incorporate uses clauses on packages that it determines may having pinning issues—which we did not do in Chapter 5, because we knew that pinning would not be a problem thanks to size. BundlorEclipse also will not detect the need for clauses like import-scope:=application. Much as in Bundlor's command-line version, you as the creator of the bundle will have the best vantage point for what should and shouldn't be included in a bundle's MANIFEST.MF.

If you prefer that EclipseBundlor generate a bundle's MANIFEST.MF as you are introducing the bundle's source code, choose the Enable Incremental Generation of MANIFEST.MF File option from the Spring Tools menu.

I recommend you use BundlorEclipse in either of its two modes—especially for large bundles—since this will save you time creating a bundle's MANIFEST.MF. Afterward, you can visually inspect the bundle's MANIFEST.MF to determine if BundlorEclipse's generation rules are within your criteria, and if not, tweak the MANIFEST.MF manually.

Dependency Graphs and Overviews

As an application grows, it can become difficult to visualize the many dependencies its parts have between one another. Visualizing such dependencies can make it easier to debug and test applications. The dm Server Tools—included in STS or available as a plug-in in Eclipse—provide a special section in which you can visualize an application's dependencies.

Available in the Servers area under the Bundle Dependency Graph tab, this dm Server Tools feature allows you to view dependency graphs for both packages and services belonging to applications deployed on the dm Server. Figure 8-2 illustrates the main screen of the Bundle Dependency Graph tab.

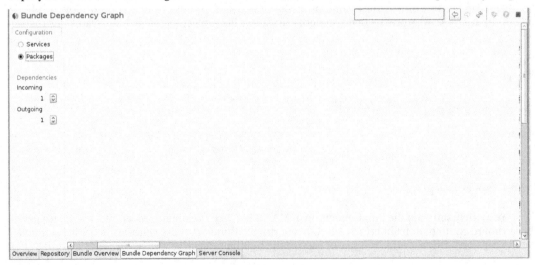

Figure 8-2. *The Bundle Dependency Graph tab of dm Server Tools*

The Bundle Dependency Graph has two parameter sections. On the left side you can choose to display either services or packages for applications, in addition to specifying the number of incoming and outgoing dependencies. Limiting the number of dependencies can be especially helpful if you have many applications running on the same dm Server instance.

In the top-right corner, you will find a text box that can be used to further filter the names of services or packages generated in a graph—also very helpful if you have a large set of applications. There is a group of buttons similar in function to those of a browser, a Back and Forward button to scroll through different graphs, as well as a Refresh button to generate a graph from the applications running on the server at any given moment. And finally, you will find three dm Server-related buttons, to start, stop, or start it in debug mode.

I will now illustrate how to generate a dependency graph for the application developed in Chapter 5. Once the application is deployed, in the filter text box of the Bundle Dependency Graph tab enter com.apress; this will limit the results of the dependency graph to those bundles you created. Next, click the Refresh icon to generate the dependency graph. Figure 8-3 illustrates the generated dependency graph.

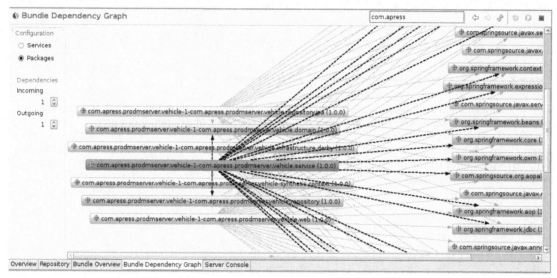

Figure 8-3. *A bundle dependency graph for the vehicle application*

Initially, the dependency graph, including bundles and arrows, will be drawn in gray. But as you can see in Figure 8-3, clicking a bundle highlights the bundle in green, demarcates its dependency arrows in black, and highlights dependent bundles in lighter green tones. In this case, clicking the com.apress. prodmserver.vehicle.service bundle will display two dependencies on bundles belonging to the application, com.apress, as well as a series of Spring-related bundles to the right, which belong to the Spring library also used by the selected bundle.

If you double-click the selected bundle, an isolated dependency graph is drawn with the selected bundle drawn at the center. This graph is illustrated in Figure 8-4.

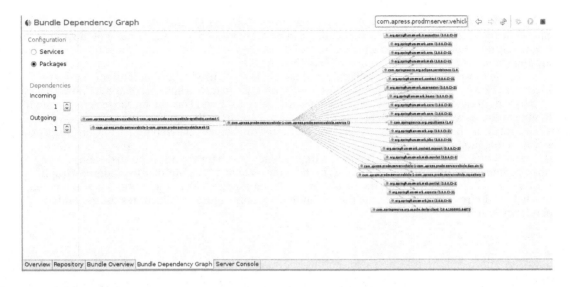

Figure 8-4. *An isolated bundle dependency graph for the vehicle application*

Finally, it's worth mentioning that right-clicking while on a dependency graph will generate a pop-up menu from which you can zoom in or out on the elements of a dependency graph.

If you're not visually inclined or simply prefer a more data-intensive way to analyze the complex interactions a bundle can have, dm Server Tools also offers a bundle overview feature. Right next to the Bundle Dependency Graph tab in the Servers area, click the Bundle Overview tab and you will see a window like the one illustrated in Figure 8-5.

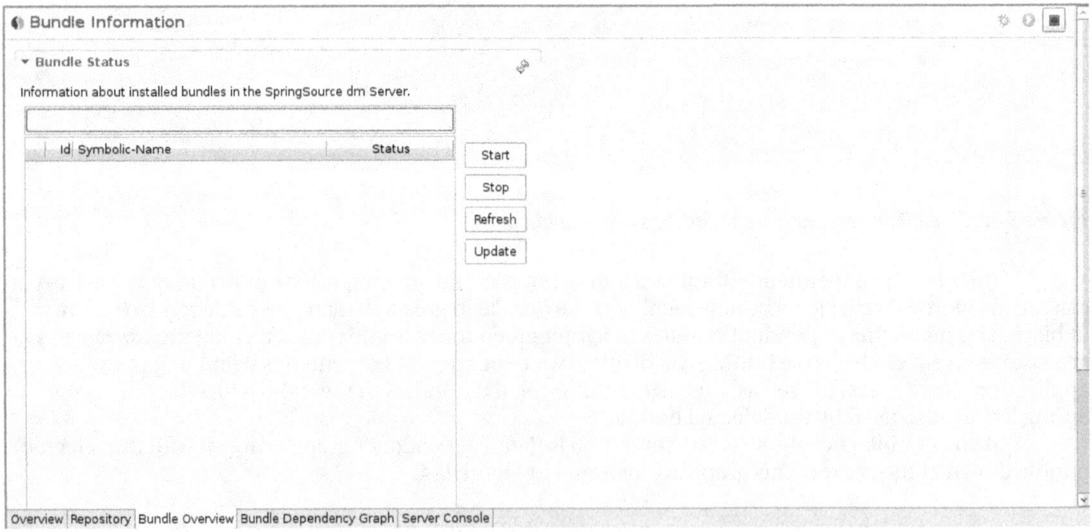

Figure 8-5. *The Bundle Overview tab in dm Server Tools*

On the left side, you will find a text box that can be used to filter the names of bundles installed on the dm Server—a helpful feature if you have a large set of installed bundles. In the same rectangle, in the top-right corner is a Refresh button that can be used to generate a list of bundles running on the server at any given moment. In addition, the Start, Stop, Refresh and Update buttons can be used to perform any of these actions on a selected bundle. And finally, in the far top-right corner you will find three dm Server-related buttons, to start, stop, or start it in debug mode.

Let's now see how to use the bundle overview feature for the application developed in Chapter 5. Once the application is deployed, click the Refresh icon to generate the dependency graph. This will generate a list of over 100 bundles, which include application bundles, preinstalled bundles, and bundles belonging to libraries, as well as dm Server system bundles.

Clicking any bundle on the list will generate an additional rectangle with information about the bundle's package exports and imports, services, `MANIFEST.MF` file, and other details. In addition, the buttons Start, Stop, Refresh, and Update will be activated in case you want to perform one of these OSGi lifecycle events on the bundle.

But before selecting any bundle, make use of the filter text box by entering `com.apress` to limit the bundle list. Next, select the `com.apress.prodmserver.vehicle.service` bundle. Figure 8-6 illustrates what the generated Bundle Overview tab looks like after this selection.

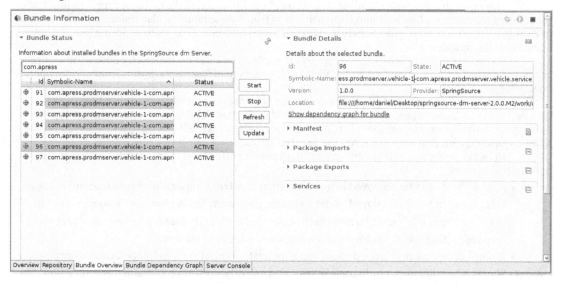

Figure 8-6. *A bundle overview for the vehicle application*

You can see that the lifecycle buttons are activated to modify a selected bundle's state, but also notice the generated Bundle Details rectangle. The first section contains the bundle's Id, State, Symbolic-Name, Version, Provider and even installation directory. Next, you see a link to generate the selected bundle's dependency graph.

The remaining tabs are hidden but can be expanded by clicking any title. These tabs include a bundle's `MANIFEST.MF` file, an associative list of package imports and exports used in the bundle, and the services that have some relationship with the bundle.

Next, we will explore another set of scenarios that may be of interest once your dm Server outgrows its basic configuration setup. These are based on the SpringSource Slices project.

SpringSource Slices for Managing Growth

If you've done Java web development, you are probably familiar with how applications start to grow organically. Once you put the finishing touches on an application and deploy it, the continuous feedback loop begins from users, requiring modifications: add a new set of images, add a new subsection at an internal URL, reuse content among sections, and the list goes on.

Java web applications rely on a particular construct named ServletContext to share information between elements. This mechanism greatly simplifies accessing existing resources in an application.

Servlets and Java Server Pages (JSPs)—which are converted to Servlets—generally form the backbone of most Java web applications and all have a ServletContext. By accessing a Servlet's or a JSP's ServletContext, you gain access to session data, configuration properties, and other such resources belonging to a particular Servlet or JSP. This practice can be pretty common in medium-sized to large applications, which can have dozens or hundreds of Servlets and JSPs, making it easier to share resources.

In applications designed for the dm Server, using a construct like ServletContext can be problematic because of the way OSGi works. While using a ServletContext is straightforward between elements contained in the same bundle, problems arise when the situation requires intra-bundle ServletContext access.

The same stringent class loading and visibility qualities that make OSGi an excellent foundation for creating modular applications and supporting Java run-time versioning also make it difficult to share resources through something like ServletContext between bundles. That's where SpringSource Slices comes into the picture.

SpringSource Slices is a dm Server project that allows OSGi-compliant web bundles intra-bundle access to ServletContexts. If you're familiar with OSGi's concept of fragments, SpringSource Slices operate on similar principles.

If you use SpringSource Slices in a dm Server application, you will have a slice host (a web bundle) and several slices (also web bundles) attached to the host. This parent/child relationship works as a way to centralize and share a ServletContext. A ServletContext will belong to a slice host, and the slices associated with that host will share the ServletContext.

In its current state, the SpringSource Slices project offers two main features with this parent/child model:

- A slice (child) can be deployed in a context (that is, a URL) under a slice host (parent) context URL. If a slice host is deployed under a context like /vehicle/, a slice can be attached to run under contexts like /vehicle/management/, /vehicle/distributors/, and /vehicle/partners/, thus separating and enhancing the management of related contexts.

- A slice can access resources present in a slice host. Content such as images, Cascading Style Sheets (CSS), licenses, configuration files, and any other resource contained in a slice host can be easily accessed from a slice. This avoids duplication and enhances the management of related contexts.

As a consequence, this parent/child model requires some forethought about which web bundle will serve as a slice host. A slice host will tend to have the most resources to share with other web bundles or slices, in addition to defining the top-level context URL used by multiple slices.

Now that you know the purpose of the SpringSource Slices project and its high-level design, I will describe how you would incorporate SpringSource Slices into the vehicle application described in Chapter 5.

Installing the SpringSource Slices Subsystem

Because the SpringSource Slices project isn't a feature that will necessarily be used by every dm Server application—and because it is still in heavy development—the dm Server needs to be configured to run

SpringSource Slices as a subsystem. To configuring a dm Server subsystem, you modify the dm Server's `kernel.properties`, located in the top-level `config` directory. In this file, you will need to modify the line beginning with `profile.subsystems` to reflect the following:

`profile.subsystems=com.springsource.server.web,com.springsource.osgi.slices`

By default, the dm Server is equipped with one subsystem, `com.springsource.server.web`, to which the SpringSource Slices subsystem, `com.springsource.osig.slices`, needs to be added by means of a comma.

The syntax `com.springsource.osig.slices` tells the dm Server to load a subsystem located in the `/repository/bundles/subsystems/com.springsource.osig.slices/` root directory of the dm Server.

The actual structure of a subsystem need not concern you, since it is simply a series of bundles and a configuration file provided by SpringSource. The book's accompanying source code includes this subsystem, which you can simply unpack into the directory cited in order to run SpringSource Slices on the dm Server.

Given the active state of development in the SpringSource Slices project, though, it may be convenient for you to build this subsystem on your own, in order to reflect the latest SpringSource Slices features that might have been incorporated since this book went to press.

To put things into perspective, the SpringSource Slices project at that time included support for the following:

- JSPs, Servlets, and Servlet mappings
- Spring MVC
- Slice-local sessions and automatic fallback to an application-wide session
- Slice-local resource lookups via `ServletContext` and automatic fallback to resource lookup in the host
- Explicit host resource lookup using `host:`

Ongoing developments that may be included in the SpringSource Slices project by the time you read this could include the following:

- Filters and filter mappings in slices
- Listeners in slices
- User Interface (UI) composition framework
- Tiles 2 integration
- SpringSource Tool Suite integration

If you decide to go ahead and build the subsystem on your own, building the SpringSource Slice subsystems will require you to install a few tools like Git and Apache Ant. Git is a source-code management control tool that you can download at `http://git-scm.com/download`. Apache Ant is a general-purpose build tool for Java, which you can download at `http://ant.apache.org/bindownload.cgi`.

Once you have Git and Apache Ant, execute the following instruction on your workstation:

`git clone git://git.springsource.org/slices/slices.git`

The SpringSource Slices project will be downloaded to your workstation. Once the download has completed, descend into the `slices/build-slices` subdirectory and invoke the command `ant clean jar package` to trigger the building of the subsystem.

Once the build process is complete, a SpringSource Slices subsystem will be generated under `target/artifacts/springsource-slices-BUILD-<timestamp>.zip`. Finally, it's just a matter of unzipping this last file in the root directory of the dm Server in order for the SpringSource Slices subsystems to be installed. The zip file already has the required directory structure built-in, so it can unzip in the root directory.

Adapting a Web Bundle into a SpringSource Slice Host

The process of adapting a standard web bundle into a slice host is designed to be as unobtrusive as possible. In fact, the process consists of simply adding a few configuration lines to a web bundle's web.xml file and MANIFEST.MF file.

The first step consists of incorporating the slice host filter into a web bundle's web.xml file, as illustrated next:

```
<filter>
  <filter-name>host-filter</filter-name>
  <filter-class>com.springsource.osgi.slices.core.SliceHostFilter</filter-class>
</filter>
<filter-mapping>
    <filter-name>host-filter</filter-name>
    <url-pattern>/*</url-pattern>
</filter-mapping>
```

This filter allows a slice host to delegate requests to its attached slices. This delegation model is dependent on how slices are configured, which is explained in the next section on configuring web bundles as SpringSource Slices.

Notice that the filter is no different than any other Java filter you would declare in a web.xml file. Similarly, this statement has no influence over any other functionality or statements you would typically use in a web bundle's web.xml file (e.g. Servlets, Servlet mappings, other filters, and so on).

Once a web bundle is configured with the slice host filter, it's necessary to add the filter's package to the bundle's MANIFEST.MF file, as illustrated next:

```
Import-Package:com.springsource.osgi.slices.core;version=[1.0.0,2.0.0)
```

Adding this statement will give the web bundle visibility to the SpringSource Slice's core package, which contains the filter and is located in the Slice's subsystem bundles installed earlier.

This is all that is required to set up a slice host. Next, you'll see how to transform a web bundle into a slice so that it can be attached to a slice host.

Transforming a Web Bundle into a SpringSource Slice

As with the design principles of a slice host, a web bundle can be transformed into a slice with minor modifications to its structure. This allows you to use the same design principles as a standard web bundle and deploy this same functionality as a SpringSource Slice if the need arises.

The first step in transforming a web bundle into a slice consists of modifying its MANIFEST.MF file. This allows a slice to be attached to a particular slice host. The following listing illustrates the additional declarations needed in a MANIFEST.MF file to transform a web bundle into a slice:

```
Slice-Host: com.apress.prodmserver.vehicle.web;version="[1.0, 2.0)"
Slice-ContextPath: /management
```

The SliceHost value represents the Bundle-SymbolicName of the slice host to which a slice will be attached. In this case, if a web bundle contains the previous statement, upon deployment the dm Server will attempt to attach it to a slice host with a Bundle-SymbolicName value of com.apress.prodmserver.vehicle.web and a Bundle-Version value between 1.0 (inclusive) and 2.0 (exclusive), which in this case represents the vehicle application's web bundle.

The Slice-ContextPath value represents the context path (URL) that is to be reserved by the slice host for the slice. In this case, since the slice host will be equipped with the statement Web-ContextPath: vehicle, the Slice-ContextPath: /management statement tells the slice host to filter all requests in the context path /vehicle/management and delegate them to the slice.

This process illustrates the purpose of configuring the slice host filter. As each new slice is attached to a slice host, new filter patterns are added to the slice host in order to delegate calls to new slices.

However, you shouldn't lose sight of the fact that SpringSource Slices only solve the delegation process. You still need to ensure that a slice—like any web bundle—is equipped to process requests at the cited context or URLs.

So for example, even though a slice host will filter requests in the form /vehicle/management and delegate them to the slice, the slice receiving such requests needs to be configured with a Servlet or other resource to attend such requests. The following listing illustrates what a web.xml statement in a slice web bundle would look like:

```
<!-- Handles all requests into the application -->
    <servlet>
            <servlet-name>managementServlet</servlet-name>
            <servlet-class>
             org.springframework.web.servlet.DispatcherServlet
            </servlet-class>
            <load-on-startup>1</load-on-startup>
    </servlet>

    <!-- Maps all requests / to the DispatcherServlet for handling -->
    <servlet-mapping>
            <servlet-name>managementServlet</servlet-name>
            <url-pattern>/*</url-pattern>
    </servlet-mapping>
```

This listing illustrates how a slice would define a Servlet (managementServlet) to handle all incoming requests(as specified by/*) that are delegated from a slice host. From this point, the DispatcherServlet would further define actions to handle incoming requests for a slice.

In addition to this delegation model, a slice can also be set up to access resources present in a slice host via ServletContext. This process is achieved using the same sequence as in standard Java web development. For example, if a Servlet in a slice requires access to a resource contained in its slice host web bundle, you would use a statement like the following:

```
ServletContext context = getServletContext();
context.getResource("/WEB-INF/messages.xml");
```

By default, when a resource lookup occurs, a slice will first attempt to find it within the slice's own resources. If the resource isn't found, then a lookup on the slice's host bundle is performed. This default behavior raises an interesting question, though: what happens if both a slice and its slice host have a resource at /WEB-INF/messages.xml, and you require access to the one on the host web bundle?

For such cases, SpringSource Slices support a special notation to specifically indicate the resource lookup be performed on the host slice. This is achieved using the host: prefix as illustrated next:

```
ServletContext context = getServletContext();
context.getResource("host:/WEB-INF/messages.xml");
```

Summary

In this chapter, you learned more advanced techniques for managing the growth of application deployed on the dm Server.

You saw how the dm Server supports application deployment using plan files, which offer a more general approach to using PAR files. In addition, you learned about Configuration Provisioning and how it complements the use of plan files, providing the capability to assign parameters via static files.

Next, you learned about the dm Server's support for cloning, which aids in the resolution of pinning or uses conflicts, which are a common occurrence for large OSGi developments in general. You saw how the dm Server automatically provides cloning functionality when it detects certain application patterns; you can also rely on the explicit use of OSGi headers to support cloning.

You then met Bundlor, a tool designed to make the migration of JARs to OSGi compliant bundles easier. You explored Bundlor's template system, how it's applied to JAR files, and how Bundlor can be invoked from tools like Apache Ant, Maven or the command line. Next, you also learned about the BundlorEclipse functionality in dm Server Tools and about dependency visualization, which allows you to determine a bundle's dependencies more easily.

Finally, you encountered the SpringSource Slices project and how it can associate various web bundles to work in a parent/child relationship. The end result is the capability to run nested contexts for web bundles (in our example, vehicle, vehicle/management, vehicle/users) and to share resources among web bundles via ServletContext.

Index